Bislama Reference Grammar

Oceanic Linguistics Special Publication No. 31

Bislama Reference Grammar

Terry Crowley

University of Hawai'i Press

Honolulu

© 2004 University of Hawai'i Press
All rights reserved
Printed in the United States of America
09 08 07 06 05 04   6 5 4 3 2 1

Library of Congress Cataloging-in-Publication Data

Crowley, Terry.
 Bislama reference grammar / Terry Crowley.
  p. cm. — (Oceanic linguistics special publication ; no. 31)
 Includes bibliographical references and index.
 ISBN 978-0-8248-2880-6 (alk. paper)
  1. Bislama language—Grammar.   I. Title. II. Series.

PM7895.B4C73 2004
427'.99595—dc22

2004044096

Camera-ready copy for this book was prepared under the
supervision of the series editor.

University of Hawai'i Press books are printed on acid-free paper and meet the
guidelines for permanence and durability of the Council on Library Resources.

Printed by IBT Global

CONTENTS

LIST OF TABLES x
PREFACE xi
ACKNOWLEDGMENTS xiii
MAPS xiv

1: BACKGROUND TO BISLAMA 1
  1.1 Bislama: An Independent Language 1
  1.2 Bislama in Vanuatu Society 3
  1.3 Historical Background 4
  1.4 The Vocabulary of Bislama 5
  1.5 Varieties of Bislama 7
  1.6 What Kind of Grammar is This? 9

2: PRONUNCIATION AND SPELLING 11
  2.1 Consonants 11
  2.2 Vowels 15
  2.3 Expanded Sound Systems 16
  2.4 Spelling 18
  2.5 Stress 21
  2.6 Intonation 22
  2.7 Syllables 23

3: PARTS OF SPEECH 24
  3.1 Nouns 25
  3.2 Pronouns 26
  3.3 Prepositions 27
  3.4 Verbs 28
  3.5 Noun Modifiers 28
    3.5.1 Number Markers 29
    3.5.2 Adjectives 29
  3.6 Adverbs 30
  3.7 Other Modifiers 31
  3.8 Interrogatives 31
  3.9 Complex Sentence Markers 32
  3.10 Interjections and Vocatives 32
  3.11 Words with Several Functions 33

4: NOUNS AND NOUN PHRASES 37
  4.1 Nouns 37
    4.1.1 Simple and Complex Nouns 37
    4.1.2 Compounding 38
      4.1.2.1 Adjective + Noun 38
      4.1.2.2 Noun + Postmodifier 39
      4.1.2.3 Verb + Noun 39
      4.1.2.4 Noun + Noun 39
    4.1.3 Reduplication 40
    4.1.4 Affixation 41

CONTENTS

- 4.1.4.1 The Suffix *-wan* 42
- 4.1.4.2 The Prefix *eks-* 43
- 4.1.4.3 Emerging Suffixes? 44
- 4.2 Pronouns 45
- 4.3 Noun Phrases 50
  - 4.3.1 Quantifiers + Nouns 50
  - 4.3.2 Pronouns + Quantifiers 56
  - 4.3.3 Adjectives 59
    - 4.3.3.1 Reduplication 59
    - 4.3.3.2 The Suffix *-fala* 60
    - 4.3.3.3 Compounding 63
  - 4.3.4 Noun Postmodifiers 64
  - 4.3.5 Demonstratives 64
  - 4.3.6 Nouns Modified by Sentences 65
- 4.4 Noun Phrases Linked by *blong* 67
  - 4.4.1 Possession 68
  - 4.4.2 Other Functions of *blong* 69
- 4.5 Coordinate Noun Phrases 70

5: VERBS AND VERB PHRASES 72
- 5.1 Verbs 72
  - 5.1.1 Reduplication 72
  - 5.1.2 Compounds 76
  - 5.1.3 Affixation 77
    - 5.1.3.1 Transitive Suffix 77
    - 5.1.3.2 Directional Suffixes 82
      - 5.1.3.2.1 *-Daon* 83
      - 5.1.3.2.2 *-Aot* 83
      - 5.1.3.2.3 *-Raon* 83
      - 5.1.3.2.4 *-Bak* 83
      - 5.1.3.2.5 *-Ap* 84
- 5.2 Complex Verbs 85
- 5.3 Verb Phrases 88
  - 5.3.1 Imperatives, Prohibitives, and Hortatives 89
  - 5.3.2 The Forms *i* and *oli* 92
  - 5.3.3 Tense 92
  - 5.3.4 Negative Markers 95
  - 5.3.5 Auxiliaries 96
    - 5.3.5.1 *Mas* 97
    - 5.3.5.2 *Bin* 97
    - 5.3.5.3 *Jas* 98
    - 5.3.5.4 *Stap* 98
    - 5.3.5.5 *Save* 99
    - 5.3.5.6 *Wantem* 100
    - 5.3.5.7 *Sud* 100
    - 5.3.5.8 *Kanduit* 101
    - 5.3.5.9 *Kam* and *Go* 101
    - 5.3.5.10 *Stil* 102

- 5.3.6 Post-Verbal Modifiers 102
- 5.3.7 Modifiers of Manner 105

6: SIMPLE SENTENCES 108
- 6.1 Statements 108
  - 6.1.1 Predicate Sentences and Predicate Markers 109
  - 6.1.2 Non-Predicate Sentences 113
    - 6.1.2.1 Presentative Sentences 114
    - 6.1.2.2 Equational Sentences 115
    - 6.1.2.3 'Ought to' Constructions 116
  - 6.1.3 Constituent Order 117
    - 6.1.3.1 Transitive and Intransitive Constructions 117
      - 6.1.3.1.1 Meteorological Expressions 118
      - 6.1.3.1.2 General States 118
      - 6.1.3.1.3 The Existential Verb *gat* 119
      - 6.1.3.1.4 Negation of Incomplete Sentences 120
      - 6.1.3.1.5 Actions without Causers 120
    - 6.1.3.2 VERB + NOUN Constructions 122
  - 6.1.4 Double Object Constructions 125
  - 6.1.5 Prepositional Phrases 127
    - 6.1.5.1 Basic Prepositions 127
      - 6.1.5.1.1 *Blong* 127
      - 6.1.5.1.2 *From* 128
      - 6.1.5.1.3 *Wetem* 128
      - 6.1.5.1.4 *Wetaot(em)* 129
      - 6.1.5.1.5 *Olsem* 129
      - 6.1.5.1.6 *Long* 130
    - 6.1.5.2 Verbal Prepositions 133
      - 6.1.5.2.1 *Kasem* 133
      - 6.1.5.2.2 *Bitim* 134
      - 6.1.5.2.3 *Ronem* 134
      - 6.1.5.2.4 *Agensem* 135
      - 6.1.5.2.5 *Raonem* 135
      - 6.1.5.2.6 *Folem* 135
      - 6.1.5.2.7 *Tokbaot* 136
      - 6.1.5.2.8 *Yusum* 136
    - 6.1.5.3 Position of Prepositional Phrases 137
    - 6.1.5.4 Complex Prepositions 137
  - 6.1.6 Adverbs 139
    - 6.1.6.1 Adverbs of Place 139
    - 6.1.6.2 Adverbs of Time 140
    - 6.1.6.3 Adverbs of Manner 141
    - 6.1.6.4 Miscellaneous Adverbs 142
    - 6.1.6.5 Placement of Adverbs and Post-Verbal Modifiers 146
- 6.2 Questions 147
  - 6.2.1 Yes-No Questions 147
  - 6.2.2 Content Questions 150
    - 6.2.2.1 *Wanem* 150

CONTENTS

- 6.2.2.2 *Se* 151
- 6.2.2.3 *Huia* 151
- 6.2.2.4 *Hamas* 153
- 6.2.2.5 *Hameni* 153
- 6.2.2.6 *Wijwan* 154
- 6.2.2.7 *Waswe* 154
- 6.2.2.8 *Watfo* 155
- 6.2.2.9 *Wataem* 155
- 6.2.2.10 *We* 155
- 6.2.2.11 *Wehem* 156
- 6.2.2.12 *From* 157
- 6.2.2.13 *From wanem* 157
- 6.2.2.14 *Olsem wanem* 158
- 6.3 Fronted Noun Phrases 159

7: COMPLEX SENTENCES 166
- 7.1 Serial Verbs 166
  - 7.1.1 Directional Verbs 167
  - 7.1.2 Manner Constructions 170
  - 7.1.3 Causative Constructions 171
  - 7.1.4 Sequential Actions 172
- 7.2 Coordination 172
  - 7.2.1 *Mo* 172
  - 7.2.2 *Be* 174
  - 7.2.3 *(N)o* 175
- 7.3 Subordination 175
  - 7.3.1 Juxtaposition 176
  - 7.3.2 Subordinator Constructions 177
    - 7.3.2.1 Simple Subordinators 178
      - 7.3.2.1.1 *Blong* and *Long* 178
      - 7.3.2.1.2 *Se* 182
      - 7.3.2.1.3 *We* 184
      - 7.3.2.1.4 *Nogud* 186
    - 7.3.2.2 Complex Subordinators 187
      - 7.3.2.2.1 *From* 187
      - 7.3.2.2.2 *Kasem* 187
      - 7.3.2.2.3 *Olsem* 187
      - 7.3.2.2.4 *Taem* 188
      - 7.3.2.2.5 *Tetaem* 188
      - 7.3.2.2.6 *Sapos* 189
      - 7.3.2.2.7 *Nomata, Nevamaen, Nating,* and *Iven* 189
      - 7.3.2.2.8 *Afta* and *Bifo* 190
      - 7.3.2.2.9 Question Words as Subordinators 191
- 7.4 Sentences in Discourse 192
  - 7.4.1 The Sequencing of Events 192
  - 7.4.2 Cause and Effect 195
  - 7.4.3 Contrary to Expectation 196
  - 7.4.4 The Pragmatic Particle *ia* 196

CONTENTS

APPENDIX: PREVIOUS STUDIES OF BISLAMA GRAMMAR 199
REFERENCES 201
INDEX 203

LIST OF TABLES

2.1 Consonants 12
2.2 English and French Consonants in Bislama 12
2.3 Vowels 16
2.4 English and French Vowels in Bislama 17
3.1 Stronger and Weaker Interjections 34
4.1 Pronouns 46
5.1 Reduplicated Intransitive Verbs 75
5.2 Transitive Verbs with -*ap* 86
5.3 Transitive Main Verbs Used in Verb Complexes 87
5.4 Intransitive Main Verbs Used in Verb Complexes 88

PREFACE

This volume has been more than a quarter of a century in the making. Since I first arrived as a linguistic fieldworker in Vanuatu in 1976—then known as the New Hebrides—Bislama has become a major part of my linguistic repertoire, not only during my periods of residence in Vanuatu (1976-78, 1983-90) but also when interacting with Ni-Vanuatu during my time in Papua New Guinea (1979-83) and New Zealand (1991-2004), as well as during my frequent—and often lengthy—return visits to Vanuatu. It is the language through which I have made many friends from all different parts of the country.

I initially had no intention whatsoever of writing a volume such as this. In the beginning, I saw Bislama as just a tool that I was using to gain access to the Paamese language, which was my primary research interest at the time. Later, I used Bislama as a means for investigating other languages in the country, from the islands of Erromango and Malakula. However, as soon as I started establishing friendships through Bislama, the language became rather more than just a tool, and eventually it became a major research interest, along with my interests in other Vanuatu languages. I produced a dictionary of Bislama to coincide with the tenth anniversary of Vanuatu's accession to independence (Crowley 1990a). This was then substantially improved and expanded a few years later (Crowley 1995), and yet another update has just appeared (Crowley 2003).

In 1987, some years before the appearance of these dictionaries, I also produced a grammatical account of Bislama, with the title *Grama blong Bislama*. This was written as part of a set of distance-teaching materials offered through the Pacific Languages Unit of the University of the South Pacific. As the title suggests, this was a description of Bislama that was written *in* Bislama. That task turned out to be extraordinarily difficult to do, as there was no ready-made terminology in Bislama for talking about grammatical topics, such as 'noun', 'preposition', or 'transitive verb'.

In terms of gaining academic kudos and achieving public accessibility, producing that volume was also not very wise. USP was not cooperative in allowing its course materials to be made publicly available except to students formally enrolled in its courses. I was also unable to persuade an academic publisher to take on the task of producing and distributing the grammar. *Pacific Linguistics*, the foremost publisher of material relating to Pacific languages, was unwilling to publish the volume in Bislama because of the limited size—and limited purchasing power—of the Bislama-speaking market.

So, I have finally decided to write this grammar in order to reach a wider audience. Although not aimed specifically at academic linguists, it is certainly hoped that they will find significant interest in this grammar. It is, in fact, aimed at a rather broader audience than just academic linguists. I hope that new arrivals in Vanuatu who are learning the language will also gain from this volume, in the same way that they have hopefully gained from the published dictionary. Obviously, nobody can learn a language from scratch from a grammar book—there is a set of basic published lessons to help people here (Tryon 1987)—but once somebody has gained a substantial foothold in learning a language, a grammar such as this provides a good way to learn more about how people use the language.

PREFACE

I would also like to think that Ni-Vanuatu who speak (and write) Bislama on a regular basis will also find value in this grammar. At the moment, Bislama has no place within the formal education system, though there has been debate in recent years relating to a possible place for both the local languages and Bislama within schools. Various suggestions have been made for a legitimate place for Bislama in schools, ranging from its possible use as a medium of instruction for initial primary education for some schools, to the teaching of Bislama as an academic subject at secondary level.

However, even if Bislama fails to gain a major role in the formal education system, it is hoped that this grammar may find a legitimate place. Many people in Vanuatu still harbor suspicions that Bislama, given its earlier history of use by uneducated plantation laborers, is somehow "deficient" as a language. Showing that Bislama has a grammar of considerable complexity is one way in which I hope that I am able to demonstrate fallacy of such assumptions.

And in purely practical terms, in describing the grammatical patterns of Bislama, I hope that I am able to offer some valuable guidance about what constitutes "good usage" in Bislama for people who are involved in the development of written materials in the language. Too often, materials that are written in Bislama have been produced with some kind of assumption that what is good in English must also be good in Bislama. In many respects, the two languages have very different ways of saying things, and I hope that this grammar serves to capture the essential genius of Bislama, and to show how different Bislama is from English.

This volume is aimed primarily either at people who already have a fair amount of familiarity with Bislama, or at people who are linguistically sufficiently sophisticated that they can work out some things for themselves. I do not intend, therefore, to explain every detail of every example that I have used to illustrate my points. Ultimately, however, every pattern that appears in my examples is accounted for within the pages of this grammar. While many grammars provide "literal" translations of all words in example sentences alongside a "free" translation of the sentence, I have provided only free translations. An example sentence such as *Traem givim faeawud i kam* may therefore be translated only as 'Please give me the firewood'. If there is no immediate need to say that *traem* literally means 'try' and *i kam* is used to express motion towards the speaker, I will leave discussion of these specific points for elsewhere in the grammar, and I will assume that a motivated or linguistically informed reader will be able to locate these discussions in the relevant sections of the grammar elsewhere.

Terry Crowley
Hamilton (New Zealand)
March 2004

ACKNOWLEDGMENTS

This grammar builds on the work of many others over the years who have published on different aspects of the grammar of Bislama. Names that come immediately to mind include Bill Camden, Jean-Michel Charpentier, Ross Clark, Jacques Guy, John Lynch, Miriam Meyerhoff, Jeff Siegel, and Darrell Tryon, and to each of these authors a debt of thanks is due.

In a moment of boredom in the middle of 2002, I was seeking suggestions via email from John Lynch about what I could do to fill in the rest of the week. He jokingly suggested that if I was so bored, I should sit down and write a Bislama reference grammar. I had resisted such a suggestion in the past, but this time the idea hit home and I started work on this volume immediately. I should therefore specifically thank John Lynch for persuading me to finally get this volume out of my system. Thanks are also due to John Lynch and Elizabeth Pearce for their helpful comments on earlier drafts of this grammar.

A grammar of a language often also calls for the expression of a debt of gratitude to one's various "informants." In this case, my debt is pretty well impossible to express given that practically everyone with whom I have ever established and maintained a friendship through the medium of Bislama has contributed to this volume in one way or another, usually without that person—or me—necessarily realizing it at the time.

From se i no gat ol stret man o woman we mi save talem tangkyu long yufala from help we yufala i bin givim long saed blong buk ia, ating bae mi jas talem bigfala tangkyu long yufala evriwan raon long Vanuatu stat long yia 1976 i kam kasem tedei. Fasin blong yumi we yumi stap stori oltaem long Bislama i mekem se ol kaen Bislama we yufala evriwan i stap toktok long hem i stap insaed long buk ia. Fulap ol fren blong mi, yufala i stap long taon blong Vila. Be mi glad tu we mi gat plante fren bakegen we yumi bin stap tugeta long olgeta aelan blong Paama, Erromango, mo Malakula. Ol toktok blong yufala evriwan i kam olsem stamba blong buk ia.

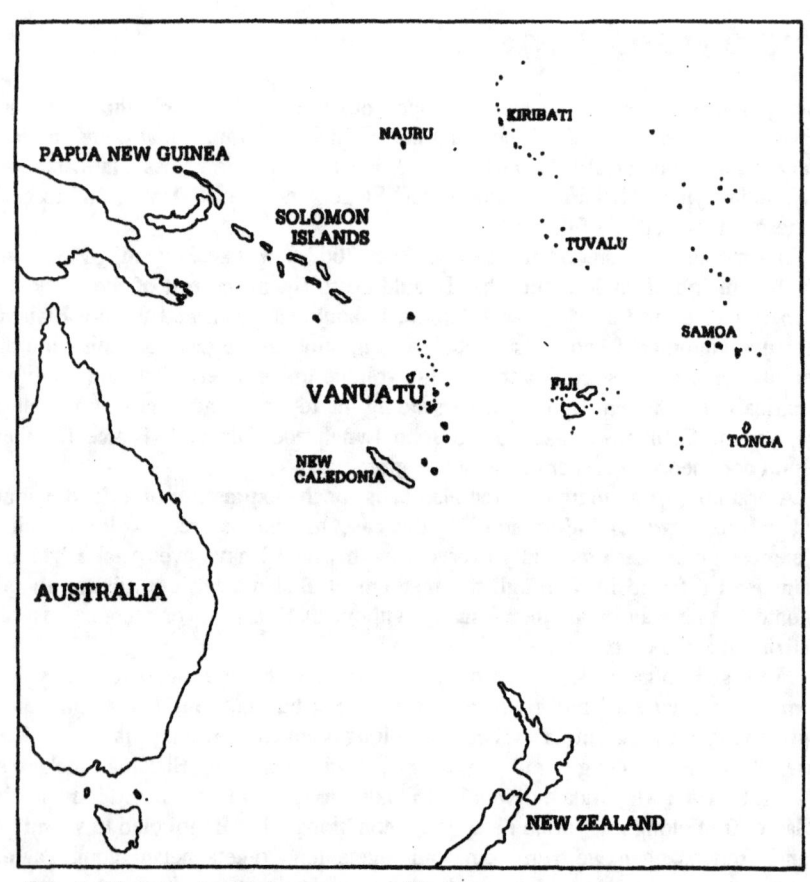

Map 1: Vanuatu in the southwestern Pacific

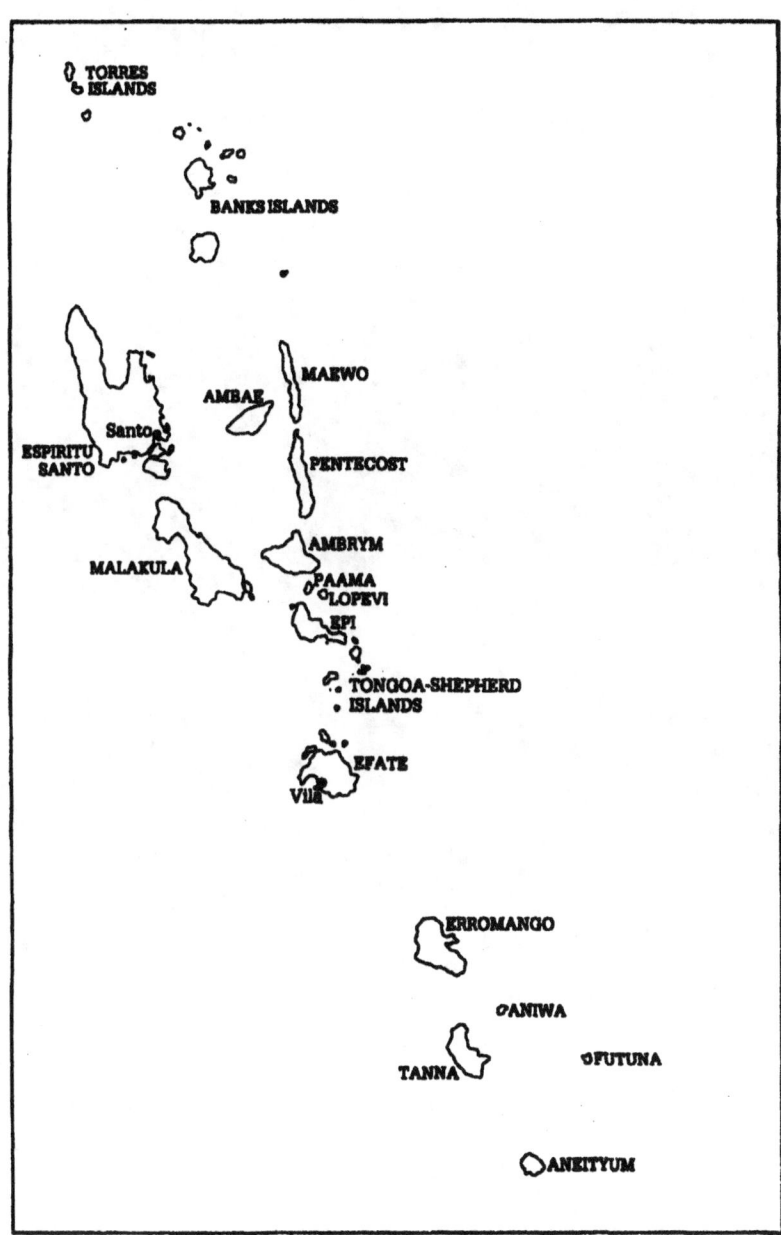

Map 2: The Republic of Vanuatu

1: BACKGROUND TO BISLAMA

1.1 Bislama: An Independent Language

Bislama is one of the newest languages in the world. It didn't exist at all in 1840. By 1890, it was widely spoken in many—though by no means all—coastal communities around Vanuatu. Today, of course, it is spoken by people in just about every part of the country. By way of contrast, English evolved out of Anglo-Saxon and French out of Latin about a thousand years ago. While Bislama clearly developed in some sense out of English, this happened much more quickly, and much more recently.

Soon after the appearance of the earliest form of Bislama, it very quickly developed into a completely separate language in its own right. In the middle of the nineteenth century, Bislama began as something very much like "broken English." However, Melanesians on the plantations of Queensland in the late nineteenth century, and later also in Vanuatu, came to rely on this "broken English" as an important means of communication with each other, rather than just with Europeans. In the process, they molded the language in such a way that it acquired new features that made it a very different language from English.

It is obvious that many of the words in use in Bislama today look very much like words in English. Thus, *dog* means *dog*, *ren* means *rain*, and *kon* means *corn*. However, the ways in which words of English origin are actually used in sentences is often very different between Bislama and English. A verb like *belong* in English, for example, has become the preposition *blong* in Bislama, while the preposition *along* in English has acquired a much wider range of functions in the Bislama preposition *long* that derives from it. The pronunciations of Bislama words are also often somewhat different to the pronunciations of the English words that they are derived from. The English word *fish*, for example, is pronounced in Bislama as *fis*, and *six* has come to be pronounced in Bislama as *sikis*.

While the pronunciations of words in Bislama are often influenced by people's various local languages, and the grammar of Bislama is clearly influenced in quite significant ways by widespread patterns found in local languages, it is sometimes harder to see direct evidence of influence from local languages in the vocabulary itself. However, the influence is there nonetheless. The vocabulary that is used to express family relationships, for example, is particularly strongly influenced by the ways that corresponding words are used in local languages in different parts of Vanuatu. For instance, the word *papa* refers both to one's biological father and to one's father's brothers, while one's mother's brothers are referred to by a different word, i.e., *angkel*. This follows the widespread pattern in local languages for maternal and paternal uncles to be expressed differently, and for paternal uncles to be referred to by the same word that is used for father.

Bislama and English have developed in different directions to the point where a newly arrived New Zealander or Australian who speaks only English will simply not understand a casual conversation between two ordinary Ni-Vanuatu speaking Bislama. At first exposure, casual Bislama may well sound as foreign to a speaker of English as a conversation taking place between two people speaking German or Dutch. In the same way, a conversation between two Australians speaking English will not be understood at all by a Ni-Vanuatu who has not first learned English at school. This shows that Bislama and English are now quite different languages, and it is a serious mistake to speak of Bislama today as if it were any kind of "broken English." Bislama is now as much a separate language from English as German is from Dutch, or as Italian is from Spanish.

However, although Bislama is a distinct language, it does fall into a special category of languages, which linguists refer to as pidgin or creole languages. These are languages that typically emerge rapidly in situations where speakers of many different local languages come together—often on plantations—without an adequate opportunity to learn each other's languages. What typically happens in such situations is that the plantation workers seize upon the restricted amount of vocabulary that they hear from their overseers and they build a completely new language out of this, based in part on widely distributed features in their own local languages.

New languages that have arisen in comparable situations are spoken in many different parts of the world. West African slaves in Haiti, when exposed to French vocabulary several hundred years ago, eventually came up with a new language that was based on French vocabulary. People in Vanuatu will be familiar with the modern version of this language through the words of Haitian Zouk musicians or those old *Compagnie Créole* favorites. A similar kind of language also developed more recently out of French vocabulary in New Caledonia in the small community of St. Louis outside Nouméa.

In Nigeria, a new language has been formed on the basis of English vocabulary in ways that are similar to what has happened in Vanuatu. There are also cases where new languages have been formed based on Spanish, Portuguese, and Dutch vocabulary. There are even places where non-European languages have been taken as the basis for new languages of this type. In the British colony of Papua in the late 1800s, for example, police recruits from Solomon Islands and various parts of Papua often communicated with each other in a new language of their own creation that was derived from the local Motu language of the colonial capital, Port Moresby. The language that these policemen developed came to be known initially as Police Motu, and later as Hiri Motu, and this continues to be used as a common language in much of southern Papua New Guinea today.

Bislama shares much of its history with the development of Tok Pisin in Papua New Guinea and Pijin in Solomon Islands. Speakers of Bislama, Tok Pisin, and Pijin can generally understand each other, which means that they are effectively speaking three dialects of a single language, which we could refer to generically as Melanesian Pidgin. However, because each of these three national varieties has its own distinct name and because each is used according to its own written standards in each country, people often speak of these instead as if they are three separate languages.

In 1980, the former New Hebrides gained its political independence to become the separate nation of Vanuatu. At the same time, what had previously been looked down upon as Pidgin English finally in a sense gained recognition as an independent language, which we now know as Bislama. Just as Vanuatu has become an independent nation, Bislama is now undeniably an independent language. It is only right, therefore, that the grammar of Bislama should be described in its own terms without being described primarily in comparison to English. That is what this grammar sets out to do.

1.2 Bislama in Vanuatu Society

The New Hebrides renamed itself in 1980 as Vanuatu, a word that derives from widely distributed words in local languages of the shape *vanua* 'land' and *tu* 'stand'. This new name was intended to symbolize the independent status of the new republic. Vanuatu is a highly multilingual nation boasting at least 80 actively spoken languages distributed across a population of about 200,000 (Crowley 2000a). It has the most complex linguistic demography of any country in the world in terms of the number of languages per head of population.

At independence, Bislama was declared in Vanuatu's newly promulgated constitution to be the national language, largely in order to avoid the need to make what would at the time have been a politically divisive choice between English and French. This declaration makes Vanuatu unique among the countries of the world in that a former pidgin language has higher constitutional status than a former colonial language. English and French are recognized alongside Bislama as co-equal "official languages," and they—but not Bislama—are also declared to be "languages of education". However, in most situations Bislama is effectively the default language throughout the country. When people speaking different local languages come together—sometimes even English- and French-speaking Europeans who don't speak the other language—it is generally Bislama that people feel most comfortable using.

Although Bislama began its life as a plantation pidgin performing a fairly restricted range of functions—and having, therefore, a relatively restricted vocabulary—it has over the last few decades dramatically expanded the range of contexts in which it is used. It is now widely used as a language—particularly in urban areas—of religious worship, national and local politics (including parliamentary debate), the bureaucracy, the courts and the police, shopping, work, sport, the radio, friendship and romance, and even family life. As a result, the vocabulary of Bislama has expanded dramatically to allow its speakers to meet a wide variety of new needs. Much of this expansion has been met by borrowing from English (*palemen* 'parliament') or, to a lesser extent, French (*lepap* 'pope' from *le pape*), and occasionally even some of the local languages (*tuki* 'fight, brawl'). However, a fair amount of new vocabulary has also developed spontaneously on the basis of original Bislama roots (*mama loa* 'constitution' from *mama* 'mother' plus *loa* 'law').

A national identity for the new Republic of Vanuatu is currently being forged, but this is largely expressed through the medium of Bislama rather than any of the local languages, or through English or French. Accompanying this development—and associated to a significant extent with the relatively young urban population in the main centers of Vila and Santo (known more formally as Port-Vila and Luganville respectively)—is a very rapid stylistic expansion of the language into areas of youthful enthusiasm and adventure. Since independence, there has been a dramatic resurgence of traditional kava drinking, and kava-bar conversations are largely carried out through the medium of Bislama. Patterns of youthful indulgence in alcohol, partying, and dancing, along with urban issues such as unemployment and inter-communal disputes, have also brought Bislama into new social domains for which its speakers have needed to acquire new vocabulary and stylistic variation.

CHAPTER 1

Nearly all children in Vanuatu these days attend English- or French-medium primary schools for six years where metropolitan languages represent the dominant (or only) medium of instruction, and smaller numbers proceed to secondary and even tertiary education. However, neither English nor French has any significant use informally among most Ni-Vanuatu. These formerly colonial languages function effectively as "high" languages in what linguists refer to as a kind of diglossic relationship at the national level. These high languages are reserved largely for written or official purposes, and Bislama is the language of choice even for most tertiary-educated Ni-Vanuatu in informal spoken contexts.

Although Bislama began its history as nobody's first language, it has gradually been acquiring small numbers of first-language speakers. Possibly as much as ten percent of the population today grows up speaking Bislama and no local vernacular, largely as a result of marriages between people from different language groups living in urban centers or on plantations. Because of this, some linguists insist on referring to Bislama as a "creole" rather than as a "pidgin." In reality, this distinction is almost meaningless in the Vanuatu context, as there are no clearly recognizable features by which Bislama acquired as a second language and Bislama acquired as a first language can be distinguished.

1.3 Historical Background

The earliest developments in the history of Bislama took place outside of Vanuatu. Soon after the establishment of the British colony of New South Wales in 1788, a pidgin developed that was used between settlers and Aboriginal peoples along the ever-expanding frontier of colonial settlement (Baker 1993). Features of this pidgin soon made their way into what is often referred to as South Seas Jargon. This was a rather basic sort of means of communication that was only used for short-term communication needs between the crews of passing vessels and people on shore in different islands around the Pacific Ocean in the early 1800s. However, it was never used by more than a small handful of local people (Clark 1979-80, Keesing 1988).

South Seas Jargon first became established in southern Vanuatu and in the Loyalty Islands on trading stations established by Europeans from around the mid-1800s (Crowley 1990b: 60-65). Europeans at the time were engaged in a three-way trade that involved sandalwood and sea slugs (or beche de mer) for sale in China, tea from China that was sold in the Australian colonies, and iron, cloth, and other trade goods from the colonies of eastern Australia that were traded for sandalwood and sea slugs in southern Melanesia.

The European traders employed substantial numbers of people from different islands on their shore stations in Vanuatu with the result that these stations were linguistically very mixed. The rather unstable and rudimentary South Seas Jargon fairly quickly became the basis for a new variety of contact language on these stations. This began to stabilize during the 1850s-1860s and acquired a number of distinct local characteristics that distinguished it from South Seas Jargon in general. Given its association with the sandalwood and beche de mer trades, it came to be known as Sandalwood English or Beche-de-Mer English. The name Sandalwood English soon disappeared and the name Beche-de-Mer English was shortened to

Beach-la-Mar. This eventually became Bislama, the name by which the language is generally known in Vanuatu today in both English and Bislama. (In French, however, it is known as *bichelamar*.)

While Bislama began its development in the Loyalty Islands and in southern Vanuatu in association with the trade in sea slugs and sandalwood, the language was introduced to the islands from Efate northward in the 1870s–1890s with the recruitment of large numbers of people to work on the sugar plantations of Queensland. However, while Bislama spread throughout Vanuatu during this era, it underwent contraction in the Loyalty Islands of New Caledonia, and it was replaced there as the common language by French in the decades after France established itself as the colonial power in 1853 (Crowley 1990b: 65–70).

Workers on plantations in Queensland again found themselves in multilingual situations, needing to communicate not only with people from other islands of Vanuatu, but also with other labor recruits from Solomon Islands and parts of Papua New Guinea. The contact language from the early years of Vanuatu continued to develop new features as more and more people came to use it as their means of communication on the Queensland plantations.

There was a constant flow of laborers between Vanuatu and Queensland in the late 1800s. A plantation economy also became established in some parts of Vanuatu during this same period, and many of those who were recruited to work locally had previous experience in Queensland. This resulted in the spread of Bislama as a plantation language on islands such as Efate, Malakula, and Espiritu Santo. When Queensland entered the new Commonwealth of Australia in 1901, further labor recruitment from Vanuatu was prohibited. Many plantation laborers were returned to their home islands, and this increased the proportion of people in Vanuatu who were familiar with Bislama.

It was not until 1906 that colonial government was established in Vanuatu, making the islands probably the last part of the world to be placed under any kind of official government authority. The system of government that was established was also unique in that the New Hebrides was jointly administered by Britain and France as a "condominium." The plantations established in the late 1800s continued to develop in the early 1900s, promoting the continued movement of people between the islands of Vanuatu, and therefore also promoting the continued spread of Bislama.

By the early 1900s, speakers of Bislama had been largely cut off from contact with Solomon Islanders and Papua New Guineans, and it began to acquire some of the unique features that distinguish it from Tok Pisin and Pijin today. Many of the plantations in Vanuatu were French owned, and this provided a major source of new vocabulary in Bislama that was not available to Solomon Islanders and Papua New Guineans on plantations there. In the early decades of the twentieth century, Bislama underwent a variety of changes in its grammar and its vocabulary, but between the First and Second World Wars, it had acquired all of the basic features that we find in Bislama today.

1.4 The Vocabulary of Bislama

Although the vocabulary of Bislama is predominantly English in origin, there is nevertheless a substantial minority of words from other languages. About 3.75% of

CHAPTER 1

the total number of Bislama words derive from local languages (*nakamal* 'meeting house', *nawita* 'octopus', *nawimba* 'Pacific pigeon'), while between 6% and 12% derive from French (*masut* 'diesel' from *mazout*, *pamplimus* 'grapefruit' from *pamplemousse*, and *ale* 'and then' from *allez* 'go!'), and about 0.25% of the lexicon derives from a variety of other sources (*pikinini* 'child' ultimately from Portuguese *pequenho* 'small' via South Seas Jargon, *burao* '*Hibiscus tiliaceus*' from Tahitian *purau*, *nalnal* 'club' from Early Australian Aboriginal Pidgin *nalanala*). The range of 6–12% for words of French origin—rather than a fixed figure—is because the forms of a substantial number of words are ambiguous betweeen an English and a French origin. Thus, *sigaret* could come equally from English or French *cigarette*, *plastik* could come from English *plastic* or French *plastique*, and *letrik* could come from English *electric* or French *électrique*.

Words from local languages are most widely encountered referring to things for which neither English nor French provided terms that were readily accessible to people in the early contact situation (or since). We therefore find a substantial number of names for local flora and fauna being expressed by means of words of local origin, e.g., *nakavika* 'Malay apple', *nakatambol* 'dragon plum', *nangae* 'native almond', *natora* 'island teak', *nasiviru* 'coconut lory'. Terminology relating to things of importance in Melanesian culture is also often expressed by words of local origin (*nakaemas* 'sorcerer', *nakamal* 'meeting house', *nimanggi* 'grade-taking ceremony', *nanggol* 'land-diving', *nasama* 'outrigger (of canoe)', *natamap* 'castrated boar'). Of course, local styles of cooking—*laplap*, *tuluk*, *simboro*, *nalot*—are also often expressed by words of local origin. Nouns in Bislama of local origin often—though by no means always—begin with the syllable *na-*, which derives from a widespread noun marker in local languages.

Words of French origin express a wider range of meanings, making it more difficult to predict which meanings are likely to be expressed by words from English and which will be expressed by words from French. Some words of French origin clearly relate in a variety of ways to the French colonial presence through administrative terminology such as *delege* 'French district agent' from *délégué* and *lameri* 'town hall' from *la mairie*; terminology associated with catholicism (associated overwhelmingly with French missionaries in Vanuatu) such as *lames* 'mass' from *la messe* and *per* 'priest' from *père*; or terminology associated with fine cuisine and restaurant dining such as *lae* 'garlic' from *l'ail*, *pima* 'chilli' from *piment*, and *gato* 'cake' from *gateau*. Nouns from French are often incorporated into Bislama with the preceding definite article *le* or *la* attached as an inseparable part of the noun itself as initial *le-* or *la-*.

However, other meanings seem to be fairly unpredictably expressed by means of words of French or English origin. It is difficult, for example, to see why the children's game of tag should be referred to in Bislama as *lelu* (from French *le loup*) rather than by a word of English origin, or why some playing cards are referred to by words of French origin (*las* 'ace' from *l'ace*, *pik* 'spades' from *pique*) while others are referred to by words of English origin (*daemen* 'diamonds', *hat* 'hearts'). There are also a substantial number of synonymous pairs involving words of both English and French origin (*ariko* from French *haricot* and *bin* 'bean', *pistas* from French *pistache* and *pinat* 'peanut', *lapul* from French *l'ampoule* and *glob* 'light globe'). In some cases, both words can be used interchangeably, while in other cases individual speakers may prefer words of either English or French origin.

The bulk of Bislama words, however, are clearly of English origin. In some cases, either the form or the meaning of a word—or both—in English has been substantially changed in Bislama. We therefore find examples such as *purumbut* 'step on' (from *put 'im foot*), *kolta* 'bitumen' (from *coal tar*), *solmit* 'slut' (from *salt meat*). In some cases, the English word from which a modern Bislama word is derived may no longer be current in English, such as *giaman* 'tell lies' (from nineteenth-century Australian English *gammon*) or *masket* 'rifle' (from the old-fashioned word *musket*).

In some cases, while the English source of a Bislama word may be immediately obvious, the meaning may have been substantially modified under direct influence from patterns in local languages. Thus, Bislama *han* comes from English *hand*, but it translates as both 'arm' and 'hand', following the widespread use of the same term for these two meanings in local languages. In the same way, Bislama *mama* covers the meaning of both 'biological mother' and 'mother's sister', as local languages usually use the same word for both.

There is also a substantial component of the vocabulary involving words that are ultimately based on English sources yet which have been compounded creatively to express meanings without having to resort to directly borrowing from English. Local flora and fauna often came to be referred to by means of such compounds, for example *blufis* 'parrotfish' from *blu* 'blue' plus *fis* 'fish'; *redwud* 'Java cedar' from *red* 'red' plus *wud* 'wood'. Items of cultural importance for which English does not provide ready-made words may also be expressed in the same way, such as *bolpig* 'uncastrated boar' from *bol* 'testicle' and *pig* 'pig'. Unfamiliar technology can also be expressed in this way too. During the Second World War, when Ni-Vanuatu were first exposed to grenades through their association with American troups, they coined their own term, *hanbom* from *han* 'hand/arm' plus *bom* 'bomb'. This is very much an ongoing process in Bislama, and the same pattern has been used for the more recent coinage *roketbom* 'missile' from *roket* 'rocket' plus *bom* 'bomb'.

1.5 Varieties of Bislama

No language on earth is used in the same way by all of its speakers in all situations in which it is used. Languages can vary according to the geographical origin of their speakers, much as we find with speakers of English from New Zealand and from Canada. Languages can also differ according to the level of education or the wealth of their speakers. A wealthy and better-educated New Zealander, for example, will often speak English in ways that are different from a less well-off and lesser-educated person. Any individual will use a language slightly differently depending on whether they are speaking with a close friend or a family member as distinct from a stranger. And we also use different forms of our language depending on whether we are speaking or writing the language.

This grammar does not set out to reflect *all* varieties of Bislama. Apart from anything else, no comprehensive study has ever been carried out on the full range of variation to be found in Bislama. I have set out to concentrate on the kind of lan-

CHAPTER 1

guage that is spoken in everyday informal contexts by people of fairly average levels of education. My focus has not been exclusively on urban Bislama or on rural Bislama, and I have tried to draw on varieties encountered in a broad cross-section of the community. At the same time, however, I discuss quite a number of points where we do find variation between different groups of speakers. A fully detailed grammar of a language would set out to find out precisely what kinds of speakers use which particular variants, and what sorts of considerations determine the kinds of choices that people make.

Some features of Bislama are known to be restricted to people of particular geographical origins (or to people of particular local language backgrounds). For example, people from Malakula commonly use the word *salsal* to refer to a temporary shelter, *navas* to refer to a wild yam, and *malmal* for 'naked', but these are words that are not used at all on many other islands. Regionally distributed features are more likely to represent items of vocabulary rather than grammatical features, though grammatical patterns can be distributed geographically as well. For instance, while most speakers of Bislama would say something like *Hemia sop we bambae mi wasem plet long hem* 'That is the detergent that I will wash the dishes with', it is common for people on Malakula to say instead *Hemia sop we bambae mi wasem long plet*.

People's Bislama also varies to some extent on whether they have grown up in a rural village or in town. Many people comment that there is a major difference between "island Bislama" and "town Bislama", with urban Bislama showing much more evidence of influence from English (and French). In reality, the major difference is probably more due to differences of educational level. Lesser-educated town-dwellers share more in common with lesser-educated rural speakers than with their better-educated urban counterparts in terms of the kinds of pronunciation, grammar, and vocabulary that they use.

Bislama that is spoken informally is often quite different from varieties that are used in more formal contexts, and written Bislama is often quite different from the way that people speak. If an expatriate were to learn to speak Bislama only from a hymnbook, from articles in a newspaper, or from news broadcasts on the radio, he or she would end up sounding like a very strange conversationalist indeed. There are some features of Bislama that almost never appear in print yet which are extremely common in the colloquial spoken language. This grammar sets out to make people aware, for example, that *save* 'know', *stap* 'stay' and *long* 'on, in, at' are very often pronounced rapidly in informal speech as *sae*, *sta*, and *lo* respectively, even though they are seldom written that way.

In some cases, I have made observations about correlations between the use of particular grammatical patterns and different kinds of social considerations. However, this is an area in which a great deal more research needs to be done before we can offer more definitive statements about what kinds of people make use of which particular grammatical patterns. To provide this kind of detailed information would call for a major study by a sociolinguist—or a team of sociolinguists—which would require large amounts of funding and probably many years to conduct. That kind of study is beyond my own level of funding, dedication—and even interest—so we will have to wait to see if somebody else is able to fill in these gaps in our knowledge.

1.6 What Kind of Grammar is This?

There is no single way to write a grammar of any language. The particular kind of grammar that is written is going to depend largely on what kind of person is expected to be reading it. It would be necessary to write one kind of grammar for an audience of academic linguists, and another quite different sort of grammar for expatriates attempting to learn Bislama. A different kind of grammar yet again would be required for an intended readership of well-educated adult Ni-Vanuatu wanting to learn something about Bislama, and still another kind of grammar for people involved in writing, editing, and translating into Bislama from English or French.

In fact, even a volume aimed just at academic linguists would have to make particular kinds of choices, potentially leaving some readers less than fully satisfied. Some might argue that a grammar should represent a quantitative variationist study of different patterns based on a carefully assembled corpus of data, with all examples derived from actual usage. Others might argue that speaker intuitions about what represents "real" Bislama and what does not should be the basis of the grammar, with examples possibly being made up to illustrate points.

The title that I have chosen —*Bislama Reference Grammar*—says something about the kind of grammar that I have set out to write. The inclusion of the term "reference" in the title means that this is intended to be a grammar book that a wide variety of people may want to actually *refer* to when they want to know something about the grammar of the language. This is intended to differentiate this grammar from the kind of account that I might have written specifically for an audience of academic linguists. Academic linguists make regular use of specialist grammatical terminology that I have been very cautious about using in this book. Where I do use such terminology, it is because it has been unavoidable, and I make sure that I give detailed explanations of what a term means first, along with any relevant examples.

In saying that this grammar is not aimed primarily at an academic readership, I have little doubt, however, that linguists will be able to make good use of it. It should therefore be of interest to pidgin and creole specialists in general, and to those interested in Melanesian Pidgin and other Pacific pidgins and creoles in particular. Linguists conducting research on the local languages of Vanuatu should also find value in this volume, and possibly even linguists with broader interests in linguistic universals and issues relating to linguistic theory.

In keeping with my goal of writing for a general rather than an academic audience, I have for the most part avoided making detailed in-text reference to the views of other writers, particularly on those points where there is common agreement about particular patterns. Even where there are competing views, I have avoided the temptation to load the text with evaluations of these different perspectives because of the distraction that I fear this may bring to non-specialists. However, where there are contentious issues—and there certainly are some—or where there are additional sources that I suspect an academic readership may be particularly interested in, this will be indicated separately in footnotes rather than being incorporated within the main text. I have also provided an appendix that briefly describes the content of some of the main contributions that have been made in the study of Bislama grammar to date.

CHAPTER 1

This grammar is not based on a finite corpus of taped material that has been transcribed, quantified, analysed, and then stored in an archive. Nor is it based on formal elicitation derived from translations from English, or contrived sentences that have been presented to speakers by a linguist for grammaticality judgements. Rather, this grammar is based on more than a quarter of a century of personal observation of the spontaneous use of Bislama in natural conversational contexts. This has proved to be ample time to be exposed to a wide range of patterns from which appropriate examples of usage can be drawn.

It is also necessary to decide how prescriptive an approach one should adopt when writing a grammar. Ideally, a grammar of a language should reflect how speakers of that language actually use the language in their daily lives, and it should avoid telling people how they should—or should not—speak where genuine choices are available. However, no grammar of any language to date has succeeded in completely accurately describing *every* aspect of the use of any language. For purely practical reasons, written grammars always have to be somewhat selective about what patterns to include and what patterns to ignore. I have certainly not tried to describe Bislama as if it were a monolithic entity that is subject to a single set of unbending rules. People familiar with grammars of English or French may find this approach difficult to accept because such grammars typically filter out anything but the formal written varieties. Such grammars, for example, will generally allow for *want to* but not contracted forms such as *wanna*, even though most speakers of English systematically use both alternatives in different situations. However, while such an approach is common in written grammars, the resulting linguistic descriptions are arguably the poorer for it. I have chosen to reflect Bislama as a living and flexible language rather than one that is stiff and unresponsive to people's social needs.

2: PRONUNCIATION AND SPELLING

While this volume sets out primarily to describe the grammar of Bislama, it is important also to have an idea of how words are pronounced and how these pronunciations are represented in writing. This chapter provides some of the relevant background to the pronunciation and spelling of words in Bislama.

In discussing pronunciation, it is unfortunately not possible to completely avoid the use of specialist phonetic terminology, as well as phonetic symbols. Readers who find such terminology and symbolism unfamiliar or distracting may therefore wish to skip substantial portions of this chapter.

2.1 Consonants

Most people use the consonants *b, d, f, g, h, j, k, l, m, n, ng, p, r, s, t, v, w,* and *y*. These are set out in Table 2.1. To those who are familiar with phonetics, the sounds are displayed according to their places and manners of articulation.

The consonant *r* is phonetically normally an alveolar flap in Bislama, though an occasional trilled articulation can be heard as a free variant. Some speakers produce instead a retroflex flap for this sound. However, people often poke fun at speakers with this pronunciation, which is associated particularly with people from parts of Pentecost and from northern Efate. Particular note should be made of the fact that the consonant *j* is generally pronounced as a voiceless post-alveolar grooved affricate, i.e., [tʃ], though there is often a slightly fronted pronunciation, i.e., [ts].

Words from local languages tend to be adopted into Bislama with minimal change in shape, as the consonant system of Bislama very closely resembles consonant systems that are widely distributed in Vanuatu languages. Given that the number of consonants in Bislama is substantially reduced in comparison to what we find in English and French, a number of contrasts are systematically merged in Bislama. In particular, the contrasts between /s/, /z/, /ʃ/, and /ʒ/ in English and French are typically merged as /s/, for example *saen* 'sign', *saen* 'shine'; *dresa* 'dresser', *resa* 'razor'; *sondam* '(French) policeman' from *gendarme*. The contrasts in English between /t/ and /θ/ on the one hand and /d/ and /ð/ on the other are merged as *t* and *d* respectively in Bislama, for example *tin* 'tin' and *tingting* 'think'; *dis* 'dish' and *disfala* 'this'. The contrast between voiced and voiceless segments is lost word-finally in Bislama, with only voiceless segments being found. Thus, the contrast between English *dog* and *dock* results in a homophonous form that could be written as *dok* in Bislama meaning 'dog' and 'warehouse' (from *dock*) in Bislama. (Despite the widespread lack of contrast, as pointed out in §2.4, this difference is generally maintained in the spelling system for Bislama.)

The ways in which the consonantal contrasts of English and French are reflected in Bislama can be captured in the form of a series of general statements, as represented in Table 2.2. In these examples, a word from English, with the corresponding Bislama word, is presented first. A word originating from French

CHAPTER 2

Table 2.1 Consonants

	Labial	Alveolar	Palatal	Velar	Glottal
Voiceless stops	*p*	*t*	*j*	*k*	
Voiced stops	*b*	*d*		*g*	
Nasals	*m*	*n*		*ng*	
Voiced fricatives	*v*				
Voiceless fricatives	*f*	*s*			*h*
Rhotic		*r*			
Lateral		*l*			
Glides	*w*		*y*		

Table 2.2 English and French Consonants in Bislama

Eng.	Fr.	Bis.	Source word	Bislama word	
p	p	*p*	*place*	*ples*	'place'
			pistolet	*pistole*	'pistol'
t	t	*t*	*tongue*	*tang*	'tongue'
			tricot	*triko*	'sweater'
k	k	*k*	*kitchen*	*kijin*	'cook-house'
			claquettes	*klaket*	'flip-flops'
b	b	*b*	*book*	*buk*	'book'
			barre à mine	*baramin*	'crowbar'
d	d	*d*	*dog*	*dok*	'dog'
			dame-jeanne	*damsen*	'flagon (of wine)'
g	g	*g*	*girl*	*gel*	'girl'
			délégué	*delege*	'district agent'
m	m	*m*	*man*	*man*	'man'
			manivelle	*manivel*	'starting handle'
n	n	*n*	*knife*	*naef*	'knife'
			cochonet	*kosone*	'jack (in bowls)'
—	-aɲ	-*aen*	*champagne*	*sompaen*	'champagne'
ŋ	—	*ng*	*tongue*	*tang*	'tongue'
l	l	*l*	*light*	*laet*	'light'
			le loup	*lelu*	'tag (game)'
rV	rV	*rV*	*right*	*raet*	'right'
			robinet	*robine*	'tap'
—	Vr	*Vr*	*arrière*	*arier*	'reverse'
h	—	*h*	*house*	*haos*	'house'
f	f	*f*	*friend*	*fren*	'friend'
			profiter	*profite*	'take advantage'
v	v	*v*	*vinegar*	*viniga*	'vinegar'
			avocat	*avoka*	'lawyer'
θ	—	*t*	*think + think*	*tingting*	'think'
ð-	—	*d-*	*this + fellow*	*disfala*	'this'

PRONUNCIATION AND SPELLING

Eng.	Fr.	Bis.	Source word	Bislama word	
-ð-	—	-t-	brother	brata	'brother'
s	s	s	saucepan	sospen	'saucepan'
			lycée	lise	'secondary school'
z	z	s	razor	resa	'razor'
			mazout	masut	'diesel'
ʃ	ʃ	s	ship	sip	'ship'
			bouchon	busong	'cork, stopper'
ʒ	ʒ	s	decision	disisen	'decision'
			gendarme	sondam	'French police'
tʃ	tʃ	j	church	jej	'church'
			caoutchouc	kaojuk	'rubber'
dʒ	—	j	judge	jaj	'judge'
w	w	w	west	wes	'west'
			oui + oui	wiwi	'French (arch.)'
j-	—	y-	you	yu	'you (sg.)'
—	-Vj	-Ve	l'ail	lae	'garlic'

and its corresponding Bislama form are presented below this. A dash in the chart indicates the absence of that sound in either English or French. In Table 2.2, commonly used phonetic symbols are used to refer to the pronunciations of words in English and French.

It is generally possible to predict by the correspondences in Table 2.2 the shape of a newly incorporated word of English or French in Bislama. However, these correspondences are not completely regular. Thus, while English /tʃ/ generally corresponds to Bislama *j* as in *jej* 'church', in *sakem* 'throw (from *chuck*)' it idiosyncratically appears as *s*. Also, while English /r/ is the primary source of Bislama *r*, there are some forms in which *r* between vowels unexpectedly derives from other sounds, as in *griri* 'greedy' (where /-d-/ appears as *r* rather than *d*), *wora* 'water' (where /-t-/ appears as *r* rather than *t*), and *narafala* (where /-ð-/ appears as *r* rather than *t*). However, not all instances of the sounds /-d-/, /-t-/, and /-ð-/ in English between vowels correspond to *r* in Bislama, as evidenced by forms such as *hotel* 'hotel' and *lada* 'ladder', which are never pronounced as **horel* or **lara*. (Keep in mind that a word marked by an asterisk does not exist in Bislama.)

Although many speakers of Bislama operate with the consonants in Table 2.1, there is individual (and regional) variation in the maintenance of these contrasts with particular words. No comprehensive regional study of phonological diversity has been carried out on Bislama, nor has there been any empirically based quantitative study of variation in pronunciation. Different pronunciations are often also related in informal comment to the language of education—whether one is considered to be 'anglophone' or 'francophone'—though such claims have once again not been subjected to detailed empirical scrutiny.

It is difficult to make general statements that cover all possibilities regarding variation from this basic pattern of consonant contrasts in Bislama given that there is such a wide range of possibilities. A number of observations can be

CHAPTER 2

made about the loss of contrasts between consonants from the basic set, though some additional mergers may be encountered among small groups of speakers, or in particular sets of vocabulary items with some speakers:

- The contrast between voiced and voiceless stops is not always made by all speakers of Bislama. For some speakers, there appears to be little contrast at all, with only voiceless unaspirated stops being found in all environments. It is far more common, however, for a contrast to be made, but only with some words, and for the contrast to be lost with other words. That is, while some speakers may contrast *dok* 'dog' and *tok* 'talk' on the one hand and *draem* 'dry (something)' and *traem* 'try' on the other, other speakers may merge *dok* and *tok* as *tok* while maintaining a contrast between *draem* and *traem*. Others, however, may merge *draem* and *traem* as *traem* while contrasting *dok* and *tok*. If any merger takes place, it is most likely to be in the direction of the voiceless stops rather than the voiced stops.

- The contrast between *v* and *f* is also not very stable. The consonant *v* is not nearly as widely distributed as *f* in any case, and some speakers lose the contrast entirely, having only *f*. This results in alternations in pronunciation such as *Vanuatu* and *Fanuatu* 'Vanuatu' between different speakers, and sometimes even within the speech of a single individual.

- For many—perhaps even most—speakers, the contrast between voiced and voiceless stops is lost in homorganic nasal-stop clusters, this time in the direction of phonetically voiced segments. Thus, while for some speakers there may be a voicing difference in pairs such as *stampa* 'base (from English *stump*)' and *namba* 'number', most people pronounce *stamba* and *namba* respectively.

- A small minority of speakers may go further than this in tending to lose the contrast between voiced and voiceless stops *and* homorganic nasal-stop clusters, pronouncing all as voiced prenasalized stops, particularly in word-initial position. Thus, a word that will be pronounced by many as *pima* 'chili' may occasionally be encountered as *mbima*.

- There is also a substantial amount of unpredictable alternation between voiceless bilabial stops and the corresponding voiceless fricatives, with *pik* 'pig' and *faea* 'fire' occasionally being heard as *fik* and *paea* respectively. Such variation with some words is often viewed negatively, but it may be quite widespread with other words.

- There is a tendency for the distinction between *j* and *s* to be lost in the direction of *s* among some speakers, or with some words, resulting in alternations such as *jalus* and *salus* 'jealous' and *jenis* and *senis* 'change'.

- The consonant *h* is often lost. This is especially frequent between vowels with pronunciations such as *biaen* 'behind' being far more common than *bihaen*. However, *h* can also be lost at the beginnings of words, resulting in alternations such as *harem* and *arem* 'hear' and *hem* and *em* 'he, she, it'.

PRONUNCIATION AND SPELLING

Some hypercorrective insertion of *h* with words beginning with vowels also results in occasional alternations such as *ae* and *hae* for 'eye'.

Given that for the vast majority of speakers, Bislama is acquired after learning to speak a local language, these kinds of mergers, as might be expected, correspond to some extent to the distribution of features in local languages. It has been noted, for example, that in a number of languages from the island of Malakula, while there is a prenasalized /ᵐb/ phoneme, there is no corresponding plain voiceless /p/. It is precisely with speakers of such languages that more widely distributed pronunciations such as *pima* 'chili' in Bislama are encountered as *mbima*. The retroflex flap articulation of *r* that was mentioned earlier also appears to correspond closely to the distribution of retroflex rather than alveolar flap pronunciations of /r/ in local languages.

Having pointed to a correlation between variations from the basic pattern described above and differences between local vernacular sound systems, we should exercise some caution in assuming that *all* regional variation in the pronunciation of consonants shares this explanation. Not only do we have an inadequate knowledge of the distribution of variants to this basic sound system of Bislama, but we have a detailed knowledge of the sound systems of only a small number of local languages (Lynch and Crowley 2001: 14–19).

Even with the limited knowledge that we do have, it is not difficult to point to features of the sound systems of local languages that are *not* carried over into Bislama. In the Paamese language, for instance, there is a loss of contrast between /p/ and /v/ at the ends of words, with free variation between stop and fricative pronunciations. However, this does not seem to correspond to any observable tendency among speakers of Paamese to lose their contrast between *p* and *v* or *f* at the ends of words when they are speaking Bislama. Thus, people continue to pronounce *kap* 'cup' and *laf* 'laugh' and do not say **kaf* or **lap*.

2.2 Vowels

Bislama is also usually described as having the five vowels set out in Table 2.3. There is a tendency for rural or lesser-educated speakers from Tanna to phonetically lengthen stressed vowels in words of two syllables, reducing unstressed vowels in closed final syllables to a high central vowel [ɨ], resulting in variation in the pronunciation of *apol* 'apple' as [ápol] and [á:pɨl]. Such pronunciations, however, are strongly stigmatized, and it is certainly not the case that all people from Tanna speak like this.

As we find with the consonants, there are some fairly regular correspondences between the vowels in Bislama words and the vowels of the English or French words from which they are derived. Given that Bislama has only five vowels, there is, of course, substantial reduction in the number of vowel contrasts from English and French. English /a:/, /æ/, /ʌ/, and word-final /ə/, for example, regularly correspond to just *a* in Bislama, for example *mak* 'mark', *man* 'man', *tang* 'tongue', *mobeta* 'better'. New words are constantly being incorporated into Bislama from English and French by generalizing on these kinds of correspondences.

CHAPTER 2

Table 2.3 Vowels

	Front	Back
High	i	u
Mid	e	o
Low		a

This is not to say that the vowels of Bislama words can be unfailingly predicted from the shape of an English word. There are substantial numbers of unpredictable shifts such as *talem* 'tell' (rather than **telem*), *rusum* 'roast' (rather than **rosem*), and *flaek* 'flag' (rather than **flak*). The most regular patterns of correspondence between English and French vowels on the one hand and Bislama vowels on the other are set out in Table 2.4. Non-final schwa tends to be variably reflected in Bislama as *o*, *e*, or *a*, for example *ofisol*, *ofisel*, or *ofisal* 'official'. The long central vowel /ɜ:/ is also unpredictably reflected, sometimes appearing as *o*, for example *bon* 'burnt' and *wok* 'work', and sometimes as *a*, for example *tanem* 'turn'. In other cases, we find an even wider variety of competing reflexes in Bislama, for example *set*, *sat*, or *sot* 'shirt'.

Words in English containing diphthongs beginning with mid vowels and ending in a high vowel of the same value for frontness and roundedness tend to be somewhat variable in Bislama. Word-medially, such diphthongs are generally reflected simply as mid vowels with no off-glide. Thus, English /oʊ/ and /eɪ/ correspond to Bislama *o* and *e*, as in examples such as *post* and *cake*, which appear in Bislama as *pos* and *kek* respectively.

At the end of a word, there is more variation between pure vowels and diphthongs, with /oʊ/ sometimes appearing as *o* and sometimes as *ou*, and /eɪ/ appearing as either *e* or *ei*. Thus, *blow* corresponds to either *blo* or *blou*, while *day* corresponds to either *de* or *dei*. Word-final diphthongs beginning with a mid vowel and having a schwa off-glide— corresponding to post-vocalic /r/ in rhotic dialects of English—also vary in their Bislama reflexes between a simple mid vowel and sequences of *ea* and *oa*. Thus, English *more* and *where* correspond variably to Bislama *mo* or *moa* and *we* and *wea* respectively.

2.3 Expanded Sound Systems

In addition to the mergers described in §2.1 and §2.2, some speakers operate with somewhat expanded consonant and vowel inventories, at least for some words. This corresponds to some extent to a higher command of English or French. With such speakers, we find that not only is the contrast between *s* and *j* maintained, but there is a tendency also to distinguish between /s/ and /ʃ/. Thus, we may encounter different pronunciations in *sup* 'soup' and *shus* 'shoe'.

There is also a tendency among better-educated speakers for the contrast between long (or diphthongized) and short (or pure) vowels in English—which is ordinarily lost in Bislama—to be maintained in Bislama in the form of a tense-

Table 2.4 English and French Vowels in Bislama

Eng.	Fr.	Bis.	Source word	Bislama word	
i	i	i	leak	lik	'leak'
			pique	pik	'spades (in cards)'
I	I	i	lick + him	likim	'lick'
			quitte-à-quitte	kitkit	'draw (in sport)'
—	e	e	pétanque	petong	'French game of bowls'
ɛ	ɛ	e	leg	lek	'foot, leg'
			arrière	arier	'reverse'
æ	—	a	man	man	'man'
a	a	a	mark	mak	'mark'
			mazout	masut	'diesel'
ʌ	—	a	tongue	tang	'tongue'
-ə	—	-a	together	tugeta	'together'
o	o	o	sauce	sos	'sauce'
			gateau	gato	'cake'
ɔ	ɔ	o	salt	sol	'salt'
			pilote	pilot	'tug boat'
u	u	u	boot	but	'boot'
			bouton	butong	'button'
ʊ	ʊ	u	cook	kuk	'cook'
			gourmand	gurmong	'sucker (of plant)'
—	y	i	putain	piteng	'whore'
—	ʏ	i	butteur	biter	'shooting marble'
—	ø	e	monsieur	misie	'sir'
—	œ	e	butteur	biter	'shooting marble'
—	ɛ̃	eng	putain	piteng	'whore'
—	ɔ̃	ong	bouchon	busong	'cork, stopper'
—	ã	ong	croissant	kwasong	'croissant'

lax distinction. Thus, while *set* for many speakers is the pronunciation for 'shirt' and 'agreed' (from *set*), some speakers contrast /sɛt/ 'agreed' and /set/ 'shirt'. This, however, has not been noted in any other account of the language and study by a well-trained phonetician is needed to verify (or disconfirm) this.

Another area of uncertainty involves the relationship between vowel quality and contrastive voicing with stops at the ends of words that come from English. It was indicated in §2.1 that there is no contrast in Bislama at the ends of words between *p, t,* and *k* on the one hand and *b, d,* and *g* on the other, with contrasting pairs of words in English ending up the same in Bislama. Although I am fairly confident that there is indeed no final voicing contrast in Bislama for many speakers, it may be worth investigating the possibility that there may be some kind of surviving contrast in the nature of the preceding vowel. My suspicion is that there may be some kind of acoustically detectable laxness in the vowel of forms such as *pik* 'pig' in contrast to a more tense vowel in *pik* 'plectrum (from *pick*)'. (Of course, such tests would need to be carefully constructed to ensure that they are based on natural speech without any possibility of contamination from spelling pronunciations.)

2.4 Spelling

Bislama is now a written language with a spelling system that has been developing for several decades. The written form first developed with the greater use of the language for religious purposes, with the first translations of the gospels being produced in the 1970s, leading up to a translation of the entire Old and New Testaments by 1997. The 1970s also saw a rise of political consciousness associated with a sense of nationalism. The struggle for independence—along with political debates and campaigns afterwards—were conducted largely through the medium of both spoken and written Bislama.

In general, Bislama spelling reflects the way that words are pronounced. This means that there are no 'silent letters', so a word such as 'night' is simply spelled *naet*. The same sound is written in the same way wherever it occurs, so words like *centimetre*, *send*, and *scent*, which are spelt differently at the beginnings of the words in English, all begin with *s* in Bislama, i.e., *sentimeta*, *sendem*, *senda*. Bislama does not make use of double letters to represent single sounds, so *Tanna* is spelled exactly as it is pronounced, i.e., *Tana*.

The rules of Bislama spelling state, basically, that each distinct contrasting sound should be consistently represented by means of the written symbol that is used to represent that sound in most Vanuatu vernacular spelling systems. This means that letters should be pronounced according to vernacular phonetic values rather than English or French values. The letter *u*, for example, should be pronounced rather like in English *put*, and never as in *but*.

Sequences of letters should normally be interpreted as representing two separate sounds in Bislama. Thus, for example, the letters *oa* are used to represent the sound *o* followed by the sound *a*, as in *loa* 'law'. This sequence of letters is never used in Bislama to spell a word like *boat* in English, for which the correct spelling is *o*, as in *bot*. Similarly, the letters *sh* in Bislama represent a sequence of *s* followed by *h*, as in the Bislama name of the odd group of people who run on Mondays to get healthy and then drink copious amounts of beer afterwards to get unhealthy, i.e., the *hashas* 'Hash House Harriers'.

Aspects of Bislama spelling worthy of special note are discussed below.

- *Ng*

The single sound at the end of the word *rong* 'wrong' is written with two letters in Bislama, i.e., *n* followed by *g*. This is so even when there is a following *k* or *g*. This means that these sequences of sounds are written *ngk* and *ngg* respectively, as in *angka* 'anchor' (not *anka) and *fingga* 'finger' (not *finga). In the small number of words where the single sound *ng* and a sequence of separate *n* followed by *g* are distinguished in Bislama pronunciation, forms containing the latter sequence of sounds are written as two words. Since *nk* can never be am-

PRONUNCIATION AND SPELLING

biguous, there is no need to write forms containing this sequence as two words. Thus: *han gan* (and not *hangan*) 'pistol', *hankaf* (and not *han kaf*) 'handcuff', *angka* (and not *anka*) 'anchor' and *hanga* 'coathanger'.

- *J*

This letter is used to represent a sound that is pronounced very much like the sound that is represented as *ch* in English words like *church*. Although this is the same letter that is used to represent the sound in English words like *jury*, it is not pronounced this way in Bislama.

- *Diphthongs*

These are sequences of vowels that appear together in a word. The diphthongs in English words such as *high*, *boy*, and *town* are written as *ae*, *oe*, and *ao* respecttively in Bislama, i.e., *hae* 'high', *boe* 'boy', and *taon* 'town'. Other diphthongs are written in Bislama exactly as they are pronounced, for example: *pua* 'poor', *loa* 'law', *jea* 'chair'.

- *Y/i* and *w/u*

There is a contrast in Bislama between the vowels *i* and *u* on the one hand, and the sounds *y* and *w* on the other. In accordance with widespread usage, words containing the sounds *w* and *y* are spelled as follows:

(a) The sound *w* is spelled as *w* everywhere except between the vowels *a*, when the sequence is spelled as *aoa*. Thus: *twin* 'twin', *swet* 'sweat', *gwava* 'guava', *kwestin* 'question', *wota* 'water', *rikwes* 'request', *waswe* 'how come', *tawi* 'brother-in-law', *namemiwa* 'kind of tree', *awe* 'wow', *awo* 'wow', *tawel* 'towel', *flaoa* 'flower', *paoa* 'power'.

(b) The sound *y* is spelled as *y* at the beginning of a word, and in the middle of a word when there is a break between two meaningful parts of the same word. Thus: *yad* 'yard', *stokyad* 'stockyard', *fulyia* 'whole year', *yes* 'yes', *yis* 'yeast', *yosi* 'exclamation of surprise', *yu* 'you'.

Although the word meaning 'this, that, here' is clearly pronounced as *ya*, the spelling that was endorsed in a previously published dictionary (Crowley 1995) seems to have had no impact in tempting people away from their determination to write this overwhelmingly as *ia*. I have therefore been advised to bow to popular preference in using spellings such as *ia* for /ya/ 'this, that, there', *yia ia* for /yia ya/ 'this year', and *ia ia* for /ia ya/ 'this ear'.

(c) The sound *y* occurring between either of the vowels *o* and *a* and the vowel *a* is spelled as *e*. Between *u* and *a*, it is spelled as *i*. Between any other vowels, the sound *y* is spelled as *y*. Thus: *faea* 'fire', *loea* 'lawyer', *baeawin* 'sail with wind', *huia* 'who', *naoia* 'now', *saye* 'that's it', *soyu* 'soy sauce', *siyu* 'cheerio'.

(d) After consonants, the sound *y* is spelled as *i*. Thus: *tangkiu* 'thanks', *arier* 'reverse', *giaman* 'lie', *piano* 'piano', *storian* 'chat', *babakiu* 'barbecue', *nius* 'news', *tamiok* 'small axe'.

CHAPTER 2

- *B, d* and *g*

Although the general rule states that words are spelled as they are pronounced, a major exception involves words that end in the sounds *p, t,* and *k*. When such words derive from English words that end in *b, d,* and *g* respectively, they are spelled in Bislama according to the pronunciation of the final sound in English, not as they are pronounced in Bislama. Thus, although the final sounds in the words *dog* 'dog' and *dok* 'storage shed (from *dock*)' in Bislama are often the same, they are spelled differently, according to how they are written and pronounced in English.

The question of what we should write as single words, and what should be written as separate words is an issue where English speakers find it difficult to apply consistent rules even in their own language. People write *paper mill* as two words, *sawdust* as one word, and are probably fairly inconsistent when it comes to writing *woodchip, wood-chip,* or *wood chip*. People seem to find it just as difficult to decide where to write one word and where to write two words in Bislama.

A working group on Bislama spelling that met prior to the preparation of the Bislama dictionary (Crowley 1995, 2003) decided to recognize word boundaries on the basis of the pronunciations of words. Thus, when a form is stressed as if it were a single word, then it has been written as a single word. Thus, the word *redae* 'conjunctivitis' is stressed only on the first syllable, i.e., *rédae*. When there is separate stress on each word, the form is written as two words. Thus, because *mán bús* 'inland person' is pronounced with two stressed syllables, so this is written as two separate words.

This means that all NOUN + MODIFIER (§4.1.2.2) constructions, whether the modifier is itself a noun or a member of another part of speech, are written as separate words, for example *man bus* 'inland person', *bubu woman* 'grandmother', *masket led* 'air rifle', *kava tudei* 'kava with two-day effect', *yam ariko* 'yam with tiny tubers', *haos timba* 'timber house'. MODIFIER + NOUN constructions are sometimes treated as constituting two separate words and sometimes behave as a single unit of pronunciation. When the modifier is a noun and both nouns occur frequently in the language independently of the compound construction, both are written as separate words, for example: *bensin mases* 'cigarette lighter', *aelan dres* 'Mother Hubbard dress', *wota taro* 'swamp taro', *stamba tingting* 'basic idea, motivation'. Also, in the few instances in which nouns are derived from a verb as the preceding modifier, the compound is treated as two separate words: *bagaremap nat* 'pipe wrench', *jenis ki* 'change of key (in tune)', *daeva glas* 'diving goggles'.

However, when the modifier is a noun that occurs only rarely on its own, or not at all, apart from in that particular compound construction, then the two are treated as a single unit. For example, while *man* 'man', *yad* 'yard', and *sus* 'shoe' are freely occurring forms, *stok* does not occur independently in Bislama, so we use spellings such as *stokman* 'stockman', *stokyad* 'stockyard', and *stoksus* 'riding boots'.

When a freely occurring independent noun behaves as a modifier in a compound but it only enters into a single compound construction, or at best only a very small number of compounds, these compounds are also written as single words, especially when the meaning of the compound is relatively opaque. For example, while *ti* 'tea', *ketel* 'kettle', *spun* 'spoon', and *tawel* 'towel' are all widely used words, *ti* only enters into compounds with these few words, so these particular compounds are treated as single units. Thus: *tiketel* 'kettle', *titawel* 'tea towel, hand towel', *tispun* 'teaspoon'.

Compounds involving an initial adjective (§4.1.2.1) are generally written as single words, for example: *bigbol* 'coconut crab', *redae* 'conjunctivitis', *blutin* 'Fosters beer', *grinsnel* 'green snail'. Compounds involving ADJECTIVE + NOUN constructions can often alternate between a single word structure such as that just illustrated and a genuinely phrasal construction in which the adjective carries the suffix *-fala* (§4.3.3.2). Although the same roots are involved and the same meanings are being expressed, the first construction must be written as a single word and the second as two words. Thus: *sotleg* but *sotfala leg* 'emerald dove' and *bigmane* but *bigfala mane* 'expensive'.

There are other words that, on the basis of their pronunciation, behave as single words or as phrasal units in violation of the generalizations just made. Such words are spelled in this grammar as they are pronounced. In many such cases, the unpredictability in Bislama mirrors similar unpredictability in English.

Having said that the Bislama spelling system closely reflects the pronunciation, it should be pointed out that there are some very common pronunciations that are seldom—if ever—reflected in the established spelling system. In particular, there are some very commonly used words with established spellings that represent pronunciations that are not at all common in ordinary casual speech. The prepositions *long* and *blong* (§6.1.5.1), for example, are not commonly pronounced with the final consonant that is represented in the spelling, being far more commonly pronounced as *lo* and *blo* (and sometimes even as *l-* and *bl-* before a following word that begins with a vowel). We therefore commonly find pronunciations such as *lo graon* 'to the ground' and *l-aelan* 'to the island' for what would normally be written as *long graon* and *long aelan* respectively. For the most part, such colloquial pronunciations are not represented in this grammar unless particular attention is drawn to that feature.

2.5 Stress

The position of stress within a word in Bislama is not predictable. Although this means that stress is phonemically contrastive, I am not aware of any pair of words that differ in meaning solely in the position of stress. However, there are cases in which stress appears in different syllables in words of very similar shape. Thus, it appears on the first syllable in *nákamal* 'meeting house', *kálabus* 'prison', and *píkinini* 'child', on the second syllable in *Novémba* 'November' and *nabángga* 'banyan', and on the third syllable in *demonstrésen* 'demonstration' and *nakatámbol* 'dragon plum'. There are even words in which stress appears on the final syllable, for example *lakaskád* 'waterfall'. Although stress is not predictable in Bislama, there is no tradition in the writing system for marking the

CHAPTER 2

position of stress. Stress will not be marked in this grammar, and it is likewise not marked in the dictionary (Crowley 1995, 2003).

To talk about stress, it makes more sense to subdivide the vocabulary of Bislama into words deriving from different languages, treating words of English, French, and Melanesian origin separately. Words originating from local vernaculars behave overwhelmingly according to the pattern that we find in local languages whereby stress is systematically applied to the second-last syllable. This would therefore account for the position of stress in words such as *nabángga* 'banyan' and *nakatámbol* 'dragon plum' presented above. Following widespread patterns in local languages, a diphthong in a final closed syllable is also stressed in Bislama, for example *namaláos* '*Garuga floribunda*'. Where two syllables appear to have been reduplicated, the second element does not count for syllable-counting purposes, which means that stress is found on the second-last syllable of the unreduplicated root, for example *napíripiri* 'sea hearse tree', *nadúledule* 'red silkwood'.

However, the generalizations just presented represent strong tendencies in Bislama rather than exceptionless rules, and some forms originating from local languages exhibit stress patterns that vary from these. We sometimes find that the initial syllable is stressed, for example *námarae* 'eel', *nákamal* 'meeting house', while in other cases the second syllable is stressed, for example *namáriu* 'acacia tree'. These irregularities are unlikely to derive from divergent patterns in the substrate languages, so there seem to have been genuine unpredictable shifts of stress in these cases.

Words of French origin are often found with stress on the final syllable, which is what we would expect given the stress pattern of the source language. Thus: *glasóng* 'ice block' (from *glaçon*), *restoróng* 'restaurant', *limonád* 'soft drink (from *limonade*)', *maratóng* 'running shoes (from *marathon*)'. However, final stress in words of French origin is again not universal, and we do find forms in which stress has shifted, for example *kálsong* '(mens') underpants' (from *caleçon*), *pétong* 'French bowls (from *pétanque*)', *bóndi* 'criminal (from *bandit*)'.

Finally, we have the English-derived bulk of the lexicon. Unlike French and the Melanesian languages, stress is not predictable in English, and this unpredictability is mirrored in words of English origin in Bislama. For the most part, the position of stress in Bislama can be deduced directly from the position of stress in English, for example *pálamen* 'parliament', *haebískis* 'hibiscus', *demonstrésen* 'demonstration'.

2.6 Intonation

One feature of Bislama that is immediately obvious to even a new learner of the language is its intonation pattern. Not only is the primary intonation pattern of Bislama clearly different from that of English and the various local languages, but it is also quite distinct from what we find in closely related Solomons Pijin and Papua New Guinea Tok Pisin.

PRONUNCIATION AND SPELLING

In talking about Bislama intonation, it is difficult to go beyond vague impressions, but there does seem to be a substantially greater rise toward the end of a statement, followed by a much more noticeable drop immediately afterwards at the end of the statement than we find in any of the other varieties of Melanesian Pidgin, as well as English. This gives the impression that Bislama has something of a "sing-song" intonation. My only suggestion for a possible explanation is that it may reflect a French source, though this is little more than an impression that would need to be verified by checking against a detailed empirical study of the intonation patterns of both languages.

2.7 Syllables

It is only occasionally necessary to refer to syllables when writing a grammar of a language. In the section above on stress (§2.5), for example, there was specific reference to which syllable in a word receives stress. However, that discussion only requires readers to intuitively recognize how many syllables a particular word has, which is usually not all that difficult.

In the discussion of reduplication (§4.1.3, §5.1.1), however, it is necessary for people to have an appreciation not just of how many syllables a word contains, but where the boundaries are between those syllables. This is an area in which people's intuitions are sometimes less forthcoming, so this short section has been included to enable people to break words up into their constituent syllables.

We can recognize the number of syllables in a word by counting the number of vowels, though sequences *ae*, *ao*, *oe*, *ei*, and *ou* should be counted as single syllables. All other vowel sequence—*ie*, *ia*, *io*, *iu*, *ea*, *oa*, *ua*, *uo*—should be counted as two separate syllables. Where a word consists of only vowels and single consonants, we can separate syllables after each vowel. Words of this type can therefore be broken up into syllables as follows: *ti-ja* 'teacher', *sa-ve* 'know', *pi-lo* 'pillow', *a-bu* 'grandparent', *ka-kae* 'eat', *Jae-na* 'China', *gi-a* 'gear', *he-a* 'hair', *pu-a* 'poor'.

If a word ends in a consonant (or more than one consonant), then those consonants will belong to the final syllable of the word. Similarly, if a word begins with two (or more) consonants, then the entire sequence of consonants will belong to the first syllable of the word. Thus: *sti-a* 'steering wheel', *tro-ka* 'trochus', *sto-a* 'shop', *stu-den* 'student', *tra-bol* 'trouble'. Sometimes, a word may be pronounced by different speakers—or by the same speaker on different occasions—as either a single syllable or as two syllables. We therefore find alternations between *boks* and *bo-kis* 'box', *siks* and *si-kis* 'six', *fens* and *fe-nis* 'fence', *smol* and *si-mol* 'small', and *blu* and *bu-lu* 'blue'.

Where two (or more) consonants come together in the middle of the word, the rule for dividing the word into syllables requires us to assign the first of the consonants to the preceding syllable, while the second consonant (along with any others) belongs to the following syllable. Thus: *kap-ten* 'captain', *mas-ket* 'rifle', *han-kaf* 'handcuff', *mi-nis-ta* 'minister', *kol-ta* 'asphalt, bitumen, tarseal', *stam-ba* 'base', *stren-ja* 'stranger', *as-prin* 'aspirin', *dis-trik* 'district'.

3: PARTS OF SPEECH

Knowing how to speak a language obviously involves much more than just knowing how to pronounce the words and what they mean. If this were the case, a language learner would only need a dictionary and a pronunciation guide and nothing else. Of course, it is also necessary to know the very complicated set of rules that allow people to put meaningful elements together to make up words, and to then put those words together to make up sentences, and even longer utterances. These rules are referred to as the grammar of the language, and it is the nature of these grammatical rules of Bislama that is the subject of the major part of this book.

In any language, there will be many words that behave in the same sorts of ways as each other, while other words may behave in quite different ways. In a dictionary of Bislama, there are thousands of separate words, but these certainly do not all behave in exactly the same ways. This means that things that we can do with some words cannot be done with other words. For instance, the words *kuk* 'cook' and *sut* 'shoot' behave alike in that they can be followed by a form that we can write as *-um*, to give us the words *kukum* and *sutum*, as in sentences such as the following:

Hem i stap kuk long kijin.
'(S)he is cooking in the kitchen.'

Hem i kukum taro long sospen.
'(S)he cooked taro in the saucepan.'

However, not all words in Bislama can have this *-um* added to them. While there is a word *mun* 'moon' and a word *bul* 'ball (in French bowls)', there are no corresponding words **munum* and **bulum* in Bislama (keeping in mind the fact that asterisks are used to indicate unacceptable Bislama).

This means that in a grammar of Bislama, *kuk* and *sut* belong to the same part of speech, and that the words *mun* and *bul* belong to another part of speech. In this chapter, I will talk about the various parts of speech into which all of the words in Bislama must be divided, along with the various aspects of their behavior which allow us to recognize each part of speech.

English and French have been studied and described for centuries, and a whole set of specialist terminology has developed so that we can describe the grammars of these languages. In English, for example, we have words such as 'noun', 'verb', 'article', 'adjective', 'comparative', 'superlative', 'adverb', 'transitive verb', 'intransitive verb', 'pronoun', and so on. If we want to say why it is better to write *he sings well* than *he sings good*, we can use this sort of terminology to do this. The explanation in this case would involve the statement that a verb (for example *sings*) in acceptable written English should be modified by an adverb (for example *well*) rather than an adjective (for example *good*).

Because we already have an established set of grammatical terminology in English, it is very tempting to say that we should simply adopt these terms wholesale when talking about Bislama. To some extent, it is possible to use words like 'noun' and 'verb', which we already need to talk about English, to talk about Bislama also. However, it is important to be careful in the use of some such

PARTS OF SPEECH

terminology. For one thing, what is a noun in one language is not going to automatically be a noun in another language. For another thing, there are some words in Bislama that behave in ways that are quite different to anything that we find in English. We will therefore need to come up with completely new names for parts of speech in such cases.

This short chapter is not intended to represent a fully detailed description of the various parts of speech that are found in Bislama, as the detailed behavior of words is basically what the rest of this volume is all about. However, it is going to be inevitable from time to time to use words like 'noun', 'pronoun', or 'intransitive verb', and this chapter is intended to provide definitions of the main terms that will be needed for the rest of this grammar to be understood.

In setting out the various parts of speech that we need to set up for Bislama, I have also provided in this chapter some of the main tests by which each of these parts of speech can be recognized. I have deliberately avoided defining nouns, for example, as "naming words" as is often done in traditional grammars of English. Because we are on such slippery ground when defining parts of speech solely on the basis of meanings in this way, I will be defining parts of speech strictly according to the behavior that words exhibit in Bislama speech. A noun in Bislama, for example, can be defined by the fact that (among other things) it can be preceded by the number marker *ol*. This is why we say that *haos* 'house' is a noun, but *karem* 'take' is not a noun, as we can say *ol haos* 'houses', but we cannot say **ol karem*.

3.1 Nouns

Any word that can function as a verbal subject or object (§6.1.1) or which can appear after a preposition (§6.1.5), and which can be preceded by an adjective (§4.3.3) is described as a noun in Bislama. The following examples, therefore, indicate that the word *raes* 'rice' is a noun (with the word class in question in each case being presented in bold type):

Raes *i dan finis.*
'The rice is cooked.'

Hem i kakae **raes.**
'He ate the rice.'

Kakros i haed long **raes.**
'The cockroach is hiding in the rice.'

Mi no stap kakae doti **raes.**
'I don't eat dirty rice.'

The particular distinguishing characteristics of nouns in Bislama are:

(a) A noun can precede the words *i* or *oli* in a sentence:

Solwora *i raf tumas long taem blong hariken.*
'The sea was very rough during the cyclone.'

CHAPTER 3

*Plante **man** oli singsing long skul.*
'Many people sang in church.'

(b) Nouns can precede the word *ia* 'this, that', as in the following example:

*Mi no wantem luk **boe** ia from we hem i jikim mi oltaem.*
'I do not want to see that boy because he always pokes fun at me.'

(c) Nouns can appear before the word *blong* 'of', for example:

*Hemia nao **haos** blong mi.*
'That is my house.'

(d) Nouns can follow the words *wan* and *ol* or *olgeta*, as in the following:

*Wan **man** i stap dring kava long nakamal.*
'One man is drinking kava in the kava bar.'

*Mi les long harem noes blong ol **man** we oli drong.*
'I'm sick of hearing the noise of drunk men.'

(e) Nouns can follow any word that ends in the suffix *-fala*. This includes words such as *gudfala* 'good', *sotfala* 'short', *niufala* 'new', *narafala* 'other', *samfala* 'some', *sikisfala* 'six', *strongfala* 'strong, hard', and so on. Thus:

*Gudfala **man** ia hem i tekem wan strongfala **tamiok**.*
'That good man took a strong axe.'

*Hem i nilim wan narafala **kapa** long haos blong hem.*
'He nailed another roofing sheet on his house.'

(f) Nouns can follow any of the following words: *long* 'to, in, at, from', *blong* 'of, for', *olsem* 'like', *from* 'because of' and *wetem* 'with', for example:

*Bae mi karem sam vatu long **bang**.*
'I will get some money from the bank.'

*Hemia trak blong **woman** ia.*
'This is that woman's car.'

*Saki i singsing olsem **Fred Maedola** nomo ia.*
'Saki sings just like Fred Maedola.'

*Mi kam long Vila from kos long saed blong **Franis**.*
'I came to Vila because of a French course.'

*Mi nomo slip wetem **abu** blong mi.*
'I don't live with my grandmother any more.'

3.2 Pronouns

There is a set of pronouns in Bislama that make reference to person (first, second and third), number (singular, dual, trial, and plural) and inclusive vs. exclusive (§4.2). These include forms such as those in bold below:

Olgeta oli singsing.
'They were singing.'

Bae yumi go.
'We (including you) will go.'

Hem i stap slip wetem tufala.
'He lives with the two of them.'

Pronouns in Bislama in many respects behave like the nouns that were described in §3.1. However, they differ from nouns in that they cannot be preceded by words carrying the suffix *-fala*. Thus, contrast the following:

Mi luk wan strongfala dog.
'I saw a strong dog.'

Mi luk wan strongfala **hem.*

Pronouns differ also in their meanings from nouns. The noun *puskat* in Bislama always refers to a particular kind of animal (i.e., a 'cat'). However, the pronoun *yu* changes in its meaning depending on who it is being used to refer to. When I say *yu* to Tamata, it means 'Tamata', but when I say *yu* to Clarence, it refers instead to somebody quite different, i.e., 'Clarence'. This means that there is not a constant thing to which a pronoun such as *yu* refers.

3.3 Prepositions

Prepositions are those words that precede a noun in a sentence and which indicate a range of functions played in the sentence by the thing referred to by the noun phrase (§6.1.5). There is only a small class of such words in Bislama, of which the most frequently occurring are *long* 'to, in, at, on, from', *blong* 'of, for', *olsem* 'like', *wetem* 'with', and *from* 'because of'.

Many meanings expressed by prepositions in English are expressed not by prepositions in Bislama but by a different kind of word. These differ from prepositions in that they can be used on their own without a following noun phrase. A word that behaves like this in Bislama is *antap* 'above', as in the following:

Pijin i flae antap.
'The bird is flying above.'

When there is a following noun phrase associated with words like this, the adverb and the noun must be linked by the genuine preposition *long*. Thus:

*Pijin i flae **antap long** haos.*
'The bird is flying above the house.'

Above in English is a preposition, as can be seen from the translation of the example just presented, as it appears before a noun phrase in *above the house*. In Bislama, however, a word such as *antap* is not a preposition because we cannot say things like the following:

Pijin i flae **antap haos.*

CHAPTER 3

3.4 Verbs

Verbs constitute a very large part of speech in Bislama. A verb is any word in Bislama that behaves in the following ways:

(a) It follows *i* or *oli* in a sentence:

Olgeta man oli resis long kenu.
'The men raced in the canoes.'

Tamata i talem long mi se bae mi no kam.
'Tamata told me that I should not come.'

(b) It follows words such as *save* 'be able to', *bin* 'past tense', *mas* 'must', *stap* 'continuous, habitual' or *wantem* 'want to':

Taso i no save dring fo sel kava.
'Taso cannot drink four shells of kava.'

Huia i bin kam long ofis blong mi long moning?
'Who came to my office in the morning?'

Arei i mas nilim niufala kapa long haos blong hem.
'Arei has to nail the new roofing iron on his house.'

Lino i wantem mared, be olfala blong hem i no letem.
'Lino wants to get married but his father won't let him.'

Selina i stap toktok wetem bos blong hem.
'Selina is talking with her boss.'

There is a small subset of verbs in Bislama that can function as both transitive and intransitive verbs with no change in form. Such verbs include *dring* 'drink', *kakae* 'eat', *welkam* 'welcome', and *singaot* 'call', for example:

Man ia i stap singaot.
'The man is calling.'

Man ia i stap singaot mi.
'The man is calling me.'

Most verbs, however, need to be specified as either intransitive verbs or transitive verbs. An intransitive verb is one that cannot take a following object, while a transitive verb can be followed by an object noun phrase. Most—but, as I have just indicated, not all—transitive verbs in Bislama carry a suffix that has the basic shape -*Vm* (§5.1.3.1).

3.5 Noun Modifiers

The class of noun modifiers includes all forms that can be used to further restrict the reference of a noun. Noun modifiers in Bislama fall into two main subclasses: number markers and adjectives.

3.5.1 Number Markers

Number markers, such as *ol* 'plural', *olgeta* 'all', *wan(fala)* 'one', *sam(fala)* 'some', *plante* 'many', *tumas* 'too many', *staka* 'many', *evri* 'every, each', *hamas* 'how much, how many', *smol* 'few', and *lelebet* 'quite a few' can all precede a noun. Thus:

Mi luk plante man long futbol.
'I saw many people at the football.'

I gat smol man nomo long nakamal.
'There were only a few people at the kava bar.'

Numerals constitute a particular subset of number markers, sharing the characteristic that they can appear before a noun. In this respect, then, they behave like adjectives. Numerals differ from adjectives in that they can also occur after pronouns, for example:

I gat sikis man long haos.
'There are six people at home.'

Mifala sikis i stap long haos.
'Six of us were at home.'

3.5.2 Adjectives

Adjectives are words that can be used either as a modifier to a noun—in which case we say that the adjective is being used attributively—or they can be used on their own in a sentence after the words *i* or *oli*—in which case we say that they are being used predicatively. When occurring before a noun, adjectives fall into two major subcategories (§4.3.3):

- those that can be marked with the suffix *-fala*, for example *big*, *bigfala* 'big';
- those that cannot be marked with the suffix *-fala*, for example *rabis* 'terrible', but not **rabisfala*.

This subcategorization of adjectives is a part of the grammar of Bislama in which there is considerable variability between speakers. For some speakers, for example, *smol* 'little' falls into the first subclass, while for others it belongs in the second subclass, which means that some speakers will use this adjective with the suffix *-fala*, while others never do.

Most adjectives in Bislama precede the noun, though there is a handful of adjectives, including *nogud* 'bad', *nating* 'unimportant, inconsequential', and *olbaot* 'ordinary, plain', which follow the noun (§4.3.4). Thus, compare the two different kinds of adjectives in the following examples:

Hem i wan gudfala man.
'He is a good man.'

Hem i wan man nogud.
'He is a bad man.'

CHAPTER 3

Some adjectives appear much more frequently in predicative rather than attributive constructions. In such cases, it is often difficult to decide whether we are dealing with an adjective or an intransitive verb. However, there are some specific tests to determine whether a word is an adjective or a verb. One test involves the behavior of the form *stap*, as this varies in meaning depending on whether the following word is an adjective or an intransitive verb. When *stap* precedes an intransitive verb, it expresses the meaning of either 'continuous' or 'habitual' (§5.3.5.4), whereas before an adjective it can only mean 'habitual'. Thus, compare the following in which *toktok* 'talk' is a verb and *sik* is an adjective:

Sarah i stap toktok.
'Sarah is talking.'

Sarah i stap sik.
'Sarah is (habitually) sick.'

Another distinguishing characteristic of predicative adjectives is that they can be followed by *i stap* whereas genuine intransitive verbs cannot (§7.1.1). Compare, therefore, the following:

Olgeta lif i wetwet i stap from ren.
'The leaves are wet from the rain.'

Trak blong mi i rosta i stap long yad.
'My car is rusty in the yard.'

Maket long Vila i fasfas i stap evri taem nomo.
'The market in Vila is always busy.'

Naef blong mi i sap i stap.
'My knife is sharp.'

However, *i stap* cannot be used in this way with intransitive verbs, as in the following:

Masin ia i wok long moning nomo.
**Masin ia i wok i stap long moning nomo.*
'That machine just works in the morning.'

Paul i spaeglas long wok.
**Paul i spaeglas i stap long wok.*
'Paul avoids work.'

Finally, predicative adjectives can be preceded by *kam* to express the meaning of 'become' or 'get' (§5.3.5.9) whereas intransitive verbs cannot. Thus:

Vila i stap kam bisi sapos i gat turisbot i stap long wof.
'Vila gets busy if there is a tour ship at the wharf.'

3.6 Adverbs

Many adjectives can be used not only as noun modifiers but they can also be used as adverbs to qualify verbs (§6.1.6). Usually an adjective that functions as an adverb appears in its basic root form, i.e., without the suffix *-fala* if it is one of those adjectives that accept this suffix. Thus:

Man ia i toktok krangki.
'That man is talking crazily.'

Hem i katem strong faeawud blong mifala.
'He vigorously chopped our firewood.'

Notice that the word *strong* can be replaced with the same word carrying the suffix *-fala* in the last example. However, it must then be interpreted rather differently, as *strongfala* is an adjective whereas *strong* is an adverb. Thus:

Hem i katem strongfala faeawud blong mifala.
'He chopped our hard firewood.'

There are some other words appearing in a variety of positions in a sentence that cannot be defined with reference to any other part of speech. This includes forms such as *tu* 'also', *nomo* 'only', *bakegen* 'again', *oltaem* 'always', *samwe* 'approximately'. We can include within this category a number of forms that refer to time, for example *naoia* 'now', *yestedei* 'yesterday', *tumoro* 'tomorrow', *fastaem* 'before', and so on. Such words can also be regarded as kinds of adverbs.

3.7 Other Modifiers

There are a number of small sets of other modifiers that typically occur immediately before or after members of particular parts of speech. A modifier that appears before other words is referred to as a premodifier, whereas a modifier that appears after a word is a postmodifier. We need to distinguish between the following subcategories of modifiers:

- *Noun premodifiers*: occurring at the beginning of a noun phrase before the noun and any accompanying adjectives (§4.3.1). These typically function as quantifiers, for example *ol yangfala man* 'young men', *evri haos* 'every house'.

- *Pronoun postmodifiers*: occuring after pronouns and generally functioning as quantifiers (§4.3.2), for example *olgeta plante* 'lots of them', *tufala evriwan* 'both of them'.

- *Preverbal auxiliaries*: occurring between the predicate markers *i* and *oli* and the verb itself (§5.3.5), for example *Kalo i stap toktok* 'Kalo is talking', *Olgeta oli mas kam* 'They must come', and so on.

- *Verb postmodifiers*: occurring after a verb (§5.3.6), for example *Kalo i kam finis* 'Kalo has come', *Marita i toktok yet* 'Marita is still talking'. There is only a handful of words in Bislama that behave in this way.

3.8 Interrogatives

Such forms do not constitute a clearly definable word class but they are labeled together in this way because they all share the common characteristic that they can occur in isolation as minimal utterances that seek information (§6.2.2). Such items include simple forms such as *wanem* 'what' and *hu* 'who', as well as phrasal interrogatives such as *wanem taem* 'when', *olsem wanem* 'how', and *from wanem* 'why'.

3.9 Complex Sentence Markers

Under this heading is included a mixed collection of forms that are used to link short sentences together into longer and more complex sentences (§7.3.2). Words of this type include *mo* 'and', *be* 'but', *blong* 'in order to', *taem* 'when', *from* 'because', and *sapos* 'if'. Sentences illustrating the use of such words include:

Mi kam be yu no stap.
'I came but you were not in.'

Mi stap slip taem yu kam.
'I was sleeping when you came.'

Bae mi wet long yu sapos yu talem long mi.
'I will wait for you if you tell me to.'

3.10 Interjections and Vocatives

Vocatives are words that are intonationally and structurally set off from an utterance and which are used as terms of address to people, for example *tawi!* 'brother-in-law', *brat!* 'bro'. (Note that such expressions are written here with exclamation marks to represent the special way that they can be used as utterances in their own right.) Many nouns and noun phrases with nominal modifiers can also be used either jokingly or as insults, such as *bigbel!* 'big belly' or *stingas!* 'stinking arse'. A particular feature of vocatives is the fact that they can be followed by *o*, pronounced with a high intonation and lengthened vowel, when calling to someone, for example:

Kalteri o!
'Hey, Kalteri!'

Interjections are words that are normally used in isolation and which are not incorporated into the grammatical structures of sentences. For the most part, they express emotions experienced by the speaker and range in strength from the innocuous such as *olala!*, *awe!*, *kwan!*, and *maewad!* to the rather more forceful (or obscene). In this section, many interjections are not translated. This is because it is often nearly impossible to find a close equivalent to a Bislama interjection in English. Other interjections vary in strength according to the speaker's awareness of a word's source. Thus, for some people *longkile!* is as mild as 'oh my goodness' in English, while for others it is regarded as being as crude as the French *l'enculé!* from which it is derived (and which corresponds very roughly to *up yours!* in English).

Some interjections have stronger and weaker forms, where the stronger form is clearly obscene or blasphemous and the corresponding weaker interjection represents a partial imitation of the sound of the stronger form. Table 3.1 sets out a number of pairs of interjections which differ in this way.

Many words used as interjections in Bislama also have particular intonation patterns that are difficult to represent in written form. The Bislama expression *yu fakem!*, for example, has to come at exactly the right moment in a conversation and with exactly the right intonation to function effectively as a conversational retort.

3.11 Words with Several Functions

While the discussion in the preceding sections sets out various tests for part-of-speech membership for any word, there is one feature of Bislama grammar that frequently makes the task of assigning a word to a particular part of speech rather difficult. Let us take the word *skul* as an example. Look at the following sentences:

Codrington i go long wan narafala skul.
'Codrington goes to a different school.'

Codrington i stap skul long saed blong Franis.
'Codrington goes to a French school.'

The word *skul* appears in both of these sentences, but it performs quite different kinds of functions in each case.

In the first example, *skul* clearly functions as a noun. We can say this because it behaves in ways that are typical of nouns (§3.1), including the following:

(a) It appears before *i*:

Wan niufala skul i stap finis long Ambae.
'There is a new school on Ambae.'

(b) It appears before *ia*:

Skul ia nao, Codrington i stap go long hem.
'That is the school that Codrington goes to.'

Pikinini blong mi i no wantem go long skul ia.
'My child doesn't want to go to that school.'

(c) It appears before the word *blong*:

Codrington hem i go long skul blong olgeta blong Anglikan.
'Codrington goes to an Anglican school.'

(d) It appears after words like *ol* and *olgeta* or *wan*:

Wan skul i stap klosap long ples blong hem.
'There is a school near his village.'

Ol REO oli stap visitim olgeta skul olbaot.
'The Regional Education Officers visit schools everywhere.'

(e) It follows words that end in *-fala*:

Malapoa College hem i wan gudfala skul.
'Malapoa College is a good school.'

CHAPTER 3

Table 3.1 Stronger and Weaker Interjections

Stronger Interjections	Weaker Interjections
Basted!	*Basting!*
Kan!	*Kastom!*, *Kas!*
Fak!	*Fas!*, *Pak!*
Kok!	*Kos!*
Bagrit!	*Bagraes!*
God!	*Gos!*

(f) It follows any of the prepositions:

Haos ia i luk olsem skul stret.
'This building looks just like a school.'

Buk blong mi i stap long skul naoia.
'My book is at the school now.'

Despite all of these clear indications that *skul* is a noun, there are other sentences that indicate that the same word can also function as a verb. Look at the following:

Codrington i stap skul long saed blong Franis.
'Codrington goes to a French school.'

In this sentence, *skul* follows the word *stap* 'continuous, habitual' and this fact indicates that *skul* is behaving like a verb (§3.4) rather than a noun. There are many other facts about the behavior of *skul* which indicate that it can also be considered to be a verb:

(a) It can follow *i* or *oli*:

Ol pikinini oli skul long Inglis.
'The children go to an English school.'

(b) It can come after words like *save*, *bin*, *mas*, and *wantem*:

Mi bin skul long Vureas bifo.
'I went to Vureas school before.'

Yumi evriwan i mas skul gud blong kasem save.
'We must all study well to learn.'

Boe blong Taso i no wantem skul long aelan.
'Taso's son doesn't want to go to school at home.'

This means that we must treat the word *skul* as effectively representing two different words that just happen to have the same shape. On the one hand we have the word *skul* that functions as a noun meaning 'school', while on the other we have the word *skul* that functions as a verb with the related meaning of 'study' or 'go to school'.

There are many other words in Bislama that behave like *skul* in that they have more than one function in this way. In fact, sometimes a word of the same shape may even appear more than once in the same sentence with different functions. Look at the behavior of *stap* in the following sentence:

*Johnnah i **stap stap** long Namburu.*
'Johnnah lives in Namburu.'

The first instance of *stap*—expressing the meaning of 'habitual'—belongs to the part of speech referred to above as preverbal auxiliaries under the general heading of "other modifiers" (§5.3.5.4), along with other auxiliaries such as *mas* 'must', *bin* 'past tense', and so on that could be substituted for it. The second instance of *stap*—expressing the meaning of 'live'—is an intransitive verb (§3.4), which means that it could be substituted by any other verb, such as *wok* 'work', *prea* 'pray', or *kakae* 'eat'. The sentence above, therefore, follows exactly the same pattern as:

*Johnnah i **mas wok** long Namburu.*
'Johnnah has to work at Namburu.'

Another example of the same thing involves the word *finis* in the following sentence:

*Japta ia i **finis finis**.*
'This chapter is already finished.'

The first *finis* here functions as an intransitive verb meaning 'finish' and could be replaced by any other intransitive verb such as *gohed* 'continue'. The second *finis* is a post-verbal modifier meaning 'completive, already', which means that it could be replaced by another word from the same part of speech, such as *yet* 'still'. Thus, the following sentence reflects exactly the same structure:

*Japta ia i **gohed yet**.*
'This chapter is still continuing.'

For words to belong to more than one part of speech is not uncommon in the world's languages, and even in English a word like *hammer* can function as a noun (*John bought a new hammer*) as well as a verb (*John hammered the nail*). However, it is especially common in Bislama for words to belong in more than one part of speech and sometimes the boundary between adjective and noun and intransitive verb becomes particularly blurred. A form such as *bigbel* can therefore function as a noun, as in:

***Bigbel** ia i stap wokbaot i kam.*
'The person with the paunch is walking over.'

On the other hand, in the following, it looks like an adjective:

***Bigbel** man ia i stap wokbaot i kam.*
'The pot-bellied man is walking over.'

Finally, in the following, it looks like an intransitive verb:

CHAPTER 3

*Mi no wantem **bigbel** olsem man ia.*
'I do not want to have a paunch like that man.'

In such cases, it is often difficult to decide which of these functions represents the "basic" function of the word.

4: NOUNS AND NOUN PHRASES

Noun phrases are elements within a sentence that can consist of just a noun or a pronoun and nothing else. The words in bold in the following examples represent noun phrases:

Mi stap kakae tinfis.
'I eat tinned fish.'

Dog i kakae yu?
'Did the dog bite you?'

Nouns and pronouns can be associated with a variety of preceding or following words within more complex noun phrases. In the following examples, therefore, the material that is set out in bold represents a variety of different kinds of such noun phrases:

Olfala man ia i stap swim neked.
'That old man is bathing naked.'

Plante woman oli stap luk yumi evriwan.
'Lots of women are looking at all of us.'

Mifala plante i les long olgeta man blong faet.
'Many of us are sick and tired of men who fight.'

In this chapter, the internal make-up of nouns and pronouns is described, along with the rules describing the behavior of the different kinds of words that can accompany nouns or pronouns within more complex noun phrases.

4.1 Nouns

This section comprises a detailed discussion of the internal make-up of nouns, leading to a discussion of how nouns combine with words from other parts of speech to make up more complex noun phrases (§4.3).

4.1.1 Simple and Complex Nouns

Many words in Bislama consist of just a single meaningful part. Thus, words like *skul* 'school' and *mases* 'match' in Bislama cannot be broken down into smaller parts with separate meanings of their own. Such nouns can be referred to as simple nouns. Bislama words such as *bigman* 'important person' and *bigwan* 'big one', however, can be broken down into smaller elements, each of which have meanings of their own. We refer to such nouns as complex nouns. The form *bigman* is, of course, derived from the independently occurring words *big* 'big' and *man* 'man'. The word *bigwan* can also be broken down into smaller elements. There is firstly the form *big* 'big', and then there is the ending *-wan* whose function is described in more detail in §4.1.4.1.

Although many words in Bislama are clearly derived from words in English, we must be careful not to assume that just because a word in English can be broken

CHAPTER 4

down into smaller meaningful elements, the same must be true of a corresponding word in Bislama. The word *mases* in Bislama derives from the English word *matches*. The English word here consists of two meaningful parts, the root *match* and the ending *-es* (meaning 'more than one'). However, we cannot divide the word *mases* into **mas* and *-es* in Bislama, because it is not possible to speak of a single *mas*. It is also not possible to add *-es* in Bislama to make other nouns in the language plural. If we want to speak of just a single *match* in Bislama, we must still use the word *mases*, as in the phrase *wan stik mases* 'one match'. Similarly, the ending *-es* is not regularly added to other nouns in Bislama when we want to express the idea that there is more than one thing involved. This means, for example, that from a word such as *haos* 'house', we cannot derive the word **haos-es*. If we want to express that meaning in Bislama, we do so by using the separate plural marker *olgeta* with the word for 'house' remaining unchanged, as in *olgeta haos* 'houses'.

However, there are many other nouns in Bislama that *do* consist of more than one meaningful part. Such smaller elements within words are referred to as *morphemes*. In this section, I will be describing the way in which nouns are made up in Bislama when they consist of more than one morpheme. Complex nouns that are made up of more than one morpheme in Bislama fall into one of three general groupings, depending on whether they are compound nouns, reduplicated nouns or affixed nouns.

4.1.2 Compounding

Many nouns in Bislama are made up of two separate words, each of which can be used on its own with a clearly recognizable meaning of its own. The meaning of the new word that is formed out of these other words, however, is not always directly predictable from the meanings of the individual words. There is a variety of different kinds of compound nouns, depending on the kinds of words that are joined together, and the kinds of relationship that hold between the two compounded elements.

4.1.2.1 Adjective + Noun

Many compounds are made up of an initial element that is an adjective with a following noun. Thus, from the adjective *smol* 'small' and the noun *traoses* 'trousers' we can derive the compound *smol-traoses* 'underpants'. Other examples of the same process include the following: *swit* 'sweet' and *blad* 'blood' give *swit-blad* 'diabetes', *big* 'big' and *ae* 'eye' give *big-ae* 'gecko', *hot* 'hot' and *san* 'sun' give *hot-san* 'direct sun', and *dabol* 'double' and *laet* 'light' give *dabol-laet* 'hazard lights (on car)'.

A common pattern of this type involves the use of adjectives of color to represent a salient feature of the item in question. Thus: *blu* 'blue' and *tin* 'tin' gives *blu-tin* 'Fosters beer' (which comes in a blue can), *waet* 'white' and *bun* 'bone' gives *waet-bun* 'Chinese cabbage with a pale stalk,' and *grin* 'green' and *bun* 'bone' gives *grin-bun* 'Chinese cabbage with a green stalk'. Another pattern is to use the adjective *smol* 'small, little' with a kin term that may be used reciprocally to refer specifically to the younger member of the pair. Thus, while *abu* can mean both 'grandparent' and 'grandchild', to specifically express 'grandchild' it is possible to say *smol-abu*. Similarly, from *anti* 'aunt, niece' we can derive *smol-anti* 'niece'.

4.1.2.2 Noun + Postmodifier

Some compounds involve an initial noun with a following adjectival modifier. There is not a wide range of such constructions. Such compounds are restricted to either of the following patterns:

- The adjective *nogud* 'bad' following a noun indicates something that is morally reprehensible or something that is not to be referred to publicly. For example, from *sik* 'disease' we derive *sik-nogud* 'venereal disease', from *buk* 'book' we get *buk-nogud* 'pornographic book', from *kaset* 'cassette' we get *kaset-nogud* 'pornographic cassette', and from *gras* 'body hair' we get *gras-nogud* 'pubic hair'.

- A noun with a following compounded numeral. Thus, *gato* 'cake' and *eit* 'eight' produce *gato-eit* 'twisted doughnut'. *Namba* 'number' combines with *sikis* 'six' to give *namba-sikis* 'prison cell' (so called because it has four walls and a roof and a floor) and with *faef* 'five' to give *namba-faef* 'sleeping' (referring to the shape of somebody asleep in the fetal position). Note also the combination of *namba* and *haf* 'half', which gives *namba-haf* 'not quite the best', in contrast to *namba-wan* (from *wan* 'one') meaning 'the best'.

4.1.2.3 Verb + Noun

Some compounds are based on an intransitive verb that has been compounded with a following noun. Such compounds are not particularly plentiful, though the following examples illustrate this construction: *giaman* 'lie' and *stori* 'story' give *giaman-stori* 'false report', *stil* 'steal' and *man* 'man' give *stil-man* 'thief, burglar', *ren* 'rent' and *haos* 'house' give *ren-haos* 'rental house', and *daeva* 'dive' and *glas* 'goggles' give *daeva-glas* 'diving goggles'. We occasionally also find sequences of transitive verbs with a following object in such compound constructions. Thus, from *bagaremap* 'ruin' and *nat* 'nut' we find *bagaremap nat* 'pipe wrench' and from *wasem* 'rinse' and *maot* 'mouth' we get *wasem-maot* 'tasty nibbles (for cleansing the mouth after kava)'. Another rare possibility of this general type involves an intransitive rather than a transitive verb with a following noun, for example *jenis* 'change' plus *ki* 'key (of guitar)', which gives *jenis-ki* 'change of key'.

4.1.2.4 Noun + Noun

Many compound nouns consist of two nouns that are joined together. Some examples of this kind of compound are: *turis* 'tourist' and *bot* 'boat' to give *turis-bot* 'cruise ship', *stori* 'storey' and *haos* 'house' to give *stori-haos* 'multi-storey

CHAPTER 4

building', *enjin* 'engine' and *so* 'saw' to give *enjin-so* 'chainsaw'. Compounds of the NOUN + NOUN pattern fall into three different categories. In the examples just presented, the first element of the compound represents a modifier to the second element that represents the head. Thus, a *turis-bot* 'tourist ship' is a kind of *bot* 'bot' that caters to *turis* 'tourist' and a *stori-haos* 'multi-storey building' is a kind of *haos* 'building' that has a number of *stori* 'storey'.

However, in *pin-klos* 'clothes peg' we are dealing with a kind of *pin* 'pin' that is used with *klos* 'clothes' and in *sos-pima* 'chili sauce' we are referring to a particular kind of *sos* 'sauce' that is made of *pima* 'chili'. Comparing these two groups of compounds, we can say that the first group consists of an initial modifier with a following head. In the second group, however, the head comes first and this is followed by the modifier.

There is a third type of NOUN + NOUN compound in Bislama, in which the same meaning can be expressed with the head either at the beginning of the compound or as the second part of the compound. Thus, *kabis* 'cabbage' and *aelan* 'island' can be compounded to give either *kabis-aelan* or *aelan-kabis* '*Abelmoschus manihot*', while *gras* 'grass' and *nil* 'thorn' can give either *gras-nil* or *nil-gras* '*Mimosa pudica*'. Simlarly, *lif* 'leaf' and *ti* 'tea' can be combined as either *lif-ti* or *ti-lif* 'tea leaves'. In some such compounds, there is a clear distinction between a more archaic (or old-fashioned-sounding) HEAD + MODIFIER construction and a more modern-sounding MODIFIER + HEAD construction that is more commonly encountered in spoken Bislama today. Thus, from *bang* 'bank' and *buk* 'book' we commonly encounter the compound *bang-buk* 'passbook', though occasionally the archaic form *buk-bang* may be encountered with the same meaning from an older and less well-educated speaker, especially someone from a rural area.

Similar to these kinds of alternations are examples such as modern *skul-fi* 'school fee' and *bed-sit* 'sheets (of bedding)' corresponding to archaic alternative compounds of the shape *fi-skul* and *sit-bed* respectively. These differ from the examples described above in that while the words *skul* 'school' and *bed* 'bed' are widely used in Bislama, few people use the forms *fi* 'fee' and *sit* 'sheet' as independent forms outside these particular compounds. One possibility is that the forms *fi* and *sit* may have been more widely used in Bislama in the past than at present.

4.1.3 Reduplication

Reduplication is the term that is used to refer to words that are made up by repeating identical material within the word, whether all of the word or just part of the word. There are many nouns in Bislama which, by this definition, appear to be reduplicated in that they contain sequences of identical syllables, for example *laplap* 'pudding', *dakdak* 'duck', *parpar* 'cloth worn around waist', *pispis* 'urine', *tamtam* 'slitgong', and *sipsip* 'sheep'. However, these do not involve reduplication as part of their grammatical make-up because the unreduplicated roots do not occur independently in Bislama. Thus, corresponding to *laplap*, there is no meaningful form **lap*. Some of these seemingly reduplicated forms are clearly derived from unreduplicated forms in English. Bislama *sipsip* corresponds to English *sheep*. However, **sip* is not a meaningful form in Bislama, and this is never used to

NOUNS AND NOUN PHRASES

express the meaning of 'sheep.'[1] This means that we cannot break *sipsip* 'sheep' down into any smaller parts that are meaningful in Bislama today.

In this grammar, there is far more discussion of reduplication as it applies to verbs (§5.1.1) than in this section on nouns. This is because the process of reduplication is not very frequently used in the derivation of new nouns, whereas it is extremely commonly used in the formation of verbs.

When a noun is reduplicated, we repeat the entire root to create a new word rather than just repeating a part of the root (as is typically the case when verbs are reduplicated). The nouns *kaen* 'kind, variety' and *kala* 'color' can be reduplicated to express a multitude of varieties or colors rather than just a single variety or color. Compare, therefore, the following examples involving the plain and reduplicated forms of both of these words:

Mi no save wanem kaen nao bae mi karem.
'I don't know what kind I'll bring.'

Man ia i stap wokem kaen-kaen, mi harem mi sem blong luk hem.
'That man does any kind of thing and I feel embarrassed to see him.'

Mi no laekem kala blong set blong yu.
'I don't like the color of your shirt.'

Mi no laekem ol set we i gat kala-kala olsem ia.
'I don't like shirts with lots of different colors like that.'

The noun *saed* 'side' can also be reduplicated as *saed-saed* to express the meaning 'both sides', as in the following:

Graon blong mi i stap long saed blong reva.
'My land is on the side of the river.'

Graon blong mi i stap long saed-saed.
'My land is on both sides.'

The noun *ren* 'rain' is also sometimes reduplicated to give *ren-ren* 'communal showerhead in village', though this word seems to be commonly used only on Malakula. Apart from these few instances, however, there are no other nouns that are regularly reduplicated to create new nouns.

4.1.4 Affixation

Affixation refers to the addition of material at the ends or beginnings of words to create new words. Affixes at the ends of words are known as suffixes, while affixes at the beginnings of words are known as prefixes. In Bislama, there is one very commonly used suffix involved in the derivation of nouns, and there is one infrequently used prefix.

---

[1] There is, of course, a word *sip* in Bislama meaning 'ship', but this is unrelated to the word *sipsip* 'sheep' and the words *sipsip* 'sheep' and *sip* 'ship' have completely separate histories.

CHAPTER 4

4.1.4.1 The Suffix -*wan*

The suffix -*wan* is added to an adjective to create a noun that expresses a thing that is characterized by the quality expressed in the original adjective. A noun derived by means of the suffix -*wan* must also refer back to something that has already been mentioned, or which the person you are speaking to already knows about. This means that it is not possible to start out a completely new utterance by saying something like the following:

Riliwan i moa gud.
'The real one is better.'

A sentence like this can only be used if somebody has previously mentioned what particular real thing is being referred to, or if it hasn't already been mentioned, then the context in which the person is speaking must make it clear what is being talked about. Thus, in the following, the adjective *rabis* 'terrible' appears in the first sentence in reference to something—in this case, a car—while the derived noun *rabiswan* that appears in the following sentence referring back to the original noun that is modified by that adjective:

Mi pem wan rabis trak. Yes, trak blong yu hem i wan rabiswan.
'I bought a terrible car. Yes, your car is a terrible one.'

Of course, the adjective itself to which -*wan* is attached does not have to appear in the original noun phrase, as long as the context allows the hearer to work out what it refers to. Thus:

Mi pem wan gudfala trak. Nogat, trak blong yu hem i wan rabiswan.
'I bought a good car. No, your car is a terrible one.'

A noun derived by means of the -*wan* suffix normally refers to things rather than people. This means that it would generally only be possible to say:

Brata blong mi hem i wan longfala man, hem i no wan sotfala man.
'My brother is a tall man, he is not a short man.'

We would therefore not expect to hear people saying something like this:

**Brata blong mi hem i wan longfala man, hem i no wan sotwan.*

Occasionally, however, some speakers *do* use -*wan* to derive a noun referring to people, as in the following:

Givim long woman ia, hemia fatfatwan ia.
'Give it to that woman, the fat one.'

This means that we should not regard this rule as one that is absolutely hard and fast, though it does represent a strong tendency.

While -*wan* is normally added to adjectives, we occasionally also find it added to nouns. With MODIFIER + NOUN compound constructions described in §4.1.2.1, the second element can sometimes be replaced by -*wan* when it is clear from the context exactly what noun is being referred to. For instance, the compound *manfaol* 'rooster' can be expressed as *manwan* in a context such as the following:

*Bae yumi kilim wan faol. Bae yumi kilim wijwan? Ating **manwan** ia longwe.*
'Let's kill a chicken. Which one will we kill? Perhaps the rooster over there.'

Because *-wan* more commonly refers to non-humans, it is encountered most on adjectives that are normally not used to describe humans, such as *rostawan* 'rusty one', *jipwan* 'cheap one', or *konkonwan* 'bitter one'. Adjectives such as *jalus* 'jealous', which are nearly always used in association with humans, seldom appear with this suffix. However, any adjective that is freely used with both human and non-human nouns can appear with the suffix *-wan* to derive a noun. Some of those adjectives that are commonly found with the suffix *-wan* include *rabiswan* 'terrible', *hotwan* 'hot', *baravawan* 'real', *difrenwan* 'different, unusual', *dedwan* 'dead', *krukedwan* 'crooked', *heviwan* 'heavy', *draewan* 'dry', *kliawan* 'clear', *kolkolwan* 'cold', *fatfatwan* 'fat', *laefwan* 'alive', *rotenwan* 'rotten', *waelwan* 'wild', *riliwan* 'real', *jipwan* 'cheap', *giamanwan* 'false', *speselwan* 'special', *konkonwan* 'bitter, sour'.

Adjectives with the suffix *-fala* (§4.3.3.2) generally lose this suffix when the suffix *-wan* is added to the adjective to create a noun:

*Mi pem wan longfala rop. Rop blong mi hem i wan **longwan**.*
'I bought a long rope. My rope is a long one.'

However, some younger speakers these days use both suffixes together on the same adjective, with *-fala* preceding *-wan*. People who do this are creating a noun out of an adjective that is associated with *-fala* in its particularizing function (§4.3.3.2). Contrast, therefore, the following examples:

*Mi gat wan **big** haos.*
'I have a big house.'

*Mi gat wan **bigfala** haos.*
'I have a rather big house.'

*Haos blong mi hem i wan **bigwan**.*
'My house is a big one.'

*Haos blong mi hem i wan **bigfalawan**.*
'My house is a rather big one.'

For those who do not use forms such as *bigfalawan*, the meaning in the last example would have to be expressed in a rather different way using an adverb such as *lelebet* 'quite, rather', as in the following:

*Haos blong mi hem i wan **bigwan** lelebet.*
'My house is a rather big one.'

4.1.4.2 The Prefix *eks-*

There is one prefix that is now used fairly commonly to create a new noun out of another noun, and that is *eks-*. This derives a noun that expresses the idea that the thing that the noun refers to used to be something else. This is illustrated by the following examples:

CHAPTER 4

Barak Sope hem i wan eks-praem minista.
'Barak Sope is a former prime minister.'

Taem hariken, sam man oli bin go haed long eks-FOL.
'During the cyclone, some people went and took refuge in the old FOL.'

Man ia hem i eks-Franis polis be naoia hem i wok long VMF.
'That man used to be a French policeman but now he works with the VMF.'

4.1.4.3 Emerging Suffixes?

It is difficult in some cases to decide whether a prefix or suffix should be regarded as a genuine part of the grammar of present-day Bislama or not. I mentioned in §4.1.1, for example, that the plural marker *-es* should not be regarded as a suffix in Bislama. However, younger and better-educated speakers of Bislama are these days increasingly likely to add the suffix *-es* to nouns ending in *s* and *j*, and another variant of this suffix, *-s*, to nouns ending in other sounds when the noun is plural, usually along with the original Bislama preceding plural marker *ol* or *olgeta*. We therefore encounter variation between plurals such as *ol boe* and *ol boe-s* 'boys' and *ol risos* and *ol risos-es* 'resources'.

It could be argued, however, that at this stage this suffix has not become a regular part of the grammar and that its appearance simply represents random influence from English. Certainly, most rural and lesser-educated speakers seldom—if ever—use this suffix. Also, those better-educated speakers in town who do use it certainly do not regularly use it on all nouns. The plural suffix is more likely to appear on what we might call "educated" vocabulary, i.e., words that are less commonly encountered in everyday usage and which are more likely to be learned in school or from books rather than being learned in everyday conversation.

This suffix is also much less likely to be used with words that do not derive from English. It is therefore hard to imagine many people ever saying something like *ol nakamal-s 'meeting houses' or *ol nasiviru-s 'coconut lorys', as most people would only ever say *ol nakamal* and *ol nasiviru* respectively. There are also some words of English origin that are very unlikely to appear with the plural suffix *-(e)s*, particularly those which have undergone more substantial change in shape or meaning from the original English word, or where the source word is one that is seldom used in ordinary spoken English contexts. This would explain why most people are far more likely just to say *ol samting* 'things' than *ol samting-s, or *ol puskat* 'cats' rather than *ol puskat-s.

However, there are other suffixes that are fairly productive in English that are occasionally encountered on Bislama words, sometimes even in cases where the corresponding suffixes would not be used in English. There is, for example, a small number of very common Bislama pairs such as *tij* 'teach' and *tij-a* 'teacher' and *draev-em* 'drive' and *draev-a* 'driver' pointing to the possible existence of the suffix *-a* that derives so-called agent nouns from verbs. Some better-educated people also use this suffix in other words such as *plei-a* 'player' and *wok-a* 'worker' alongside *plei* 'play' and *wok* 'work'. However, the addition of *-a* is by no means a productive pattern in Bislama. An English noun such as *drinker* is regularly expressed in Bislama by means of a construction involving several words

NOUNS AND NOUN PHRASES

such as *man blong dring*, literally 'man of drinking'. We would therefore not expect to hear somebody express this meaning as **dring-a*.

At the same time, however, this pattern cannot be described as completely unproductive in Bislama. There is a handful of derived nouns involving *-a* that have been created by speakers of Bislama. For instance, the agent noun derived from the verb *coach* in English is irregularly unsuffixed, appearing as just *coach*, yet speakers of Bislama commonly use the transitive verb *koj-em* '(to) coach' and the derived noun *koj-a* '(a) coach' to express this meaning. In addition, we find pairs such as the following that are even used by lesser-educated people in rural areas:

flot	'float'	*flot-a*	'(a) float attached to fishing net'[2]
advaes	'advice'	*advaes-a*	'(foreign) adviser'
sek-em	'shake'	*sek-a*	'jinglestick'[3]

For some speakers, in fact, this suffix appears to be spreading as a marker of a general set of agentive and instrumental nouns, being used even on nouns that are arguably not derived primarily from verbs at all, such as *renj-a* 'pipewrench', *mold-a* 'mold (for making cement blocks)'.

There are some other productive suffixes in English that have some kind of semi-productive status in Bislama, particularly among urban and better-educated speakers. I refer in particular to the suffix *-ing* which is occasionally found to derive an abstract noun out of a verb, for example *rid* 'read' and *riding* '(Bible) reading', *tij* 'teach' and *tij-ing* 'teaching'. The Latinate suffix *-ation* of English is also found on a substantial number of Bislama nouns, for example *edukesen* 'education', *demonstresen* 'demonstration'. In many cases, the verbal root from which these forms are derived is seldom used in Bislama, but if enough pairs such as *demonstret* 'demonstrate' and *demonstresen* 'demonstration' enter the language, it is possible that this pattern may become increasingly productive in Bislama, and may eventually even become the basis for new derivations that do not derive directly from English.

4.2 Pronouns

The basic set of pronouns in Bislama is set out in Table 4.1. Some pronouns vary in their shape, as indicated by parentheses. The first person dual inclusive is most commonly encountered as *yumitu*, though *yumitufala* is occasionally used. The third person plural is usually *olgeta*, though some people use the shorter form *ol*. However, *ol* is used only as a verbal object and after a preposition, while *olgeta* can be used in any position. This means that we can expect to hear variation between the following:

---

[2] These are found washed up ashore in Vanuatu from international fishing vessels. Cut in half, they are often used as household dishes.

[3] This refers to a length of stick to which a number of bottletops have been loosely nailed. This is used as a musical instrument by local stringband groups. The jinglestick player shakes a short hand-held jingletstick or bangs a longer jinglestick made out of a broomstick on the ground to produce a rhythmic rattling noise.

CHAPTER 4

Table 4.1 Pronouns

	Singular		Dual	Trial	Plural
1	*mi*	Inclusive	*yumitu(fala)*	*yumitrifala*	*yumi*
		Exclusive	*mitufala*	*mitrifala*	*mifala*
2	*yu*		*yutufala*	*yutrifala*	*yufala*
3	*hem*		*tufala*	*trifala*	*ol(geta)*

Yumitu go!
Yumitufala go!
'Let's go!'

Hemia kakae blong olgeta.
Hemia kakae blong ol.
'That's their food.'

The pronoun system of Bislama marks a radically different set of contrasts to those categories that are expressed in English. Pronouns in Bislama have the same form regardless of whether they appear as the subject or the object of a verb, apart from the distinction between subject *olgeta* and object *ol* in alternation with *olgeta*. Thus, subject pronouns such as *I* and the corresponding object form *me* have the same shape in Bislama, as shown by the following:

Mi harem wan gel.
'I can hear a girl.'

Wan gel i harem mi.
'A girl can hear me.'

There are also no separate possessive pronouns in Bislama, with the pronouns above being used with the possessive marker *blong* (§4.4.1), for example:

Hemia blong mi.
'That's mine.'

The three-way gender distinction in English in the third person singular is not expressed, with Bislama having the gender-neutral pronoun *hem* 'him, her, it'.

The distinction in English between singular and plural has been expanded in Bislama into a four-way distinction between singular (*yu* 'you'), dual (*yutufala* 'you two'), trial (*yutrifala* 'you three'), and plural (*yufala* 'you more than three'). While many people systematically distinguish between these four numbers, it is quite common for the trial forms to be completely abandoned and for people to use the plural forms to refer to three or more.

For a small number of speakers, however, there is only a two-way distinction between singular and plural pronouns, just as we find in English. Such speakers therefore even abandon the dual forms in favor of the plural forms. Whether a speaker will operate with a two-way number distinction (singular vs. plural), a three-way number system (singular vs. dual vs. plural), or a four-way distinction (singular vs. dual vs. trial vs. plural) depends at least in part on what kind of pro-

NOUNS AND NOUN PHRASES

noun system is found in a speaker's local language, and there is considerable local variation on this point.

In the first person non-singular forms, there also is a systematic distinction in Bislama between inclusive and exclusive pronouns. The inclusive forms are used whenever the speaker is including the person (or people) being spoken to, while the exclusive forms are used whenever the person (or people) are being excluded. Thus, for example, when beseeching God in prayer, people will invariably use the pronoun *mifala* 'we (exclusive)' because in addressing God, they are excluding God. On the other hand, if you want to exhort the people you are addressing to do something with you—as we might expect from a campaigning politician, for example—it is necessary to use the pronoun *yumi* 'we (inclusive)'.

Pronouns can also be used in impersonal constructions, corresponding to the use of the impersonal pronoun *one* in some rather formal (or even pompous) varieties of English. One way of avoiding mention of any particular participant in Bislama is to make use of the subjectless predicate construction with the plural predicate marker *oli* (§6.1.1), as in:

Oli stap wokem laplap long haos.
'Pudding is being made at home.'

However, the pronoun *yumi* can sometimes also be used with generic reference. The following, for example, could be said by somebody from another island to somebody from Epi:

Yumi mas lukaot gud olgeta lanwis blong yumi long Epi.
'The languages of Epi should be taken good care of.'

Another way of expressing a similar kind of meaning when speaking very colloquially is to use the noun *man* without any accompanying modifiers. Used in this way, *man* can replace any singular pronoun as long as the context makes it clear whether it is intended to refer to a first, second, or third person form. Thus:

Man i hanggre finis o no yet?
'Are you hungry or not yet?'

Traem no werem klos blong man.
'Please don't wear my clothes.'

The English origin of the forms of the pronouns presented in Table 4.1 should be obvious, i.e., *mi* from *me*, *hem* from *him*, *yumi* from *you* plus *me*, *yufala* from *you* plus *fellows*. Many of the meanings that are expressed, however, are clearly *not* English in origin. Local languages in Vanuatu typically make exactly the same kinds of distinctions that we find in Bislama, so this aspect of the pronoun system is very likely to originate from local language patterns.

It will be obvious from the pronouns in Table 4.1 that there are some recurring similarities between different forms, suggesting that they might be broken down into smaller meaningful parts. Non-singular pronouns often—though by no means always—involve the element *-fala*, obviously deriving from English *fellow(s)*. The dual and trial pronouns all involve *-tu* and *-tri* respectively, which correspond to the numerals *tu* 'two' and *tri* 'three' in Bislama. Thus, it appears that a pronoun such as *yutufala* 'you (dual)' might be broken down *yu-tu-fala*.

CHAPTER 4

However, this kind of breakdown is not regular across all of the pronouns. The form *yumi* 'we (plural inclusive)' is plural but we never find people saying **yumi-fala*. The form *olgeta* (or *ol*) 'they (plural)' is also plural, but it is not derived in any way from the singular form *hem* 'he, she, it', and there is again no plural *-fala* involved. If the rules that I mentioned in the preceding paragraph were to apply systematically, then we would expect people to say **hem-fala* instead of *olgeta* (or *ol*), which they clearly do not.

The number-marking elements *tu-* and *tri-* have special status in that they are the only numerals that have been incorporated into the grammatical make-up of pronouns. No other numeral can be taken as the basis for the creation of new pronouns in this way. A pronoun referring to six individuals, for instance, must be expressed by means of a numeral appearing after one of the plural pronouns. Thus, while we can say *mifala sikis* 'we (exclusive) six', we cannot say **misikisfala*.

In addition to the ordinary pronouns, there are special collective third person pronouns *tugeta* and *trigeta*. These forms are used when specifically referring to two and three participants acting together rather than individually. Thus, compare the following:

Tufala i go.
'The two of them went (but not necessarily together).'

Tugeta i go.
'The two of them went together.'

While *tugeta* is quite commonly used in this way, *trigeta* referring to three participants together is quite rare and is, in fact, regarded as slightly archaic, or even as being a sign of an unsophisticated rural background. Some people, in fact, do not use the forms *tugeta* and *trigeta* at all as pronouns. In order to express the collective meanings captured by these pronouns, such people make use of *tugeta* or *wantaem* 'together' as adverbial modifiers associated with the verb. Note, therefore, the following alternatives:

Trigeta i go.
Trifala i go tugeta.
'The three of them went together.'

Tugeta i go.
Tufala i go wantaem.
'Both of them went together.

Alternatively, *tugeta* or *wantaem* may be used as modifiers after the ordinary pronouns, as in the following:

Trigeta i go.
Trifala tugeta i go.
'The three of them went together.'

Tugeta i go.
Tufala wantaem i go.
'Both of them went together.'

NOUNS AND NOUN PHRASES

The third person demonstrative pronoun *hemia* is commonly used in Bislama in ways that clearly distinguish it from the ordinary third person singular pronoun *hem*. Note the difference in meaning between the following:

Mi no laekem hem.
'I don't like him/her.'

Mi no laekem hemia.
'I don't like that one.'

Hemia has a demonstrative function, pointing directly to something that the person you are talking to can see. For this reason, we can refer to it as a demonstrative pronoun. The following dialogue is possible:

Olsem wanem long braon raes? Hem i no gud tumas.
'How about brown rice? It's not very good.'

Now examine the following exchange:

Wijwan nao i mo gud, waet o braon? Hemia i mo gud, waetwan ia.
'Which is better, white or brown? That one is better, the white one.'

In the first of these two exchanges, the person is asking a general question about rice that is brown without the rice being actually present, and the other person is giving a general answer. However, in the second exchange, the white rice and the brown rice must be present and the answer clearly points to one of the two kinds of rice with the use of the demonstrative pronoun *hemia*.

Rather than the third person singular always being marked by *hem* as indicated in Table 4.1, it is quite common for this meaning not to be expressed by a pronoun at all, as in the following:

Mi no laekem Ø.
'I don't like it.'

The object of the verb *laekem* 'like' in this case would normally not be marked by means of the pronoun *hem* at all. For most speakers of Bislama, there is a difference between pronouns with singular human reference that normally *are* marked by a pronoun and pronouns that refer to singular animals or things, which are generally not marked by means of a pronoun. Contrast the example just presented with the following:

Mi no laekem hem.
'I don't like him/her.'

The use of zero to express a pronoun with inanimate reference is encountered in a range of grammatical environments in Bislama. The examples just presented illustrate the use of zero-marked verbal objects, and the same is true of pronouns that appear after most prepositions (§6.1.5), for example:

Mi stap sidaon wetem hem.
'I am sitting with him/her.'

Mi stap sidaon wetem Ø.
'I am sitting with it.'

CHAPTER 4

In fact, even with verbal subjects, the pronoun *hem* can be deleted under the same kinds of conditions. Look at the following sentence:

Mi luk wan man wetem wan dog mo Ø i bin kakae mi.

Most people would interpret this as meaning: 'I saw a man and a dog and it (i.e., the dog) bit me'. But now look at the following:

*Mi luk wan man wetem wan dog mo **hem** i bin kakae mi.*

In this case, it is more likely that this would be understood with the man doing the biting rather than the dog.

There is one environment, however, in which *all* third person singular subjects, regardless of whether they refer to humans or non-humans, must be expressed by means of *hem*, and that is after the prepositions *long* (§6.1.5.1.6) and *blong* (§6.1.5.1.1). These two prepositions differ from verbs and from all of the other prepositions in the language in that they cannot be "stranded" without some kind of object immediately following them. Thus:

*Bae mi givim buk long **hem**.*
*Bae mi givim buk long Ø.
'I will give the book to him/her.'

*Mi bin putum buk long **hem**.*
*Mi bin putum buk long Ø.
'I put the book on it.'

4.3 Noun Phrases

In this section, I will describe the kinds of constituents that can appear in a noun phrase along with the main noun or pronoun, and where these various constituents are placed within the noun phrase with respect to the noun or pronoun itself, as well as with respect to each other. The overall structure of the noun phrase with a noun as its head can be summarized as follows:

QUANTIFIER + ADJECTIVE + **NOUN** + POSTMODIFIER + DEMONSTRATIVE

The following, by way of contrast, is a summary of the overall structure of a noun phrase that has a pronoun as its head:

PRONOUN + QUANTIFIER + DEMONSTRATIVE

The two kinds of noun phrases differ in that pronouns always appear at the beginning of the phrase, whereas nouns allow a wide range of preceding modifiers. Pronouns are also much more restricted than nouns in the kinds of modifiers that they can be associated with.

4.3.1 Quantifiers + Nouns

Nouns can be preceded by the number marker *ol* 'plural' or any of the following words that express quantity in some way, as well as any of the numerals:

olgeta	'plural, all'
tugeta	'both'
trigeta	'all three'
evri	'each, every'
fulap	'many, much'
plante	'many, much'
staka	'many, much'
eni	'any'
sam	'some'
samfala	'some'
haf	'some of, part of'
tumas	'too much of, too many'
naf	'enough'
smol	'a few, a little bit'
lelebet	'quite a few, quite a lot'

Some of these forms express the same meanings. Thus, *fulap man*, *plante man*, and *staka man* all mean 'many people, lots of people', while *sam man* and *samfala man* both mean 'some people'. The use of one option rather than another in cases such as these is partly a matter of individual choice, though some of these forms may also be partly geographically distributed.

To make a noun plural, either *ol* or *olgeta* can be placed before the noun. Thus, *ol man* and *olgeta man* both mean simply 'people'. Some speakers use the plural markers *ol* and *olgeta* more or less freely with any noun. Other speakers favor *ol* with human nouns (or with nouns referring both to people and larger animals or living things) while they reserve *olgeta* for use with inanimate objects or smaller living things. Thus, some people may say *ol man* 'people' but *olgeta haos* 'houses' rather than *ol haos*.

Tugeta can be used with a noun to express the meaning of 'both', for example, *tugeta man* 'both people'. However, this meaning is more frequently expressed by means of the numeral *tufala* 'two' appearing before the noun and with *evriwan* appearing after the noun, i.e., *tufala man evriwan* 'both people'. *Trigeta* 'all three', as in *trigeta man* 'all three men' is nowadays even less common, and most people would simply say *trifala man evriwan* to express the same meaning.

There is only one noun in Bislama that has an irregular plural and that is *samting* 'thing'. For most speakers of Bislama, *samting* is in fact perfectly regular, with the plural being expressed as *olgeta samting* 'things' (or perhaps as *ol samting*). However, for some speakers, the plural of *samting*, when it is preceded by the plural marker *ol* (but not *olgeta*, or, in fact, any other quantifier or numeral), is *ting*.[4] We therefore find examples such as the following:

Bae mi fulumap ol samting blong mi i go long sutkes.
Bae mi fulumap ol ting blong mi i go long sutkes.
'I will pack my things into the suitcase.'

---

[4] Because *ol* + *ting* appear together in such a restricted set of environments, some people prefer to write this as a single word, i.e., *olting* 'things'.

CHAPTER 4

Bae mi fulumap evri samting blong mi i go long sutkes.
**Bae mi fulumap evri ting blong mi i go long sutkes.*
'I will pack everything of mine into the suitcase.'

These plural markers are never used when there is a number accompanying the noun, or when the noun is accompanied by the quantifiers *evri* 'each, every', *eni* 'any', or *naf* 'enough'. We therefore say *sikis man* 'six people' but never **sikis ol man*. It should be noted, however, that the forms *fulap, plante,* and *staka*, all meaning 'many', as well as *tumas* 'too many' and *sam(fala)* 'some', can appear both with and without a plural marker, though the plural marker is not commonly used in such circumstances. Thus, it is possible to say *fulap man* 'many people', or occasionally *fulap ol man* 'many people'.

Olgeta can be used either as a plural marker (as already indicated) or as a quantifier meaning 'all' (though the form *ol* can only be used to mark the plural). Thus, *olgeta man* can mean either 'all the men' or simply 'men'. If the context does not make it clear which of these two meanings is involved, the meaning of 'all' can be unambiguously expressed by combining *olgeta* before the noun with *evriwan* after the noun, i.e., *olgeta man evriwan* 'all the people'.

Apart from the occurrence of *ol* along with some of these quantifiers, we normally do not find more than one member of this set appearing before the same noun. The only exception to this generalization involves the numerals, which can occur along with *olgeta* 'all' in the same noun phrase, for example *olgeta sikis man* 'all six people'.

Also included in this set of quantifiers is the interrogative *hamas* 'how much, how many' (§6.2.2.4), for example *hamas raes* 'how much rice', *hamas trak* 'how many cars'. The interrogative *hameni* 'how many' (§6.2.2.5) is also occasionally used by some speakers in order to elicit a specific number with respect to a countable noun rather than a general amount as the response, for example *hameni man* 'how many people?'

The distinction between countable and non-countable nouns also applies for some speakers of Bislama in relation to the behavior of *smol* 'little bit of' and *lelebet* 'quite a lot of'. For the majority of speakers, these forms can appear only before non-countable nouns in examples such as the following:

I gat smol raes long sospen.
'There's a little bit of rice in the saucepan.'

I gat lelebet taro i stap.
'There is quite a lot of taro left.'

However, with a minority of speakers, these can also appear before countable nouns with the meaning of 'a few' and 'quite a few' respectively. Thus:

Smol man nomo oli kam long konset.
'Just a few people came to the concert.'

I gat lelebet man long nakamal las naet.
'There were quite a few people at the kava bar last night.'

For speakers with a higher level of education in English, however, the form *fiu* may be used here instead, for example:

Fiu man nomo oli kam long konset.
'Just a few people came to the concert.'

A number of these quantifiers share an additional feature in that they can stand alone within a noun phrase without any need for an accompanying noun. This includes all of the numerals, along with the following additional members of the set of quantifiers:

fulap	'many, much'
plante	'many, much'
staka	'many, much'
sam	'some'
samfala	'some'
haf	'some of, part of'
tumas	'too much of, too many'
naf	'enough'
smol	'a few, a little bit'
lelebet	'quite a few, quite a lot'
hamas	'how much, how many'
hameni	'how many'

The use of these as nouns is illustrated by the following:

I gat smol i stap yet.
'There is still a little bit left.'

Plante oli no kam yet.
'Many have not yet come.'

Hemia tumas finis.
'That's already too much.'

Tu i go long kartong finis mo wan i stap yet.
'Two have already gone into the box and there is one left.'

Yu wantem sam, no?
'Do you want some?'

In addition to these words, which appear in exactly the same shape whether they are used as quantifiers modifying nouns, the words *eni* 'any' and *evri* 'every', when they function alone in noun phrases, have the forms *eniwan* and *evriwan* respectively, as in:

Eniwan i save kam long mared blong tufala.
'Anybody can come to their wedding.'

Evriwan i kakae mit blong totel finis.
'Everybody has eaten the meat of the turtle.'

Numerals can also be reduplicated. Like nouns—and in contrast to adjectives and verbs (§5.1.1)— numerals reduplicate fully rather than just partially. With numerals of a single syllable such as *tu* 'two' or *tri* 'three', there is no indication that there is anything different from the patterns that we find with adjectival and verbal

CHAPTER 4

reduplication when we see the corresponding reduplicated forms *tutu* and *tritri*. However, it becomes obvious that full reduplication is involved when we consider the behavior of numbers consisting of two syllables such as *seven* 'seven' and *twelef* 'twelve', which reduplicate as *sevenseven* and *twelefiwelef* respectively. We therefore do not encounter partially reduplicated numerals such as **seseven*, **levleven*, **twetwelef* or **tweltwelef*.

The function of reduplication with numerals is to indicate that a number of individuals are acting together in a group of that particular size. A reduplicated numeral can appear before a noun within a noun phrase, as in the following:

Bae i gat fofo man i go long olgeta trak.
'There will be four people in each of the cars.'

The numeral *wan* 'one' can also be reduplicated as *wanwan* to express the specific meaning of 'occasional', along with the regular meaning of 'one at a time' or 'one each', as in the following:

Bae yumi dring wanwan sel kava.
'We will drink one shell of kava each.'

A reduplicated numeral can also function as an adverb without any accompanying noun, as in examples such as the following:

Ol pikinini oli wokbaot tritri.
'The children are walking in threes.'

Ol boe wetem ol gel oli danis tutu.
'The boys and girls are dancing in pairs.'

Long kriket oli no plei tweleftwelef long wan tim be oli plei levenleven nomo.
'In cricket they don't play twelve to a team but they just play eleven at a time.'

The numerals 1–10 can also accept the adjectival suffix *-fala* (§4.3.3.2). When added to numerals, *-fala* generally indicates that the noun that the numeral is modifying has already been referred to, or that it is already known to the person who is being spoken to. Thus, we would normally open with a numeral that does not carry this suffix, but any subsequent mentions of that noun phrase are likely to be marked by *-fala*. Thus:

I gat tu trak long yad blong mi. Tufala trak ia i rosta finis.
'There are two cars in my yard. The two cars are already rusty.'

Although the numerals 1–10 behave like adjectives in marking givenness by means of *-fala* in this way, it is not possible to add the noun-deriving suffix *-wan* to these forms in the same way that we find with ordinary adjectives (§4.1.4.1). If we want to refer back to a noun phrase containing a numeral, we simply use the numeral root with no added suffix, as in the following:

I gat seven haos long pis graon ia. No, mi kaontem se sikis, i no seven.
'There are seven houses on the block of land. No, I have counted six, not seven.'

Numerals can also accept the prefix *a-* to derive forms such as *awan*, *atu*, *atri*, *afo*, etc. These forms do not modify nouns within a noun phrase; rather, they appear on their own. Numerals carrying this prefix are only ever used in playing games, in either of the following specific contexts:

- In a game of marbles, a player can use one of these forms to indicate how many marbles each player should place into the ring.
- When quoting the score between two teams in football, the prefixed numeral can be placed before an unprefixed numeral to express the scores of the opposing teams, for example *Atri wan* 'The score is three to one'.

A final way of deriving a new form out of a numeral involves the formation of compound numerals to express ordinal numerals. By this process, the noun *namba* 'number' can be compounded with a following numeral to derive an ordinal adjective, and this precedes the noun that it is associated with. Thus, from *tri* 'three' we can derive *nambatri* 'third', as in the following:

Nambatri haos hem i blong mi.
'The third house is mine.'

These are also used in expressing dates, with the derived ordinal numeral preceding the name of one of the months, for example:

Bae mi stat wok long nambaten Epril.
'I will start work on the tenth of April.'

These derived ordinals can also be used as nouns in their own right, as in:

Mi kasem pei long nambafiftin.
'I got paid on the fifteenth.'

Nambatetin hem i dei blong badlak.
'The thirteenth is an unlucky date.'

Although this construction involving *namba* is quite regular, the form *nambatu* 'second' commonly alternates with *seken*. It should also be noted that the form *nambawan* does not mean 'first' as might be predicted, but means instead 'the best' or 'excellent', for example:

Hem i kukum wan nambawan kakae.
'She cooked an excellent meal.'

The meaning of 'first' is expressed instead by means of the underived form *fes*, as in the following:

Minista hem i fes man we i kam.
'The minister is the first person who came.'

However, the form *nambawan* is used to mean 'first' when giving dates, for example:

Mi bon long nambawan Epril.
'I was born on the first of April.'

A final feature of numerals is that two numerals can appear together as a compound when modifying a noun, with the lower numeral appearing before the higher numeral. In such cases, the complex numeral expresses vagueness as to whether the first or the second numeral is the appropriate one. Very often, the two numerals involved express numbers that appear in sequence, for example:

Bae yumi wajem tutri vidio long wiken.
'Let's watch two or three videos on the weekend.'

However, sometimes non-sequential numerals can be used in the same construction, as illustrated by the following:

I gat fotififti man oli kam long miting.
'There were forty or fifty people at the meeting.'

It can be seen from the examples presented above that a numeral precedes the noun that refers to whatever it is that it is counting. However, there is a restricted set of nouns where the number and the noun can be separated by an additional noun, which can be referred to as a numeral classifier. The classifier *frut* optionally appears between a numeral and a noun referring to something small that is normally encountered together in larger numbers in a packet of some kind for sale. We find this most commonly with the words *sigaret* 'cigarette' and *mases* 'match', for example *tu frut sigaret* 'two cigarettes', *tri frut mases* 'three matches'. However, anything small from a packet that is being considered individually can be counted by means of this numeral classifier. This is most likely to happen when people in a rural village buy individual items according to need rather than buying an entire packet in order to save money, for example *tu frut asprin* 'two aspirins', *fo frut lipton* 'four tea-bags', *sikis frut draebiskit* 'six breakfast crackers'. With the word *mases* 'match', the numeral classifier is often *stik* rather than *frut*, for example *faef stik mases* 'five matches'.

4.3.2 Pronouns + Quantifiers

Pronouns differ from nouns in that quantifiers appear after forms that they modify rather than before them. Thus: *mifala sikis* 'six of us', *olgeta hamas* 'how many of them?', *yufala plante* 'many of you', *yumi smol nomo* 'just a few of us', *mifala samfala* 'some of us'. There is, however, an alternative way of expressing quantifiers with pronouns and that is for the quantifier to be placed before the pronoun, followed by the preposition *long* and then the pronoun, as in the following: *sikis long mifala* 'six of us', *sam long mifala* 'some of us'.

The quantifier *evri* that appears before nouns appears in the special form *evriwan* when used as a quantifier with pronouns. Contrast therefore *evri trak* 'each car' with *yumi evriwan* 'each of us'. Note that *evriwan* can be used with a pronoun with trial or plural reference to mean 'every, all' as well as with a dual pronoun, where it means 'both'. Thus, compare *yufala evriwan* 'all of you' and *yutrifala evriwan* 'all three of you' with *yutufala evriwan* 'both of you'. While *tugeta* 'both' is not commonly used with nouns, it is fairly commonly used with pronouns, for example *yutufala tugeta* 'both of you'. However, as just indicated, it is also possible to express this meaning by using the form *evriwan* after the pronoun, i.e., *yutufala evriwan*.

A numeral that follows a pronoun may appear either in its unsuffixed form or it may carry the suffix *-fala*. When the suffixed form of the numeral is used, a specific group of people is being referred to, whereas the unsuffixed form is associated with a non-specific group. Compare, therefore, the following:

Olgeta seven oli wokem garen.
'Seven of them made the garden.'

Olgeta sevenfala oli wokem garen.
'The seven of them made the garden.'

Note that the numerals *tu* 'two' and *tri* 'three' can redundantly follow a dual or trial pronoun, though always in their unsuffixed forms. Thus:

Tufala tu i go.
**Tufala tufala i go.*
'Two of them went.'

Mi bin luk yutrifala tri.
**Mi bin luk yutrifala trifala.*
'I saw the three of you.'

Wan 'one' has some specific functions when used after singular pronouns. It expresses firstly the idea that the action is performed by the subject 'alone' or 'by oneself', as in the following:

Mi wan mi stap sidaon.
'I am sitting by myself.'

Yu wan yu stap kukum raes?
'Are you cooking the rice by yourself?'

This meaning can be expressed alternatively by incorporating the pronoun into an adverbial phrase of the pattern PRONOUN + *wan* after the verb, or after the object noun phrase in the case of a transitive verb. Thus:

Mi stap sidaon mi wan.
'I am sitting by myself.'

Yu stap kukum raes yu wan?
'Are you cooking the rice by yourself?'

When *wan* follows a singular object pronoun that is identical with the person of the subject, this normally expresses a reflexive meaning, for example:

Mi luk mi wan long glas.
'I looked at myself in the mirror.'

The reflexive meaning can be expressed in a variety of other ways, including *nomo* 'only' or *bakegen* 'again' following the object pronoun, for example:

Yu stap luk yu nomo?
'Are you looking at yourself?'

CHAPTER 4

Mi katem mi bakegen.
'I cut myself.'

Another way of expressing the reflexive meaning is to place the suffix *-bak* on the verb (§5.1.3.2.4), for example:

Hem i kilim-bak hem.
'He killed himself.'

Finally, any or all of these can be used together to express the reflexive, e.g.,

Hem i kilim-bak hem wan nomo.
'He killed himself.'

Yu katem yu wan bakegen?
'Did you cut yourself?'

With plural reflexive constructions, the construction with *wan* is not an option, so the other options just presented must be used. Thus:

Yufala i katem yufala nomo?
**Yufala i katem yufala wan nomo?*
'Did you cut yourselves?'

Wan can also appear in this construction after a singular pronoun to express the idea that an action takes place spontaneously 'by itself', with no deliberate involvement of an outside agency, for example:

Gras i bon hem wan.
'The grass just caught on fire (without anybody apparently lighting it).'

Mi foldaon mi wan.
'I accidentally fell over (rather than being pushed over by somebody else).'

Because *wan* can only be used in association with a singular subject, the same meaning is somewhat difficult to express with plural subjects. Some speakers occasionally use *hem wan* as a generic adverbial modifier regardless of the subject, producing sentences such as the following:

Mifala i foldaon hem wan.
'We accidentally fell over.'

Most speakers, however, find such sentences to be stylistically awkward or even downright wrong, and prefer to express this meaning instead by repeating the pronoun but with following *nomo* 'only', as in the following:

Mifala i foldaon mifala nomo.
'We accidentally fell over.'

Also:

Olgeta oli singsing olgeta nomo.
'They sang by themselves.'

Bae yufala i wokem garen yufala nomo.
'Make the gardens yourselves.'

4.3.3 Adjectives

Like nouns, adjectives can be described as either simple or complex. A simple adjective is one that cannot be broken down into any smaller meaningful elements, such as *rosta* 'rusty', *braon* 'brown', and *impoten* 'important'. However, many adjectives are complex in that they can be broken down into smaller meaningful elements. Adjectives show evidence of productive reduplication, as well as affixation, and there is also some evidence of compounding.

4.3.3.1 Reduplication

Adjectives—along with verbs—undergo productive reduplication in Bislama. The patterns of reduplication for verbs and adjectives can be described in exactly the same terms, though detailed discussion of the nature of the various patterns is reserved for §5.1.1. At this point, I will only briefly point out and exemplify the various patterns of adjectival reduplication. Corresponding to complete syllable reduplication with verbs, we find the same kinds of alternations with adjectives. Note that only material within a root is affected by reduplication, so where an adjective carries the suffix *-fala* (§4.3.3.2), this does not constitute part of the reduplicated material. Thus, *smol* 'small' can reduplicate as *smol-smol*, *strongfala* 'strong' as *strong-strongfala*, *niufala* 'new' as *niu-niufala*, *yangfala* 'young' as *yang-yangfala*, and *difren* 'different' as *dif-difren*. We also find adjectives that are reduplicated according to the pattern of partial syllable reduplication. For example, *smol* 'small' can reduplicate as *smo-smol* and *strongfala* 'strong' can reduplicate as *stro-strongfala*. Finally, corresponding to the pattern of partial root reduplication, we find examples such as *simol* 'small', which can reduplicate as *sim-simol*.

Adjectives also provide evidence of an additional pattern of reduplication that is not encountered with verbs. Rather than just reduplicating the initial syllable or the first consonant of the second syllable, *difren* 'different' is frequently reduplicated with all of its first syllable, along with the first *CV* of the second syllable. This means that in addition to the possible reduplicated forms *di-difren* and *dif-difren*, which have already been accounted for, we also encounter *difre-difren*. However, this pattern has only been encountered with this single adjective, and this is not a productive pattern.

The examples presented above clearly indicate that individual adjectives can participate in more than one pattern. Considering also that some adjectives may vary slightly in their shape with the presence or absence of vowels between certain sequences of consonants, and that each of these different forms of the same adjective can be taken as the basis of reduplication, it is possible to encounter a wide variety in the shapes of reduplicated adjectives. *Smol* 'small' (which alternates with *simol*) results in the reduplicated forms *smo-smol*, *smol-smol*, *si-simol*, *sim-simol*.

The various functions associated with the reduplication of adjectives are as follows:

- *Plural.* Adjectives can be reduplicated when they modify plural nouns, whereas corresponding unreduplicated forms are associated with singular nouns. Thus:

CHAPTER 4

*Mi mas pem wan **longfala** timba blong wokem gud veranda long haos blong mi.*
'I have to buy a long piece of wood to build the verandah on my house.'

*Oli no salem ol **longlongfala** long Agathis; oli salem ol sotsotwan nomo.*
'They don't sell long pieces of wood at Agathis; they only sell short ones.'

*Hem i givim wan **doti** traoses long mi blong bae mi werem.*
'He gave me a dirty pair of shorts to wear.'

*Oli givim ol **dodotiwan** nomo se bae yumi werem.*
'They just gave us dirty ones to wear.'

- *Variety.* Adjectives can be reduplicated to indicate variety in whatever it is that the noun refers to, for example:

*Kastom blong Tana i **difren** long kastom blong Santo.*
'The traditions of Tanna are different from those of Santo.'

*Kastom blong olgeta aelan long Vanuatu i **difdifren**.*
'The traditions of all of the islands of Vanuatu are different from each other.'

- *Intensity.* A reduplicated adjective can also express an intensification of the state that is expressed by the unreduplicated form, for example:

*Yu kambak long ples blong kolkol, mi luk skin blong yu i **waetwaet** bakegen.*
'You have come back from a cold place, I can see that your skin has gone really pale again.'

4.3.3.2 The Suffix *-fala*

Certain adjectives can accept the suffix *-fala*. The suffix appears in this shape with all adjectives apart from those ending in *f*, in which case it appears as *-ala*. With a root such as *big* 'big', therefore, the suffixed form is *big-fala*, whereas with a root such as *faef* 'five', the suffixed form is *faef-ala*. The suffix *-fala* only appears on a subset of the total class of adjectives in Bislama. Adjectives with roots of just a single syllable are very commonly found with *-fala*. We therefore find forms such as the following:

big-fala	'big'
sot-fala	'short'
long-fala	'long, tall'
gud-fala	'good'
naes-fala	'nice'
strong-fala	'strong, hard'
swit-fala	'sweet'
klin-fala	'clean'
niu-fala	'new'
sap-fala	'sharp'
blak-fala	'black'
blu-fala	'blue'
grin-fala	'green'
braon-fala	'brown'

red-fala   'red'
waet-fala   'white'

Longer adjectives, however, typically do not accept this suffix. We therefore find forms such as *yelo* 'yellow' but not **yelofala*. The suffix *-fala* is also commonly found on words expressing the numbers 1–10 (§4.3.1) regardless of whether they contain just a single syllable or if they are longer, for example *tu-fala* 'two', *seven-fala* 'seven'.

There is a small subset of adjectives that vary from speaker to speaker with respect to the behavior of *-fala*. For most speakers, the adjectives *sem* 'same', *smol* 'small' and *stret* 'straight' (along with a small number of others) never accept this suffix, but some speakers do use the forms *semfala*, *smolfala* and *stretfala*.

The suffix *-fala* has a meaning that is somewhat difficult to pin down. In some cases, it indicates that the quality that is expressed by the adjective is in some way especially notable. Note, therefore, the difference in meaning between *gud* and *gudfala* in the following examples:

*Mi karem wan **gud** wok finis.*
'I have got a good job.'

*Mi karem wan **gudfala** wok finis.*
'I have got an especially good job.'

In other instances, however, *-fala* appears instead to be a marker of givenness, indicating that the noun with which a suffixed adjective is associated has previously been mentioned. This function of *-fala* is indicated by the following:

*Mi karem wan waet trak. **Waetfala** trak olsem ia i no hot tumas long hotsan.*
'I have a white car. A white car like that is not too hot in the direct sun.'

In this case, the first mention of *waet trak* 'white car' does not appear with the suffix *-fala* because the speaker has not yet established which particular kind of vehicle is being talked about. However, the second mention appears with the suffix as *waetfala trak* because the speaker is referring back to the previously mentioned kind of vehicle.

For those adjectives that do not accept *-fala*, these distinctions of meaning must be expressed in other ways. A form such as *difren* 'different, unusual' never appears as **difrenfala*, so in order to express something close to the particularizing function of *-fala*, a modifier such as *lelebet* 'rather' must be used, as in the following:

*Mi karem wan **difren** wok **lelebet**.*
'I have a rather unusual job.'

The role of expressing givenness falls entirely on the accompanying noun phrase postmodifier *ia* (§4.3.5), as in the following:

*Mi karem wan **difren** wok. **Difren** wok olsem **ia** mi laekem.*
'I have an unusual job. I like unusual jobs like that.'

With a small number of adjectives, the suffix *-fala* appears so frequently that it is almost meaningless. *Sam* and *samfala* 'some', *wan* and *wanfala* 'one' and *nara* and *narafala* 'other' appear to be completely interchangeable, with no difference in meaning. Thus:

*Mi karem wan **nara** wok.*
*Mi karem wan **narafala** wok.*
'I have another job.'

In the case of *olfala* 'old', the suffix *-fala* has become so tightly attached to the root that **ol* almost never occurs on its own with the meaning of 'old'. Note therefore the following:

*Hem i wan **olfala** dokta.*
*Hem i wan ol dokta.
'(S)he is an old doctor.'

*Hemia wan **olfala** trak.*
*Hemia wan ol trak.
'That is an old car.'

Although there is a corresponding form *olwan*, this is a derived noun that has exclusively non-human reference. To express a derived noun with human reference, the form *olfala* must be used instead.[5] Contrast, therefore, the following:

*Hem i wan **olfala**.*
'(S)he is an old person.'

*Hemia wan **olwan**.*
'That is an old one.'

    The adjectives described above precede the nouns that they modify. (Note that adjectives can never be used in association with pronouns.) We therefore find noun phrases such as the following: *stret ansa* 'correct answer', *rabis tingting* 'terrible idea', *strongfala mit* 'tough meat'. Where the noun phrase comprises both a quantifier and an adjective, the order is invariably QUANTIFIER + ADJECTIVE, as illustrated by the following: *fulap hanggri dog* 'many hungry dogs', *evri les pikinini* 'every lazy child', *tumas drong man* 'too many drunk men'.

    It is possible for several adjectives at a time to precede a noun, as we find in English with a phrase such as *big black dog*. Although this could be expressed as *bigfala blak dog*, there is a strong preference in Bislama to avoid strings of two or more adjectives before a noun. Normally, only one of these meanings will be expressed by means of an adjective, while other modifiers associated with the noun are likely to be expressed within a relative clause (§4.3.6). Thus, rather than saying *bigfala blak dog*, people are more likely to say instead *bigfala dog we i blak* 'big dog that is black.'

    In the event that two adjectives do appear together before a noun, it is difficult to spell out in what precise order they will appear. One generalization that seems to be reasonably secure is that an adjective carrying the prefix *-fala* will normally precede an unsuffixed adjective. Thus:

---

[5] The word *olfala* is also often used colloquially as a noun with the specific meaning of 'husband' or 'father'.

I gat tu sotfala krangki man i stap singaot long rod.
*I gat tu krangki sotfala man i stap singaot long rod.
'There are two short crazy men shouting on the road.'

Wan bigfala drong man i bin faetem smol brata blong mi.
*Wan drong bigfala man i bin faetem smol brata blong mi.
'A big drunk man hit my younger brother.'

4.3.3.3 Compounding

Many adjectives are derived by linking a simple adjective with a noun to derive a new compound adjective. Thus, for example *strong* 'hard' and *hed* 'head' combine to give *strong-hed* 'stubborn', *big* 'big' and *bel* 'stomach' combine to give *big-bel* 'pot-bellied', *big* 'big' and *maot* 'mouth' can be joined to give *big-maot* 'loud-mouthed', and *sat* 'shut' and *hed* 'head' can combine to produce *sat-hed* 'moronic'. That words such as these should be treated as adjectives is indicated by the fact that they can appear before a noun in the same way that an adjective qualifies the noun, as in examples such as the following:

Bigbel boe ia nao i stap wok long Centrepoint.
'The pot-bellied lad works at Centrepoint.'

Sam man oli talem se ol man Amerika ol bigmaot man.
'Some people say that Americans are loud-mouthed people.'

George hem i wan sathed presiden.
'George is a moronic president.'

Such forms are also frequently used as nouns to refer to a person who is characterized by that quality. We therefore also find examples such as the following where the same forms behave as nouns:

Yu luk bigbel ia longwe?
'Can you see the person with the paunch over there?'

Lukaot, bigmaot ia i stap kam.
'Watch out, the loud-mouth is coming.'

It is also worth noting that the adjective *sem* 'same' can be compounded with the noun *mak* 'variety' to produce *sem-mak*. Some people reduce the two instances of *m* to a single *m* when these sounds come together in the same word to produce *semak*. For some speakers, *sem* is used only as a noun premodifier, while *sem-mak* is only ever used in a predicate construction (§6.1.1). Thus:

Yumitu gat sem trak.
'We have the same car.'

Trak blong yumitu i sem-mak.
'Our cars are the same.'

However, some speakers use *sem-mak* (or *semak*) in either context, so you can occasionally also expect to hear the following:

CHAPTER 4

Yumitu gat semak trak.
'We have the same car.'

4.3.4 Noun Postmodifiers

In addition to the very large set of adjectives that precede a noun in Bislama, there is a much smaller set of adjectives that normally follow the noun instead. These forms will be referred to by way of contrast as postmodifiers. The only forms of this type are *nogud* 'bad', *olbaot* 'ordinary, plain', *nating* 'unimportant, useless, of no value' and *olsem* 'such a'. These appear in examples such as the following:

Fasin olsem i save ronem ol gel.
'Such behavior frightens off girls.'

Mi man nating be stil mi mas gat haos blong slip.
'I'm an unimportant person but I still need a house to live in.'

Of course, noun phrases of this type can accept a variety of preceding quantifiers and adjectives, as in the following:

Ol man aelan oli kam long taon mo oli wokem ol niufala haos olbaot.
'People from the islands have come to town and made many ordinary new houses.'

Fulap ol olfala man nogud oli stap wokem rabis fasin samtaem.
'Many bad old men behave inappropriately sometimes.'

Some younger speakers these days treat *nogud* and *olbaot*—but not the other two postmodifiers of this type—as if they were ordinary adjectives. This means that they occasionally place these words before a noun rather than after it. (When these forms are used before the noun, they never accept the suffix *-fala.*) We can therefore find occasional variation between sentences such as the following:

Hem i wan man nogud.
Hem i wan nogud man.
'He is a bad man.'

Hem i wokem wan haos olbaot.
Hem i wokem wan olbaot haos.
'He built an ordinary house.'

4.3.5 Demonstratives

The final element in the noun phrase is the demonstrative *ia* 'this/these, that/those'. The pronunciation of this demonstrative is actually *ya*, though there is a fairly widespread acceptance these days of the spelling *ia*, and that is the spelling that is adopted throughout in this grammar (§2.4). Note that unlike demonstratives in English, this form is identical for both singular and plural nouns, with the difference in number being marked in Bislama by means of the preceding modifier *ol* or *olgeta*. Thus: *gel ia* 'this/that girl', *ol gel ia* 'these/those girls'. Although the meaning of 'this' and 'that' is generally expressed by means of *ia*, some speakers use the longer form *hemia* in this way as well. We therefore sometimes find variation between examples such as the following:

Mi mi karem tinfis ia.
Mi mi karem tinfis hemia.
'I brought that tinned fish.'

Ia (along with *hemia*) expresses a range of meanings. It can be used as a direct equivalent to 'this' and 'these' in English, as well as 'that' and 'those'. This means that a phrase such as *man nogud ia* can be translated as 'this bad man' or 'that bad man', as well as 'these bad men' and 'those bad men'. In fact, in many cases, *ia* corresponds even to the ordinary definite article 'the' in English. Thus:

Man Niusilan ia i stap wok long wota saplae.
'The/this/that New Zealander works for water supply.'

Very often, the context in which people are speaking will make it clear which particular meaning is intended for *ia*. However, if it is necessary to make an unambiguous distinction between the meaning of 'this/these' on the one hand and the meaning of 'that/those' on the other, this can be achieved by means of *ia nao* 'this/these' and *ia longwe* 'that/those'. Thus:

Hu i save singsing? Man ia. Wijwan man ia? Man ia nao o man ia longwe?
'Who can sing? This/that man. Which man? This man or that man?'

There are some other lengthier ways of distinguishing between these meanings. For the meaning of 'this/these', it is also possible to add the phrases *long ples ia* 'in this place' or *long saed i kam* 'in this direction' after the demonstrative, while the meaning of 'that/those' may be expressed with *long saed i go* 'in that direction'. Thus: *haos ia long ples ia* 'this house', *haos ia long saed i go* 'that house'.

While on the topic of demonstratives, mention should also be made of *disfala* 'this'. This is another way of expressing the meaning of 'this/these', as in *disfala man* 'this man'. This precedes the noun as in English, rather than follow-ing it, and it is often also accompanied by *ia* as a postmodifier within the noun phrase. Thus:

Disfala man ia i save singsing.
'This man can sing.'

Disfala was not mentioned along with the other noun adjectives (§4.3.3) because it is a little difficult to be certain about its status in modern Bislama. While some people certainly do use it, it is not nearly as common as *ia*, and some people regard *disfala* either as just random influence from English *this*, or as perhaps a borrowing from similar forms that are much more commonly used in Tok Pisin in Papua New Guinea or Solomons Pijin.

4.3.6 Nouns Modified by Sentences

A noun phrase can sometimes be modified by a sequence of words that effectively corresponds to a full sentence in its own right. Look at this example:

Wan olfala we mi storian wetem hem yestedei i stap dring kava long haos.
'An old man who I was chatting with yesterday is drinking kava at home.'

The part of this example that is presented in bold could perfectly well function as a sentence on its own, i.e.,

CHAPTER 4

Mi storian wetem hem yestedei.
'I was chatting with him yesterday.'

When a complete sentence like this modifies a noun phrase—in this case *wan olfala* 'an old man'—we refer to this as a relative clause.

This example demonstrates that relative clauses follow the nouns to which they refer. A relative clause in Bislama is normally introduced by *we*, even though relative clauses referring to humans in English are marked by *who*, whereas those referring to things are introduced by *that* or *which*, and those referring to possessive noun phrases are marked by *whose*. Compare, therefore, the following in English and Bislama:

Jif we i toktok wetem mifala i stap long nakamal.
'The chief **who** spoke to us is in the meeting house.'

Haos we i stap longwe oli jas wokem nomo.
'The house **that** is over there has only just been built.'

Tija we mi karem buk blong hem i stap wet long mi long klasrum.
'The teacher **whose** book I brought is waiting for me in the classroom.'

A relative clause can always be viewed as containing a noun phrase of its own that is identical with the noun phrase that it is modifying. In the first example presented in this section, for example, the relative clause is modifying *wan olfala* 'an old man', and that relative clause can be seen as containing that same noun phrase in the form of the pronoun *hem* in *we mi storian wetem hem yestedei* 'who I spoke to yesterday'. The marking of the understood identical noun phrase in relative clauses by means of a pronoun is very much a regular feature of Bislama. Some other examples of pronouns included in relative clauses in Bislama are set out below:

Ol pikinini we yumi ronem olgeta oli stap mekem noes afsaed.
'The children who we chased away are being noisy outside.'

Haos we mi stap slip long hem i bon las wik.
'The house that I was living in burned down last week.'

Mi stap karem mane long man ia we mi wokem haos blong hem.
'I am getting money from the man whose house I built.'

It can be seen that there is a major difference between the way that the relative clause is expressed here in Bislama and in English in that there is a pronoun marking the identical noun phrase in the relative clause in Bislama, whereas in English there is no pronoun marking the understood noun phrase within the relative clause. This is why, in English, we say *the old man who I spoke to yesterday* and not **the old man who I spoke to him yesterday*.

There are, however, situations in which the pronoun within the relative clause in Bislama may be deleted. It was pointed out in §4.2 that third person singular subjects and objects are marked by *hem* when the noun phrase is human, but with inanimate noun phrases—and often also with non-human animate noun phrases—the pronoun *hem* is often absent. The same is also true of subjects and objects of verbs in relative clauses, as well as noun phrases following any of the prepositions other than *long* and *blong*. Compare, therefore, the following pairs of examples:

Bae mi luk tija we mi laekem hem.
'I will see the teacher who I like.'

Bae mi planem yam we mi laekem Ø.
'I will plant the yam that I like.'

Tija blong mi i singaotem pikinini we mi toktok wetem hem.
'My teacher called the child who I was talking with.'

Olfala i holem kruba we mi pikim hol wetem Ø.
'The old man is holding the crowbar that I dug the hole with.'

Hem is also optionally deleted when it refers to a human noun in subject position, for example:

Woman we hem i bin tijim mi i go long wan difren skul finis.
Woman we Ø i bin tijim mi i go long wan difren skul finis.
'The woman who taught me has gone to a different school.'

All of the relative clauses illustrated above contain verbs. It is also possible for the relative clause marker *we* following a noun to introduce a relative clause that does not contain a verb at all (§6.1.2). In such cases, the content of the relative clause must be a noun phrase, as illustrated by the following:

Manu i gat tu buluk we man.
'Manu has two cattle that are bulls.'

Mi mi laekem ol trak we smolwan.
'I like cars that are small ones.'

Although relative clauses are most frequently found after nouns (or noun phrases consisting of nouns and their associated modifiers), it is possible for a relative clause to modify a pronoun. In such cases, the pronoun must also be expressed within the relative clause. We therefore find examples such as the following:

Yu we yu ting se yu gat raet long graon ia yu mas putum wan klem long kot.

This kind of example is difficult to translate into English as the literal translation would be as follows:

'You who you think you have a right to this land must make a claim in court.'

This is not good in English, as relative clauses do not normally follow pronouns. A better translation would therefore be something like the following:

'Whoever thinks they have a claim to this land must make a claim in court.'

4.4 Noun Phrases Linked by *blong*

The preposition *blong* (§6.1.5.1.1) is commonly used to link two noun phrases together to make up a more complex noun phrase.

4.4.1 Possession

The primary function of *blong* in such constructions is to express possession. There are no separate possessive pronouns in Bislama such as we find in English (for example *my, your,* etc.) or in the various local languages of Vanuatu. Possession is expressed in Bislama in exactly the same way for all kinds of possessor noun phrases, whether they involve nouns or pronouns, according to the following basic pattern:

POSSESSED NOUN PHRASE + *blong* + POSSESSOR NOUN PHRASE

The following possessive constructions therefore fit this pattern: *dog blong papa* 'Dad's dog', *haos blong mifala* 'our house'. Of course, both the possessor and the possessed noun phrases may themselves be complex, consisting of a variety of associated modifiers within the phrase, for example *ol dog blong papa* 'Dad's dogs', *tufala niufala haos blong mifala evriwan* 'the two new houses of all of us'. Finally, of course, either the possessor noun phrase or the possessed noun phrase may itself involve a possessive construction, for example *dog blong papa blong mi* 'my father's dog'.

Although this possessive construction is used everywhere, there are some alternative ways of expressing possession that are occasionally encountered. These constructions tend to be restricted to people from rural backgrounds or to people from only certain parts of the country, and many people regard the use of some of these patterns as a sign of unsophistication. One of these alternative patterns involves placing a pronoun possessor, along with a preceding possessive preposition *blong,* before the possessed noun phrase rather than after it, i.e.,

blong + POSSESSOR PRONOUN + POSSESSED NOUN PHRASE

Thus, instead of saying *haos blong mi* 'my house', some people may say *blong mi haos* 'my house'. Also, when the possessor is a noun rather than a pronoun, the following pattern is sometimes used:

POSSESSOR NOUN PHRASE + POSSESSED NOUN PHRASE + *blong* + POSSESSOR PRONOUN

This means that instead of saying *haos blong papa* 'Dad's house', some people say *papa haos blong hem* to express the same meaning.

A noun phrase referring to the possessed item in a possessive construction can be left out if this is clear from the context, leaving just *blong* followed by the possessor, as in the following:

Dog blong papa o dog blong olgeta i bin kakae yu? **Blong papa i kakae mi.**
'Was it Dad's dog or their dog that bit you? Dad's (dog) bit me.'

When these reduced possessive constructions involve a pronoun as the possessor, this corresponds to the English possessive forms *mine, yours,* etc., as in the following:

Blong mi i bigwan bitim blong yu.
'Mine is bigger than yours.'

These reduced possessive constructions behave just like ordinary noun phrases. This means that they can themselves be immediately preceded by another preposition such as *long* 'to, on, at' or *from* 'because of' in a prepositional phrase, for example:

Bae mi putum kakae long blong yu?
'Shall I put food on yours (for example a plate)?'

Hem i kam from blong man ia.
'He came because of that man's (thing).'

The preposition *blong* itself has a variety of shapes. While it is normally written *blong*, it is more commonly pronounced simply as *blo*. Thus, people would normally not say *blong mi* 'mine' but *blo mi* instead. This can also be further reduced in everyday pronounciation to just *bl-* when the following word begins with a vowel rather than a consonant. Thus, *blong olgeta* 'theirs' will often be pronounced in casual speech as *bl-olgeta*. Also, given that *hem* alternates in pronunciation with *em*, *blong hem* 'his, hers, its' often appears as either *blo-hem*, or even *bl-em*. Such shortened pronunciations, however, are seldom reflected in the written form of the language.

4.4.2 Other Functions of *blong*

Exactly the same construction involving the preposition *blong* in Bislama is also frequently used to express other kinds of relationships between nouns in addition to the expression of possession. Each of these additional functions of is listed below:

- *Purpose*

The purpose to which something is put can be expressed by a following noun phrase introduced by *blong*. Thus, in *ki blong trak* 'car key', we are talking about a *ki* 'key' that has as its purpose something to do with the *trak* 'car'. Other examples of purpose noun phrases of this type are: *bed blong kopra* 'copra rack', *spia blong fis* 'fish spear'.

- *Characteristic*

A noun phrase introduced by *blong* can also express something that in some way specially characterizes the preceding noun phrase. For instance, in *ples blong ren*, we have a *ples* 'place' that is specially characterized by *ren* 'rain', hence 'rainy place'. The English agent suffix *-er* is usually expressed in this way, e.g., *man blong singsing* 'singer'. Note also: *man blong woman* 'womanizer', *man blong man* 'gay man'. A common pattern of this type involves a noun that is modified by a verb phrase, for example *pikinini blong krae* 'cry-baby', *man blong dring* 'drinker', *dog blong kakae man* 'vicious dog', *man blong kakae dog* 'dog-eater'.

- *Part-whole*

Finally, *blong* can indicate that something is part of a larger whole, as in *laet blong trak* 'lights of a car', *leg blong jea* 'chair leg', *handel blong baket* 'handle of a bucket', and so on.

CHAPTER 4

4.5 Coordinate Noun Phrases

Two noun phrases can be linked together in a coordinate construction, which means that both of the noun phrases together make up a new complex noun phrase in which the various elements are seen as functioning together as a collection of the individual parts. When two noun phrases involving nouns are linked in this way, *mo* 'and' (§7.2.1) can be placed between the two elements, for example *Kali mo Janet* 'Kali and Janet'. The preposition *wetem* 'with' (§6.1.5.1.3) can also be used to express the same meaning, as in *Kali wetem Janet* 'Kali and Janet'. Thus:

*Mi luk **Kali mo Janet** long naet.*
'I saw Kali and Janet in the night.'

***Kali wetem Janet** tufala i stap wokbaot long sanbij.*
'Kali and Janet were walking along the beach.'

Where two nouns refer to things that are very commonly encountered together as items for consumption rather than as separate items, we sometimes find that the two nouns are simply placed one after the other without either *mo* or *wetem* coming between them. We therefore find examples such as *wiski kok* 'whisky and Coke', *jin tonik* 'gin and tonic', *jikin jips* 'chicken and chips' and *hambega jips* 'hamburger and chips'.

Where a pronoun is coordinated with a noun, the same construction involving *mo* and *wetem* can again be used, producing examples such as the following:

*Mi luk **yu mo Janet** long naet.*
'I saw you and Janet in the night.'

***Janet wetem mi** i stap wokbaot long sanbij.*
'Janet and I were walking along the beach.'

However, such constructions sometimes seem to be stylistically somewhat awkward and a rather different pattern is much more commonly used in ordinary conversation. This involves taking a non-singular pronoun that represents the sum of the coordinated noun phrases in question and placing this before the other noun phrase, with the pronoun and the following noun phrase being linked by either *mo* or *wetem*. Thus, since the combination of *gel ia* 'that girl' and *mi* involves two people, and if I am talking about the two of us to a third person, I would be talking about us using an exclusive pronoun. This means that I would take the first person dual exclusive pronoun *mitufala* and place it before *gel ia* 'that girl' giving the following:

***Mitufala wetem gel ia** i stap wokbaot long sanbij.*
***Mitufala mo gel ia** i stap wokbaot long sanbij.*
'That girl and I were walking along the beach.'

In the same way, a coordinate noun phrase consisting of *hem* '(s)he' and *gel ia* 'that girl' would be expressed as follows:

***Tufala wetem gel ia** i stap wokbaot long sanbij.*
***Tufala mo gel ia** i stap wokbaot long sanbij.*
'That girl and him (or her) were walking along the beach.'

When the pronoun in question is a first or second person pronoun, there is an additional option, by which the non-singular pronoun can simply appear before the other noun phrase with no intervening *mo* or *wetem*, as in the following:

Mitufala gel ia i stap wokbaot long sanbij.
'That girl and I were walking along the beach.'

When third person pronouns are involved, it is not possible to delete *mo* or *wetem* in this way. However, there is an additional option that is not available with first and second person pronouns and that is for the non-singular pronoun that represents the sum of the coordinated noun phrases in question to be placed immediately after the other noun phrase rather than before it. Thus:

Janet tufala i stap wokbaot long sanbij.
*Tufala mo Janet i stap wokbaot long sanbij.
'Janet and him (or her) were walking along the beach.'

Kali olgeta oli stap singsing long haos.
*Olgeta mo Kali oli stap singsing long haos.
'Kali and them are singing in the house.'

5: VERBS AND VERB PHRASES

A verb phrase can consist of nothing but a verb in Bislama, as in:

Mi wekap long naen klok.
'I woke up at nine o'clock.'

Yu kukum sup o no yet?
'Have you cooked the stew or not?'

However, there is a wide variety of additional elements that can accompany a verb within a larger verb phrase, as in the following:

Manu i save draevem trak.
'Manu can drive a car.'

Mi no wantem kakae raes.
'I don't want to eat rice.'

The internal make-up of verbs along with the behavior of elements that go with verbs to constitute the verb phrase is the subject of this chapter.

5.1 Verbs

The structure of verbs is rather more complex than that of nouns in that there is a wider variety of productive processes involved in their internal make-up. The major patterns that are encountered involve reduplication and affixation, though there is also evidence of a minor pattern of verbal compounding.

5.1.1 Reduplication

While reduplication is very commonly encountered with verbs, there is considerable variation between speakers in the extent to which this process is used, as well as variation in the particular kinds of patterns that are encountered. Speakers of different languages tend to apply the different patterns of reduplication of their own languages when they are speaking Bislama. There may also be an element of individual variability involved. Reduplication is also something that is perhaps a little bit more difficult to pin down than other aspects of the grammar because sometimes the choice by a speaker to use a reduplicated form seems to be more a matter of stylistic judgment rather than of purely grammatical considerations.

Reduplication is very frequently used to derive new verbs, though it is also used with adjectives (§4.3.3.1), and very occasionally with words from other parts of speech (as indicated in §4.1.3). The reduplication of verbs is discussed separately from other parts of speech because there are some differences both in the forms that reduplication takes, as well as the functions that it expresses.

Reduplication of verbs normally does not involve repetition of an entire verb, so we typically encounter what are referred to as patterns of partial reduplication. Thus, although the noun *kala* 'color' can undergo full reduplication to give *kala-kala*, a verb of the shape *rama* 'pound' does not reduplicate as **rama-rama*. There are three different patterns of partial reduplication of verbs that are commonly encountered: complete syllable reduplication, partial syllable reduplication and partial root reduplication.

Complete syllable reduplication involves the repetition of the entire first syllable of the verb. If an initial syllable consists of just a consonant followed by a single vowel, then what is repeated is the initial *CV-*, resulting in the reduplication of *rama* 'pound' as *ra-rama*, of *tajem* 'touch' as *ta-tajem*, and of *fogivim* 'forgive' as *fo-fogivim*. Even if a root appears to involve some kind of historical process of reduplication, this is no bar to its undergoing reduplication according to this pattern, as *kakae* 'eat' can be reduplicated as *ka-kakae*.

An initial syllable may end with a consonant, in which case it is the initial *CVC-* that is reduplicated. Thus, *foldaon* 'fall' can be reduplicated as *fol-foldaon*, and *askem* 'ask' can be reduplicated as *as-askem*. An initial syllable can also begin with a sequence of consonants. If the word begins with two or more consonants before the first vowel, then all of these consonants will be reduplicated along with the first vowel, as we find with the reduplication of *brekem* 'break' as *bre-brekem*. Where an initial syllable contains two vowels in sequence, either just the first vowel can appear in the reduplicated syllable, or both vowels can be repeated together. We therefore find that *faetem* 'punch' can be reduplicated as either *fa-faetem* or *fae-faetem*, *laekem* 'like' can be reduplicated as both *la-laekem* or *lae-laekem*, and *giaman* 'tell lies' can be reduplicated variably as *gi-giaman* or *gia-giaman*.

The pattern of partial syllable reduplication differs from the first pattern described in that it involves the repetition of just the first consonant (or consonants, if the word begins with a sequence of consonants) and the following vowel, but without the final consonant of the syllable. Examples such as the reduplication of *jam* 'jump' as *ja-jam* or the reduplication of *foldaon* 'fall' as *fo-foldaon* illustrate this pattern.

By the third pattern—referred to above as partial root reduplication—what is repeated extends beyond the complete initial syllable and includes also the initial consonant of the second syllable. By this pattern, forms such as *rama* 'pound', *jenis* 'change', *fogivim* 'forgive', and *save* 'know' reduplicate as *ram-rama*, *jen-jenis*, *fog-fogivim*, and *sav-save* respectively. Where the initial syllable contains two vowels, these again both appear in the reduplicated syllable along with the following consonant, such as we find with the reduplication of *giaman* 'tell lies' as *giam-giaman*. Very frequently, transitive verb roots of a single syllable of the shape *CVC-* that carry the suffix *-Vm* (§5.1.3.1) undergo reduplication of the entire root. We therefore find that *karem* 'take' may be reduplicated as *kar-karem*, *katem* 'cut' as *kat-katem*, *faetem* 'punch' as *faet-faetem*, and *laekem* 'like' as *laek-laekem*.

When the first syllable of a verb consists of just a vowel, this cannot be reduplicated according to the pattern of initial syllable reduplication described above, as this would result in two identical vowels appearing one after the other. To prevent this, such verbs can only reduplicate by the third pattern. Thus, *arier* 'reverse' reduplicates as *ar-arier* and not as **a-arier*. There is a similar restriction against the reduplication of roots in which the initial syllable and the following syllable both begin with the same consonant. In order to prevent two identical consonants from appearing together, such forms never reduplicate according to the second pattern described above. Thus, *skrasem* 'scratch' reduplicates only as *skra-skrasem* and never as **skras-skrasem*.

CHAPTER 5

The same verb can appear in a variety of different reduplicated guises. A form such as *brekem* 'break', for example, can be reduplicated as *bre-brekem* or as *brek-brekem*, while a form such as *faetem* 'punch' can appear in any of the following reduplicated guises: *fa-faetem, fae-faetem, faet-faetem*.[1] Some verb roots may also have slightly different shapes involving the addition or modification of some sounds (as described in §2.2) that are often used by different speakers, such as we find when some speakers say *jam* 'jump' while others may say instead *jiam*. Of course, either of these forms can undergo reduplication, which means that we can expect to encounter any of the following reduplicated forms: *ja-jam, jam-jam, ji-jiam, jia-jiam, jiam-jiam*.

So far, I have just presented the forms of reduplicated verbs without mentioning the meanings that they express. There is one function of reduplication that is rather restricted in its distribution, and I will mention this first of all. With a small number of transitive verbs that have roots of just a single syllable—which are usually followed by the transitive suffix -*Vm* (§5.1.3.1)—a corresponding intransitive verb is derived by complete reduplication of the verb root, along with the loss of the transitive suffix. Table 5.1 sets out pairs of verbs that reflect this pattern. This pattern is restricted to just this small set of forms and cannot be extended to other verbs. Thus, from *kilim* 'kill (something)' it is not possible to derive the logically possible form *kil-kil 'kill (intransitively)'.[2]

In the discussion that follows, I have not attempted to ascribe separate functions to the different patterns of reduplication set out above. Whether a form such as *faetem* 'punch' reduplicates as *fa-faetem, fae-faetem*, or *faet-faetem*, appears to be largely irrelevant as far as the various functions of reduplication are concerned, with these different forms being used more or less interchangeably.

The following functions of reduplication are encountered with large numbers of verbs:

- *Random action*

A reduplicated verb can indicate that the action referred to by the verb takes place in a variety of locations. Compare, therefore, the examples on the following page, in which the same verb appears first in its unreduplicated form and then in a reduplicated form:

---

[1] Roots of a single open syllable are indeterminate between these patterns, so *go* 'go' reduplicates as *go-go*, while *rao* 'argue' becomes *rao-rao*. Such forms also technically fall under the heading of complete reduplication, as does the reduplication of verbs of a single closed syllable, such as the reduplication of *jam* 'jump' as *jam-jam* and *dring* 'drink' as *dring-dring*.

[2] Some verbs, originally only ever found with the transitive suffix (§5.1.3.1), correspond to occasional intransitive forms derived by removing the suffix and using the unreduplicated root. Thus, *fraenem* 'fry', *granem* 'grind', and *sperem* 'spear' correspond to intransitive *fraen* 'fry', *gran* 'grind', *sper* 'spear'. We therefore occasionally encounter sentences such as the following:

Man ia i stap sper long rif.
'That guy is spearing on the reef.'

Table 5.1 Reduplicated Intransitive Verbs

Transitive Verb		Intransitive Verb	
digim	'dig (something)'	*dig-dig*	'dig'
katem	'cut (something)'	*kat-kat*	'cut'
pusum	'push (something)'	*pus-pus*	'push'
sekem	'shake (something)'	*sek-sek*	'shake'
luk	'look at (something)'	*luk-luk*	'look'

Man ia i jam long fanis ia kasem graon.
'That man jumped from the fence to the ground.'

Pikinini ia i jajam olbaot long yad mo i no save stap kwaet.
'That child jumped all over the yard and he can't keep quiet.'

Hem i sakem paoda long hed blong mi long taem blong bonane.
'She tipped powder over my head at new year.'

Long taem blong bonane ol man oli saksakem paoda mo ples i waet nomo.
'At new year, people tipped powder everywhere and everything was white.'

- *Continuous/habitual action*

Actions that are either habitual or continuous can also be marked by reduplication of the verb. Thus:

Joseph i giaman long mi yestedei.
'Joseph lied to me yesterday.

Joseph i giagiaman oltaem nomo—neva bae mi bilivim samting we hem i talem.
'Joseph always lies—I will never believe anything he says.'

Tufala i rao from graon, be tufala i stretem finis.
'They argued over land, but they have settled it.'

Tufala i raorao, be toktok i no finis yet.
'They argued on and on, and the discussion isn't over yet.'

Note that habitual or continuous actions can also be expressed by means of the verbal auxiliary *stap* (§5.3.5.4).

- *Reciprocal action*

Verbs that have plural subjects expressing actions that affect the same group of subjects and objects can also be expressed by reduplicating the verb. Thus:

Franis lanwis i mekem se yumi save ol man Kaledoni.
'The French language makes it so that we can know New Caledonians.'

Bislama nao i mekem se yumi savsave yumi.
'It is Bislama that makes it so that we can know each other.'

Dog blong mi i no save kakae man.
'My dog does not bite.'

CHAPTER 5

*Tufala dog ia i stap **kakakae** tufala.*
'Those two dogs are biting each other.'

- *Intensive*

Finally, reduplication can indicate that something is characterized to a considerable extent by some quality:

Trak blong mi i fas long sofmad.
'My car got stuck in the mud.'

*Sapos yu go long New York, bae yu luk trak i **fasfas** long evri kona.*
'If you go to New York, you will see cars all clogged at every intersection.'

5.1.2 Compounds

There is a small number of verbal compounds in Bislama. The verb *save* 'know' can be used as the second part of a compound after a verb of perception to indicate the means by which the perception has been achieved. Thus, from *harem* 'hear, feel', *luk* 'see', and *smelem* 'smell' we can derive *harem-save* 'recognize by sound or touch', *luk-save* 'recognize by sight', and *smelem-save* 'recognize by smell'. For many speakers, this pattern is strictly limited to the small set of verbs just presented, and other logically possible combinations such as *likim* 'lick' and *tajem* 'touch' with *save* 'know' as *likim-save 'recognize by licking' or *tajem-save 'recognize by touch' are simply not used. However, this pattern does seem to be coming to be used more widely by some speakers, with forms such as *filim-save* 'recognize by touch' derived from *filim* 'feel', *ting-save* 'realize, be aware' from *ting* 'think', and *ridim-save* 'understand through reading' from *ridim* 'read' starting to be used.

Another pattern of verbal compounding that is encountered with a fair number of words involves the combination of the root of a transitive verb (i.e., what is left of a transitive verb after the removal of the transitive suffix -*Vm*) and a following noun. Such combinations of verbs and nouns are restricted to fixed expressions and have meanings that are often only partly predictable from the meanings of the verbs and nouns that make them up. Thus, *givim* 'give' and *han* 'hand' results in *giv-han* 'help'. The same pattern is reflected in the following additional examples: *sekem* 'shake' and *han* 'hand' giving *sek-han* 'shake hands', *wasem* 'wash' and *fes* 'face' giving *was-fes* 'wash one's face', *wasem* 'wash' and *han* 'hand' giving *was-han* 'wash one's hands', *brasem* 'brush' and *tut* 'teeth' giving *bras-tut* 'brush one's teeth', *karem* 'get' and *kil* 'injury' giving *kar-kil* 'be injured', *spenem* 'spend' and *taem* 'time' giving *spen-taem* 'spend time', *klapem* 'clap' and *han* 'hand' giving *klap-han* 'applaud', and *pem* 'pay' and *ren* 'rent' giving *pe-ren* 'pay rent'.

A particularly common pattern is for the verbs *mekem* 'make' and *tekem* 'take' to form compounds of this type. From *mekem* we encounter compounds with *noes* 'noise' to give *mek-noes* 'disturb', with *ful* 'fool' to give *mek-ful* 'ridicule', with *fani* 'joke' to give *mek-fani* 'joke', with *hed* 'head' to give *mek-hed* 'behave inconsiderately', and with *mes* 'mess' to give *mek-mes* 'muck around'. *Tekem* is compounded with *rod* 'road' to give *tek-rod* 'be on one's way', with *taem* 'time' to give *tek-taem* 'take a long time', and with *pat* 'part' to give *tek-pat* 'participate'.

5.1.3 Affixation

The final morphological process associated with verbs in Bislama is suffixation. There is a very widely distributed suffix in Bislama that can be referred to as the transitive suffix, as well as a small set of what I will refer to as directional suffixes.

5.1.3.1 Transitive Suffix

There is a frequently encountered verbal suffix in Bislama that I have referred to prior to now as -*Vm*. This suffix usually ends in *m*, but there is generally also a preceding vowel that varies in shape according to the sounds that are found in the base to which it is attached.

With verbs ending in consonants where there is either a preceding single *a*, *e*, or *o*, or there is a preceding diphthong (*ae*, *oe*, *ao*), this suffix has the form -*em*. Note, therefore, the following verbs carrying this form of the suffix, along with the roots from which they are derived:[3] *melek* 'milk' gives *melek-em*, *level* 'level' gives *level-em*, *smok* 'smoke' gives *smok-em*, *bon* 'burn' gives *bon-em*, *slak* 'loose' gives *slak-em*, *taet* 'tight' gives *taet-em*, *boel* 'boil' gives *boel-em*, and *draon* 'drown' gives *draon-em*.

If the vowel that precedes the final consonant of the root is *i* or *u*, then the suffix -*Vm* appears instead as -*im* and -*um* respectively. Thus, from *rid* 'read' we get *rid-im*, from *stil* 'steal' we get *stil-im*, from *kuk* 'cook' we get *kuk-um*, and from *rus* 'roast' we get *rus-um*.

With the addition of the various forms of the suffix -*Vm*, the consonant at the end of the root also occasionally changes. Where a root ends in *f* (and this derives from a word in English that is pronounced with a *v*-sound), then the *f* often changes to a *v* in the suffixed form of the verb in Bislama. Thus, *bilif* 'believe' gives *biliv-im*, *muf* 'move' gives *muv-um*, and *pruf* 'prove' gives *pruv-um*. However, where the source word in English ends instead with an *f*-sound, this remains unchanged in the suffixed form of the verb. Thus, *of* 'off' results in the suffixed form *of-em*.

There is some variability in the pronunciation of suffixed forms that are derived from English words ending in *b*, *d*, and *g*. The Bislama forms of such words are generally pronounced with *p*, *t*, and *k* at the end of the word (§2.1). Thus, the English word *read* is usually pronounced in Bislama as *rit*, even though it is normally still written with the letter *d*, i.e., *rid*. When the -*Vm* suffix is added to such words, the resulting form *rid-im* continues to be pronounced by some speakers as if it were spelt *ritim*. On the other hand, some speakers change the *t* at the end of the suffixed form to a *d*, resulting in alternations in pronunciation between *rit* and *ridim*.

We also encounter variation between speakers with respect to verbs that are derived from English words ending in two consonants but where the second of these consonants is regularly lost in Bislama. For example, *paint* appears simply as *pen* in Bislama, and *pump* appears as *pam*. With some words of this type—though by no means all—the deleted second consonant sometimes reappears with the addition

---

[3] The suffixed verbs are not translated at this stage, as I have not yet described the functions of -*Vm*.

CHAPTER 5

of the suffix *-Vm*. Thus, while the suffixed forms of *pen* 'paint' and *brodkas* 'broadcast' are sometimes simply *pen-em* and *brodkas-em* (as governed by the rules stated above), some speakers—particularly those who are more highly educated in English—"reinstate" the lost consonants and say *pent-em* and *brodkast-em*. This kind of reinstatement of lost consonants does not affect all words equally. The suffixed form of *pam* 'pump', for example, almost invariably remains as *pam-em* rather than becoming **pamp-em*.

When a root ends in a vowel rather than a consonant, there is a fairly complex set of variations in the shape of the suffix *-Vm*. When the final vowel is *o* (whether as a single vowel or in the sequence *ao*), then the suffix appears again as *-em*. Thus, corresponding to *dro* 'draw' we find *dro-em* and to *alao* 'allowed' we find *alao-em*. However, if the root ends in either of the single vowels *i* or *e*, or a diphthong ending in *e* (*ae*, *oe*), then the suffix takes the shape *-m* instead, without any vowel at the beginning. This pattern is encountered with roots such as *jiki* 'cheeky', which gives *jiki-m*, *pe* 'pay', which gives *pe-m*, *rere* 'ready', which gives *rere-m*, *drae* 'dry', which gives *drae-m*, and *enjoe* 'enjoy', which gives *enjoe-m*. If the vowel at the end of the root is *u*, then the form of the suffix is *-im*. Thus, *skru* 'screw' gives *skru-im*.

With words ending in a consonant followed by the vowel *a*, or by the vowel *u* followed by *a*, the suffix appears as *-rem*. Thus, *hama* 'hammer' corresponds to *hama-rem*, *ansa* 'answer' corresponds to *ansa-rem*, and *tua* 'tour' corresponds to *tua-rem*. However, when the vowel *a* appears at the end of a word and there is a preceding *e* or *o*, then the suffix again takes the shape *-rem*, though in these cases the preceding *a* is usually deleted. Thus, *pripea* 'prepare' gives *pripe-rem*, *sea* 'share' gives *se-rem*, *faea* 'fire' gives *fae-rem*, and *stoa* 'store' gives *sto-rem*. However, it is also possible for the *a* to be retained, so some people will continue to say *pripea-rem*, *sea-rem*, *faea-rem*, and *stoa-rem* respectively.

Finally, with words that end in the two vowels *-ia*, we again encounter some variability between different speakers. Sometimes, *-rem* is added to the unmodified form of the root. However, in other cases, the *a* at the end of the root is lost and the suffix takes the form *-rim* instead. We therefore find alternations such as *klia* 'clear' which results in alternation between *klia-rem* and *kli-rim* and *stia* 'steer' which alternates between *stia-rem* and *sti-rim*.

In the examples that I have presented above, both the unsuffixed and suffixed forms of these words exist independently in the language. However, there are many verbs in Bislama carrying the suffix *-Vm* for which the unsuffixed root has no independent existence. Thus, with verbs such as *kar-em* 'carry', *tal-em* 'tell', *put-um* 'put', and *har-em* 'hear', while this suffix takes the shapes predicted by the generalizations presented above, the roots to which these suffixes are added, i.e., *kar-*, *tal-*, *put-*, and *har-*, are never used on their own without the accompanying suffix.

The suffix *-Vm* has a very clearly defined function in Bislama. A transitive verb is one that can be immediately followed by an object noun phrase, and any verb of this type in Bislama requires that this suffix be added. We can see this function most clearly when we compare a number of unsuffixed intransitive verbs with the corresponding suffixed transitive form of the same verb:

Bae yumitu rus.
'We will roast (food).'

Bae yumitu rusum taro.
'We will roast taro.'

Man ia i stap stil oltaem.
'That man is always stealing.'

Man ia i stilim mane blong mi.
'That man stole my money.'

This transitive suffix is so productive that any newly introduced transitive verb from English will automatically appear with the appropriate form of *-Vm*, for example *imel-em* 'email (someone)':

Stanley i imel i kam long mi yestedei.
'Stanley emailed to me yesterday.'

Bae mi imelem yu tumoro.
'I will email you tomorrow.'

The only major exceptions are verbs ending in vowels that have been incorporated into Bislama from French, as such verbs usually do not accept this suffix. Thus, from *rato* 'rake' (which comes from the French word *rateau*), it is not likely that people will express the corresponding transitive verb as **rato-em*.[4] However, verbs of French origin with final consonants can take a transitive suffix in the normal way. Thus, from *glis* 'slip, slide' (which comes from the base of the French verb *glisser*) we can get *glis-im* 'catch side on'.

In very fast colloquial speech, especially among younger speakers of Bislama, the transitive suffix in many contexts optionally loses its final *m*. This reduction appears to be most common when the verb is directly followed by an object noun phrase, as in the following:

Mi no boele ti blong yu.
'I haven't boiled your tea.'

This reduction in the shape of the transitive suffix never takes place when the verb appears at the end of a sentence and the object is marked by zero, as described in §4.2. Thus:

Boelem!
'Boil it!'

Ti blong yu mi no boelem.
'I haven't boiled your tea.'

However, reduction of the transitive suffix takes place occasionally within a sentence when the following material does not belong to a noun phrase object. We therefore also find examples such as the following in which a variety of different following elements are preceded by a transitive verb with a reduced form of the suffix:

---

[4] See §6.1.5.1.6 for a discussion of how the object of 'to rake' can be expressed with a verb that does not accept *-Vm*.

CHAPTER 5

*Mi **hare** i hot.*
'I feel hot.'

Kare i go.
'Take it away.'

*Bae yu **hare** gud.*
'You will feel good.'

*Bae mi jas **teke** insaed.*
'I will just get it inside.'

While *-em* is very frequently reduced to *-e*, other forms of the suffix are also sometimes reduced in the same way under the same conditions as already noted for *-em*, as shown by the following:

Kompiuta i on biti hapas fo.
'The computer is on past half-past four.'

*Roses flaoa i **stiki** yu?*
'Did the rose prick you?'

***Putu** gud ol klos blong yu.*
'Tidy up your clothes.'

There is a small subset of transitive verbs that are irregular in that they do not accept any form of the transitive suffix *-Vm*. The members of this irregular set are *kakae* 'eat, bite', *save* 'know', *lego* 'leave, release', *tingbaot* 'think of, think about, remember', *tokbaot* 'talk about, discuss', *gat* 'have', *se* 'say', *somap* 'sew', and *klaemap* 'climb'. Thus, *kakae* 'eat' never appears as **kakae-m*, even when there is a following object. Compare, therefore, the following intransitive and transitive uses of some of these verbs:

*Joseph i stap **kakae**.*
'Joseph is eating.'

*Joseph i stap **kakae** raes.*
'Joseph is eating rice.'

Other verbs in this set are only ever used transitively, but they invariably appear without the transitive suffix, as illustrated by the following:

*Bae i **gat** kava long aftenun.*
'There will be kava in the afternoon.'

*Mi no save **lego** yu.*
'I cannot leave you.'

*Hem i **se** wanem?*
'What did he say?'

In addition to the set of unsuffixed transitive verbs, there is a second set of irregular verbs in Bislama. These differ from the verbs just presented in that there is at least an option for the regular suffixed forms to be used, even if these suffixed forms are in many cases only very occasionally encountered. Verbs in this set are *dring(im)* 'drink', *luk(im)* 'see, look at', *swim(im)* 'bathe', *singaot(em)* 'call, shout at', *selaot(em)* 'remove (copra)', *seraot(em)* 'share, distribute', *belaot(em)* 'bail (canoe)', *lukaot(em)* 'look for, look after', *klem(em)* 'claim', *welkam(em)* 'welcome', and *brum(um)* 'sweep'. Thus, while *dring* 'drink' occasionally appears as *dring-im*, the form that is by far more frequently encountered is *dring*:

Man ia i stap dring jus nomo.
Man ia i stap dringim jus nomo.
'That man just drinks cordial.'

The transitive verb *luk* 'see, look at' is doubly irregular in that it can appear without the transitive suffix, but when the transitive suffix is present, it has the shape *-im* rather than *-um* as we would expect. Thus:

Bae mi luk yu tumoro.
Bae mi lukim yu tumoro.
'I will see you tomorrow.'

This set also includes a number of verbs ending in *-aot*, about which there is separate discussion in §5.1.3.2.2 below. The base that remains after the removal of *-aot* often has no independent function so these forms are treated as unmarked transitive verbs. However, these are occasionally attested with the *-Vm* suffix, so we find alternations between *singaot* and *singaot-em* 'call, shout at', *selaot* and *selaot-em* 'remove (copra)', *seraot* and *seraot-em* 'share, distribute', *belaot* and *belaot-em* 'bail (canoe)', and *lukaot* and *lukaot-em* 'look for, look after'.

Finally, there is a small number of transitive verbs ending in *-m* that appear either with or without the transitive suffix *-Vm*. We therefore find alternations of the following kind:

Oli no brum ples ia yet.
Oli no brumum ples ia yet.
'This place has not yet been swept.'

Olgeta blong smolaelan oli klem graon ia.
Olgeta blong smolaelan oli klemem graon ia.
'The people from the offshore island have claimed this land.'

Hem i swim bebi blong hem.
Hem i swimim bebi blong hem.
'She bathed her baby.'

Members of this set behave unpredictably in this way, as other transitive verbs ending in the same sound invariably accept the transitive suffix. Thus:

Oli stap pamem wota long springwota.
'Water is pumped from the spring.'

Hem i stap komem hea blong hem.
'She is combing her hair.'

With these two examples, we invariably encounter *pam-em* 'pump' and *kom-em* 'comb' in transitive constructions, while the unsuffixed forms *pam* and *kom* are invariably intransitive.

CHAPTER 5

5.1.3.2 Directional Suffixes

There is an additional set of suffixes that appear after the transitive suffix -*Vm* in the case of transitive verbs, or directly on the verb root in the case of intransitive verbs. These have the shapes -*ap*, -*daon*, -*aot*, -*raon*, and -*bak*. While they perform a wide range of functions, they can all be seen generally as marking direction of one kind or another.

These directional suffixes derive from the particles *up*, *down*, *out*, *around*. and *back* that are frequently encountered in English in what are often called "phrasal verb" constructions, though they have clearly become suffixes in Bislama. We therefore find examples such as *go-bak* 'go back, return', *laen-ap* 'lined up', *res-em-ap* 'raise up', *kat-em-daon* 'cut down', *poen-em-aot* 'point out', and *put-um-bak* 'put back'. While many forms of this type correspond directly to English phrasal verb patterns, some represent genuine new creations in Bislama, such as *tal-em-aot* 'report on' (from *tal-em* 'tell' plus -*aot* 'out').

In Bislama, these forms have become completely attached to the verb. In English, it is possible to say either *I will lift up the child* or *I will lift the child up*, with the form *up* appearing either after the verb itself or after the object of the verb. In Bislama, however, the verb and the suffix -*ap* must always appear together. Thus:

Bae mi leftemap pikinini.
**Bae mi left-em pikinini ap.*
'I will lift up the child.'

Similarly, with a sequence such as *go back* in English, the two elements can be separated from a verb by an accompanying adverbial phrase, as in *He went all the way back to his house*. However, in Bislama nothing can intervene between the two parts of *go-bak*, as shown by the following:

Hem i gobak olwe long haos blong hem.
**Hem i go olwe bak long haos blong hem.*
'He went all the way back to his house.'

When the -*ap* and -*aot* suffixes—that is, those which begin with vowels rather than consonants—appear after the transitive suffix -*Vm*, the vowel of the transitive suffix is sometimes deleted, leaving just -*m*, resulting in alternations such as *pulum-aot* and *pul-m-aot* 'pull out'. It is difficult to specify the precise circumstances in which this kind of reduction may take place, though it is clear that it is not possible at all when the root of the transitive verb ends in a sequence of two consonants. Thus, *left-em-ap* 'lift up' never undergoes reduction to *left-m-ap. The reduction seems to be most frequent with transitive verb roots ending in *l*, producing alternations such as *wil-im-ap* and *wil-m-ap* 'wind up' and *pul-um-aot* and *pul-m-aot* 'pull out'. However, transitive roots ending in other consonants are occasionally followed by the reduced form of the transitive suffix, so *hip-im-ap* 'pile up' sometimes alternates with *hip-m-ap*.

While these directional suffixes are very frequently attested on transitive verbs following the transitive suffix -*Vm*, they are also found on some unsuffixed intransitive verbs, as illustrated by the following examples based on *go* 'go' and *kam* 'come': *go-daon* 'go down', *go-bak* 'go back', *go-raon* 'go around', *go-aot* 'go out', *go-ap* '(of canoe) go aground', *kam-daon* 'come down', *kam-bak* 'come back', and *kam-aot* 'come out'.

5.1.3.2.1 -*Daon*

The suffix -*daon* is used in association with a verb that expresses a downward motion. We therefore find this suffix in examples such as the following:

Hem i solemdaon meresin blong hem.
'She swallowed her medicine.'

Oli katemdaon stamba blong manggo we i stap klosap tumas long haos.
'They cut down the mango tree that was too close to the house.'

5.1.3.2.2 -*Aot*

The suffix -*aot* indicates that an action takes place away from something. Thus:

Dokta i bin pulumaot olgeta tut blong olfala.
'The doctor pulled out all of the old man's teeth.'

It can also be used to indicate that an action is performed in such a way that it makes something clear or more obvious, for example:

Hem i soemaot mak we dokta i katem hem.
'He revealed the scar where the doctor had cut him.'

Oli faenemaot finis olgeta samting we Pakoa i stilim.
'They have already discovered everything that Pakoa stole.'

Jif bae i talemaot olgeta fasin nogud blong ol yangfala long nakamal.
'The chief will report on the misdeeds of the youths in the meeting house.'

Finally, -*aot* can be used to express the idea that an action is performed in such a way that something is completely affected by the action, for example:

Olgeta oli kilimaot ol waelpig finis long aelan blong olgeta.
'They have exterminated all of the wild pigs on their island.'

5.1.3.2.3 -*Raon*

The suffix -*raon* indicates that an action takes place in such a way that the position of something is reversed, for example:

Hem i tanemraon trak long hem.
'He turned his car around.'

5.1.3.2.4 -*Bak*

The suffix -*bak* can be used to indicate that an action is performed in such a way that the object is returned to its original location, for example:

CHAPTER 5

*Glendon i **putumbak** kaset long ples blong vidio.*
'Glendon returned the cassette to the video store.'

*Bae yu **givimbak** buk blong mi wataem?*
'When will you give me my book back?'

*Joseph i no **pembak** tri taosen vatu blong mi yet.*
'Joseph has not yet repaid my 3,000 vatu.'

The suffix can also be used with a verb in which the subject and object are the same, to express a reflexive meaning (§4.3.2), for example:

*Hem i **kilimbak** hem wan wetem nivakwin.*
'He killed himself with nivaquine.'

5.1.3.2.5 -*Ap*

The last of these directional suffixes is -*ap*. It is somewhat more difficult to come up with a clear statement of the meaning of -*ap* for all of its occurrences. Another difficulty is that -*ap* is somewhat less productive than the other suffixes just described in that it tends not to be readily added to new verbs in Bislama. In some cases, however, -*ap* has a directional meaning just as we find with the other suffixes of this type, indicating that an action is performed in an upwards direction, for example:

*Yumi stap **resemap** flag evri yia long Julae 30.*
'We hoist the flag every year on July 30.'

The same suffix is also sometimes used to indicate that an action is performed in order to make something become bigger, for example:

*Bae yumi **hipimap** doti i go long saed blong rod.*
'Let's pile the rubbish up alongside the road.'

However, on many other words, it is hard to specify a particular meaning that is expressed by -*ap*, in much the same way that it is hard to see any regular function for the form *up* in the English expressions from which these verbs are derived. Thus:

*Yumi stap **miksimap** Bislama wetem Inglis oltaem nomo.*
'We are always mixing Bislama and English.'

*Mekanik ia bae i **fiksimap** trak blong mi.*
'That mechanic will fix my car.'

The suffix -*ap* offers particular problems in a grammatical description of Bislama because of the difficulty in establishing a clear set of functions. It is in addition also somewhat unpredictable in its distribution. There are probably only a couple of dozen verbs in Bislama on which this suffix is found, including *kavremap* 'cover', *ademap* 'add', *fiksimap* 'repair', *wekemap* 'wake up', *laenemap* 'align', *fomemap* 'establish', *setemap* 'establish', *leftemap* 'lift up', *pikimap* 'pick up', *putumap* 'install (as chief)', *bagaremap* 'ruin', *stanemap* 'stand up', *resemap* 'raise, hoist up', *miksimap* 'confuse', *hangemap* 'suspend', *klaemap* 'climb', *wilimap* 'wind', and *fulumap* 'fill up'. Verbs carrying the suffix -*ap* differ also from verbs carrying

VERBS AND VERB PHRASES

the other directional suffixes in that -*ap* can generally not be removed at all. While verbs such as *katemdaon* 'cut down', *putumbak* 'put back', and *karemaot* 'take out' correspond to the unsuffixed forms *katem* 'cut', *putum* 'put', and *karem* 'take' respectively, a verb such as *wilimap* 'wind up' cannot have its directional suffix removed to give *wilim in Bislama, and the same is true for most—though by no means all—of the verbs carrying the suffix -*ap*.

However, the verbs just listed are clearly transitive verbs with recognizable transitive suffixes appearing before the suffix -*ap*. This means, therefore, that the form *wilimap* can be broken down into *wil-im-ap*, in an example such as the following:

Bae yu wilimap glas blong trak.
'Wind up the car window.'

If *wilimap* could not be broken down further into smaller elements, we might have expected the transitive suffix -*Vm* to appear at the end of the verb as if *wilimap* were the root, to give the form *wilimap-em. However, the following sentence is not possible in Bislama:

**Bae yu wilimapem glas blong trak.*

There is other evidence that forms such as these can be broken down as I have described into ROOT-*Vm-ap*. For one thing, forms such as *hang-em-ap* 'hang up' and *fiks-im-ap* 'fix up' are clearly related to the intransitive roots *hang* 'hang' and *fiks* 'fix someone up (with somebody)', as well as the plain transitive forms *hang-em* 'hang' and *fiks-im* 'fix'. However, while a verb such as *hipimap* 'pile up' does not occur alongside a plain transitive form such as *hip-im, there is nevertheless a corresponding noun root of the form *hip* 'pile', as well as an intransitive root that carries the directional suffix -*ap*, i.e., *hip-ap* 'be piled up'. Table 5.2 lists a small set of similarly constructed pairs of this type, some of which are based on an unsuffixed root with a clearly related meaning, while with others there is no independently occurring root. There are also forms that end in -*ap* where the suffix clearly derives from English *up* in which -*ap* has become a completely inseparable part of an intransitive verb root in Bislama. For example, there is nothing at all in the behavior of the verb *kirap* 'get up' which points to the existence in Bislama today of any kind of boundary between *kir*- and -*ap*.

5.2 Complex Verbs

Two verbs can be placed one after the other in Bislama in such a way that they behave effectively as if they are a single verb. Such constructions can be called complex verbs.[5] With verb complexes of this type, there is a single subject preceding both verbs as well as a single object following both. There is also just a single "predicate marker" associated with these two verbs (§6.1.1).

Simple verbs are found in sentences such as the following:

---

[5] Using technical vocabulary more familiar to linguists who specialize in the languages of Vanuatu, these can also be referred to as nuclear-layer serial verb constructions.

CHAPTER 5

Table 5.2 Transitive Verbs with -ap

Root		Intransitive verb		Transitive verb	
hip	'pile'	hipap	'piled up'	hip-im-ap	'pile up'
laen	'line'	laenap	'line up'	laen-em-ap	'line up'
miks	'mixture'	miksap	'mixed up'	miks-im-ap	'mix up'
*baga[6]		bagarap	'ruined'	baga-rem-ap	'ruin'
*wek		wekap	'wake up'	wek-em-ap	'wake up'
*stan		stanap	'stand'	stan-em-ap	'stand up'
*sar		sarap	'shut up'	sar-em-ap	'shut up'

Kali i katem faeawud.
'Kali chopped the firewood.'

Kali i spletem faeawud.
'Kali split the firewood.'

The following, however, is an example of a complex verb in which *katem* 'chop' and *spletem* 'split' are linked together in a single construction:

Kali i katem spletem faeawud.
'Kali chopped the firewood in two lengthwise.'

The behavior of such sequences of verbs in an emphatic negative construction further illustrates the way in which they function in the same way as ordinary single verbs. Such constructions involve a negative element that appears before the verb (§5.3.4) and an emphatic element that appears after the verb (§5.3.6). With complex verbs, the second element of such negative constructions cannot be placed after just the first verb, but it must appear after the second verb. Thus:

Kali i no katem spletem nating wud.
*Kali i no katem nating spletem wud.
'Kali didn't chop the log in two at all.'

Complex verbs of this type differ from the very restricted pattern of verbal compounding described in §5.1.2 where we find sequences of VERB + *save* 'know'. Compounds such as *luk-save* 'recognize (by sight)' are pronounced as single words whereas such combinations of *katem* 'chop' and *spletem* 'split' in the complex verb *katem spletem* 'chop in two' are pronounced as two separate words.

There is only a restricted set of transitive verbs that can appear as the second element in complex verb constructions of this type. These typically express meanings that are clearly related to their meanings when used as verbs in their own right, though there is sometimes evidence of semantic specialization. The second element can include any of the transitive verbs set out in Table 5.3, where the first column represents the meaning associated with the verb when it appears on its own

---

[6] Corresponding to *bagarap* 'ruined' and *bagaremap* 'ruin', there is a noun *baga* 'guy, chap'. While historically related to the verbs, the meaning as a noun and as a verb are so distant that it makes little sense to include *baga* as a related root.

Table 5.3 Transitive Main Verbs Used in Verb Complexes

Main verb		Second element in complex verb
spletem	'split'	'action resulting in something becoming split'
brekem	'break'	'action resulting in something becoming broken'
klinim	'clean'	'action resulting in something becoming clean'
blokem	'block'	'action resulting in something getting in the way'
spolem	'ruin'	'action resulting in something becoming ruined'
hipimap	'pile up'	'action resulting in something becoming piled up'
fasem	'tie'	'action resulting in something being tied up'
flatem	'completely finish'	'action resulting in something being used up'
finisim	'finish'	'action resulting in completion'
panisim	'punish'	'action performed excessively, or a lot'
meksave	'do enthusiastically'	'action performed excessively, or a lot'

while the second column expresses the meaning of the same form when it appears as the second member of a complex verb.

These verbs can follow an initial verb that is either intransitive or transitive, though sequences of two transitive verbs are more common than complex verbs involving initial intransitive verbs. Examples of intransitive verbs followed by transitive verbs in this type of construction are presented below:

Hem i sidaon blokem rod.
'She sat in the way on the road.'

Fatfat man ia i slip brekem bed blong hem.
'The fat man slept on his bed, thereby breaking it.'

When two transitive verbs are combined in this way, the initial transitive verb always carries the normal transitive suffix -*Vm* (§5.1.3.1). Thus:

Rop ia i no holem fasem pig.
'This rope did not hold the pig in place.'

Drong man ia i werem spolem sus blong mi.
'The drunk man wore my shoes, thereby ruining them.'

Of course, if the second verb is one of those transitive verbs described in §5.1.3.1 as not accepting any transitive suffix, then it will appear in this construction also without any suffix, for example:

Charlie i pikimap meksave ol apol.
'Charlie picked lots of apples.'

Just as main verbs can undergo reduplication, so too can the second elements in such complex verb constructions. We therefore find examples such as the following:

Mi katkatem brebrekem ol timba.
'I cut the timber all up into little pieces.'

CHAPTER 5

Although we normally only find two verbs used together in complex verbs such as these, we sometimes encounter three verbs placed one after another, as in examples such as the following:

*Olgeta oli **blokem putum krosem** wud ia long rod.*
'They put the tree across the road, thereby blocking it.'

There is also a handful of intransitive verbs that can appear in the second position in the same construction. Table 5.4 sets out intransitive verbs found in this construction, with meanings that are again sometimes specialized in relation to their meanings when they appear as the sole verb in a verb phrase. Such verbs sometimes express the manner in which an action is carried out while others express a resulting state. The following examples illustrate the use of these verbs with a following intransitive verb:

*Man ia i stap **lukluk stil** long mifala.*
'That man was spying on us.'

*Ol boe oli stap **dring haed** long reva.*
'The youths were drinking secretly by the river.'

The same forms can also be used after an initial transitive verb, and the resulting complex verb will then be treated as a transitive construction. However, these intransitive verbs do not accept the transitive suffix -*Vm* even though they may be followed by an object noun phrase, as illustrated by the following:

*Mi **kukum haed** ol yam.*
Mi **kukum haedem ol yam.*
'I secretly cooked the yams.'

*Olgeta oli **putum redi** ol klos blong mi.*
Olgeta oli **putum redim ol klos blong mi.*
'They put my clothes so they were ready.'

Table 5.4 Intransitive Verbs Used in Verb Complexes

	Main verb	Second element in complex verb
haed	'hide'	'action performed secretly'
raf	'dishonest'	'action performed dishonestly'
stil	'steal'	'action performed dishonestly'
taet	'tight'	'action performed so that something is tight'
redi	'ready'	'action performed so that something is ready'

5.3 Verb Phrases

A verb phrase is a group of words that is tightly structured around a verb, in the same way that a noun phrase is a group of words closely linked to a noun (or pronoun). The discussion below describes the behavior of words that accompany a verb within the verb phrase. It will be seen in §6.1.1 that many of the features associated with verbs in a verb phrase can equally be ascribed to other constituents occupying the predicate position in a sentence. In a sense, then, what is being described here is really the structure of the "predicate phrase". However, verbs represent by far the most frequently encountered elements within predicates, as well as being those predicate types that allow the greatest range of associated modifiers, so this information is presented here rather than in Chapter 6.

Grammars are typically organized primarily according to the types of structures found in that language. For each particular structure, meanings associated with that pattern are then described. That has largely been the approach in this grammar. With regard to the structure of the noun phrase, for example, each distinct structural pattern corresponds closely to a distinct function. However, with the Bislama verb phrase, closely related meanings are sometimes expressed across a range of different structures. For example, it will be seen in §5.3.3 that the future is marked in a way that is grammatically quite different to the expression of the past tense. Similarly, there is a variety of quite different kinds of imperative constructions which, if described in structural terms alone, would end up being dealt with in quite different parts of this grammar.

If this grammar were organized solely in terms of structures rather than functions, connections between these features might end up being obscured, or even lost to the reader. I have therefore deliberately chosen to describe the ways in which certain functions are expressed together in a single section, though with cross-references as needed to other relevant sections of the grammar.

In talking about verb phrases, there is another problem of a rather different nature. Whereas it is generally fairly easy to determine where a noun phrase begins and ends, and therefore what belongs in a noun phrase, it is sometimes rather more difficult to determine what properly belongs in a verb phrase and what represents an element of the sentence outside the verb phrase. While some constituents are fairly closely linked to the verb and thus clearly belong to the verb phrase, there is some indeterminacy about the boundary of the verb phrase, with some pre-verbal modifiers also appearing outside the verb phrase before the subject of the verb, and some post-verbal modifiers also appearing outside the verb phrase after the object of the verb.

5.3.1 Imperatives, Prohibitives, and Hortatives

The term "imperative" is used to refer to a verb that expresses an order of some kind, such as *Go away!* or *Sit down!* Imperative verbs in Bislama can be expressed by means of a completely unmodified verb. With a singular imperative, the bare verb may be used, although the second person singular pronoun may also precede this, for example:

Go!
Yu go!
'Go away!'

It is normal for imperative verbs with non-singular subjects to be accompanied by the relevant non-singular second person pronouns. Thus:

Yufala go!
'You (plural) go away!'

CHAPTER 5

Such imperatives tend to be considered to be fairly brusque in Bislama, so they are best used either with people you know very well, or perhaps with children (or animals). For people you know less well, it is possible to make imperatives more polite by using the corresponding future form of the verb (§5.3.3) with an imperative intonation, for example:

Bae yu go!
'Go away!'

Imperatives that are even more polite can be expressed using the verb *traem* 'try' before the verb in question, either with or without a singular pronoun. Thus:

Traem go!
Yu traem go!
'Please go!'

Of course, if the subject is not singular, the appropriate non-singular pronoun must precede the sequence of *traem* with the following verb, as in the following:

Yufala traem go!
'You all please go!'

Another way to soften an imperative to make it more polite is to use the adverbial *fastaem* 'first' (§5.3.6) in association with the basic imperative form of the verb, as in the following:

Kam fastaem!
Yu kam fastaem!
'Please come!'

Yutufala kam fastaem!
'You two please come!'

A polite imperative can even make use of more than one—or even all—of these softening strategies, as in the following roughly equivalent ways of expressing a polite imperative:

Yu traem kam fastaem!
Bae yu traem kam!
Bae yu traem kam fastaem!
'Please come!'

The word *plis* 'please' can also be incorporated into imperative constructions in Bislama in much the same way that we use the equivalent word in English as a way of making instructions more polite. However, *plis* is normally placed at the beginning of the sentence in Bislama, rather than appearing either at the beginning or the end as in English. Thus:

Plis kam!
Plis yu kam!
'Please come!', 'Come please!'

This construction has been mentioned last not because it more closely resembles English, but because this is perhaps the least commonly used strategy of all for softening an imperative in Bislama. However, rather than replacing the other strategies described above for softening an imperative, the form *plis* can be used alongside these. We therefore find people occasionally softening their imperatives with constructions such as the following:

Plis yu traem kam fastaem!
'Please come!'

A final kind of imperative is the sycophantic—or begging—construction in which *plis* is used as a verb followed by *long* (§7.3.2.1.1) and then the sentence containing the action that the speaker wants to happen. Thus:

Mi plis long yu kam!
'I beg you to come.'

Closely related to imperative is the prohibitive. This is a construction that is used when we want to instruct somebody *not* to do something. Prohibitives are derived from any of the imperative constructions described above by placing a negative word such as *no* 'not' or *nomo* 'no longer' (§5.3.4) immediately before the verb. Thus:

No go!
'Don't go!'

Yufala no go!
'Don't you all go!'

Yutufala nomo go!
'Don't you two go any more!'

Some of the more polite imperatives described above correspond to the prohibitive forms below:

Yu traem no kam fastaem!
Bae yu traem no kam!
Bae yu traem no kam fastaem!
'Please don't come!'

Plis yufala nomo kam!
'Please don't you all come any more!'

Mi plis long yu no kam!
'I beg you not to come.'

Also closely related to imperatives are hortative constructions. Rather than expressing an instruction to somebody to do something, the hortative expresses a wish or a suggestion to a group of people, including oneself, to do something together. Such constructions are expressed in English by means of *let's* before the verb. In Bislama, this meaning is expressed by placing one of the first person non-singular inclusive pronouns immediately before the verb, as in the following:

CHAPTER 5

Yumi go!
'Let's go!'

It is common for the verb not to be expressed at all when it is clear what the activity is from the context. Thus, if somebody sees somebody else engaged in an activity that they want to participate in, that person can just say:

Yumitu!
'Let's do it together!'

5.3.2 The Forms *i* and *oli*

The very first element of many verb phrases in Bislama is one of the two short words *i* or *oli*. A number of examples of verb phrases presented elsewhere in this grammar have included one of these two words. Verb phrases containing these words are presented below:

Taso i go.
'Taso went.'

Ol man Ajin oli pemaot wan sip.
'The people of Atchin purchased a ship.'

I and *oli* also appear in many other examples in the sections that follow. At this stage, I do not propose to discuss their behavior other than to say that if they are present, they always appear as the very first element within a verb phrase and before the various tense markers (§5.3.3), negative markers (§5.3.4), and auxiliaries (§5.3.5) that appear within the verb phrase.

The reason that I have chosen not to describe the behavior of *i* and *oli* at this stage is that their behavior is in fact rather complex, and can only be described with reference to elements of the sentence outside the verb phrase. In particular, whether or not we find one of these two forms, and, if they do appear, whether we find *i* or *oli*, depends largely on the nature of the subject noun phrase that precedes the verb phrase. For this reason, their behavior is described in more detail in §6.1.1, which deals with the overall structure of sentences.

5.3.3 Tense

When we talk about the tense of a verb, we are talking about the time at which the situation that the verb expresses takes place, i.e., whether it takes place in the present, the past, or the future. A verb in Bislama without any associated modifiers can be used in the expression of any tense as long as appropriate contextual clues are available. A form such as *mi go*, for example, could be used to express past, present, or future tense:

Yestedei mi go long taon.
'I went to town yesterday.'

Yu singaotem mi from wanem? Mi kam ia!
'Why are you calling me? I'm coming.'

*Nekis wik **mi** go long Santo.*
'Next week I'll be going to Santo.'

If a verb is not accompanied by any clear indicators of tense or if the surrounding context does not provide any clues about tense, then the verb will normally be interpreted as present or past rather than future.

The past tense is generally not distinguished at all from the present tense in Bislama, as the context normally makes it clear which tense is involved. However, if it is absolutely necessary to indicate that something took place in the past rather than in the present, this can be marked by means of the auxiliary *bin* (§5.3.5.2). This appears between the subject and its verb, and it follows the predicate marker (§5.3.2) if there is one. Thus:

*Mi **bin** go.*
'I went.'

*Tija i **bin** go.*
'The teacher went.'

For many speakers, *bin* is an ordinary past tense marker, though, given what I have said above, it is clear that it is not used nearly as frequently as the past tense forms of verbs in English. However, some speakers of Bislama use *bin* to mark tense only with certain kinds of past tense situations. In particular, it may express what we can refer to as prior past, referring to things that happened in the past that took place before some other following event. This is something that is expressed in English as *he had eaten* in contrast to *he has eaten* or *he ate*. When we say *he had eaten*, this implies that after he ate, something else happened. For some speakers of Bislama, *bin* is only used as an equivalent to *he had eaten* and would not be used to translate *he has eaten*.

There is a final form that is used to express a past tense meaning in Bislama and that is *jas*. This also expresses the past tense, though specifically those events that have only recently taken place, so it can be referred to as a marker of the recent past. *Jas* also appears between the subject (or the predicate marker) and the verb. Note that a verb can never be marked with *bin* and *jas* at the same time. Thus:

*Mi **jas** go.*
'I have just gone.'

The form *jas* expresses some other meanings in addition to immediate past tense, though these will be discussed separately (§5.3.5.3).

Although verbs in the future tense may also be completely unmarked, the future is much more commonly marked by *bae*, or by its longer and less frequently used alternative *bambae*. When a verb has a pronoun subject, the future marker appears before the subject, as in the following:

***Bae** mi go.*
'I will go.'

***Bambae** olgeta oli go skul long nekis vilej.*
'They will go to church in the next village.'

CHAPTER 5

The future marker *bae* is fairly commonly reduced in fast speech to *ba*, and even to just *b-* when the following word begins with a vowel rather than a consonant. The following alternatives for expressing the same meaning can therefore be heard:

Bambae *oli kam.*
Bae *oli kam.*
Ba *oli kam.*
B-*oli kam.*
'They will come.'

When the subject contains a noun rather than a pronoun, the future marker can appear either before the subject, or between the subject and the verb. If it appears between the subject and the verb, the future marker differs in its behavior from the various verbal auxiliaries described in §5.3.5 in that it precedes rather than follows the forms *i* or *oli* (§5.3.2). Compare, therefore, the following:

Bae *tija i go.*
*Tija **bae** i go.*
Tija i **bae go.*
'The teacher will go.'

This kind of variation is not permitted, however, when the subject is a pronoun. Thus:

Bae *mi go.*
Mi **bae go.*
'I will go.'

Pre-verbal *bae* can combine with post-verbal *finis* (§5.3.6) to express a meaning that is somewhat different from the function of simple *bae* as a marker of the future tense in a sentence such as the following:

Bae *yumitu fidim ol pig **finis***.
'We ought to feed the pigs right now.'

This combination of *bae* ... *finis* expresses a wish that something should happen immediately. A number of other quite different structures express the same kind of meaning in Bislama. One possibility is to use the conditional marker *sapos* (§7.3.2.2.6) in the same structural position described above for *bae*, as in the following:

*Kamiong **sapos** i pas long bus antap.*
'The truck ought to pass via the bush above.'

Another possibility is to use the word *blong* in the construction described in §6.1.2.3, illustrated as follows:

*Ol pikinini **blong** swim long dei.*
'The children ought to bathe in the day.'

Finally, for some speakers at least, the auxiliary *sud* (§5.3.5.7) may also be used:

*Ol pikinini oli **sud** swim long dei.*
'The children ought to bathe in the day.'

5.3.4 Negative Markers

Mention was made of negative markers in the discussion in §5.3.1 about the prohibitive, which is expressed by a combination of a negative marker in association with an imperative verb. There are three negative markers that can appear before a verb: *no* 'no, not', *nomo* 'no longer, not any more', and *neva* 'never, not ever'. These can appear before any of the auxiliaries described in §5.3.5. Thus:

Olgeta oli no bin stap singsing.
'They had not been singing.'

Olfala ia i nomo save wokbaot.
'The old man can no longer walk.'

Mi neva toktok olsem ia.
'I never speak like that.'

There is an additional negative form that is used only by some speakers, particularly those who are better educated in English. This is *nomaj*, which also appears immediately before the predicate. *Nomaj* is only ever used to negate an adjective and it expresses the idea of 'not very'. Thus:

Buk ia i nomaj gud.
'That book is not very good.'

The majority of speakers of Bislama, however, do not use this form, and express this meaning instead simply by using the ordinary negative marker *no* along with an adjective that is modified by *tumas* 'very', for example:

Buk ia i no gud tumas.
'That book is not very good.'

Neva exhibits some differences in behavior in comparison to the negative forms *no* and *nomo*. In addition to appearing between *i* or *oli* and the verb (or its accompanying auxiliaries), *neva* also has the option of appearing outside the verb phrase altogether, being placed at the beginning of the sentence and before the subject of the verb. Sometimes, *neva* is also found between the subject and the verb phrase. Thus, compare the following alternatives:

Ol man ia oli neva save talemaot ol kastom blong bifo.
Neva ol man ia oli save talemaot ol kastom blong bifo.
Ol man ia neva oli save talemaot ol kastom blong bifo.
'Those men can never reveal the ancient traditions.'

This kind of variation is not possible with a negative marker such as *no*. Thus:

Ol man ia oli no kam.
*No ol man ia oli kam.
*Ol man ia no oli kam.
'Those men did not come.'

The negative markers *no*, *nomo*, and *neva*—but not *nomaj*—can also be used in conjunction with *nating* or *wanpis* after the verb. The resulting combinations of *no/nomo/neva* and *nating/wanpis* represent strongly emphatic negatives, as shown by the following:

*Olgeta Compagnie Créole oli **nomo** singsing **nating** naoia.*
'The Compagnie Créole don't sing any more at all now.'

When these emphatic negative elements are used in conjunction with a transitive verb that has an object noun phrase, the emphatic second element can appear either immediately after the verb, or it can appear after the verb and its following object. Thus:

*Kensen i **no** haremsave **nating** voes blong mi taem mi toktok long telefon.*
'Kensen didn't recognize my voice at all when I spoke on the phone.'

*Mi **no** faenem brata blong mi **nating** taem mi go long haos blong olgeta.*
'I didn't find my brother at all when I went to their house.'

Like *nating* and *wanpis*, the word *yet* 'still' also appears after the verb in conjunction with a pre-verbal negative marker to mean 'not yet', as in:

*Mi **no** go yet.*
'I have not yet gone.'

This form also appears either immediately after a transitive verb or after the noun phrase object to the verb, as illustrated by the following:

*Smol gel ia i **no** finisim yet wok blong hem.*
'The little girl hasn't finished her task yet.'

*Mi **no** wasem fes blong mi yet.*
'I haven't washed my face yet.'

5.3.5 Auxiliaries

There is a set of forms that appear between the negative marker and the verb, which can be referred to as auxiliaries. Verbs can be associated with more than one of these auxiliaries at a time. In terms of which auxiliaries can appear together with the same verb, and which order they appear in with respect to each other, these need to be divided into four sets:

Set I	*bin, jas, mas, sud*
Set II	*save, stap, kanduit*
Set III	*wantem*
Set IV	*kam, go*

A verb can appear with one—and only one—auxiliary from each of these sets, and they must appear before the verb in the order I–II–III–IV. This means that we can expect to encounter verb phrases such as the following:

*Yu **mas** stap go long skul.*
'You have to go to church (all the time).'

*Hem i **bin** stap wantem kakae raes.*
'She had wanted to eat rice (all the time).'

The particular functions of each of these auxiliaries are discussed in turn in the following sections.

5.3.5.1 *Mas*

Mas expresses obligation and translates into English as 'must', 'have to', or 'have got to', for example:

Mi mas go luk dokta from we mi sik.
'I have to go to see the doctor because I am sick.'

Mas does not express just personal obligation, as it can also be used to express inevitability or certainty, as in the following:

Ples i hot olsem ia, i mas ren long aftenun.
'When it's hot like this, it's got to rain in the evening.'

Mas differs from most of the remaining auxiliaries in that it can also occur alone in a verb phrase without any accompanying verb. This is only possible, however, when the meaning of the associated verb can be deduced from the context. Thus:

Yu ting se bae i ren tedei? I mas.
'Do you think it will rain today? It's got to.'

Other auxiliaries, however, must be repeated with an associated verb. Thus:

Yu ting se i save ren tedei? I save ren.
*Yu ting se i save ren tedei? *I save.*
'Do you think it could rain today? It could.'

Mas can also appear within a predicate that is made up of a noun phrase rather than a verb, as in the following:

Mi save se i mas Kalomat from mi luk mak blong sus blong hem.
'I know that it must be Kalomat because I can see his shoe prints.'

Some speakers—particularly those who are better educated in English—are likely to use the form *masbi* instead of *mas* when there is a following noun phrase, for example:

I mas Kalomat from mi haremsave voes blong hem.
I masbi Kalomat from mi haremsave voes blong hem.
'It must be Kalomat because I can recognize his voice.'

5.3.5.2 *Bin*

The functions of *bin* as either a general past tense marker or as a marker of prior past were discussed earlier in the section dealing with tense (§5.3.3). A further example is presented below:

Mi bin go luk dokta from we mi sik.
'I went to see the doctor because I was sick.'

5.3.5.3 *Jas*

Jas alternates with *jes*, and sometimes *tes*, to express the same meanings. In the separate discussion of tense (§5.3.3), I indicated that this can be used to indicate that an action took place in the recent past, as illustrated by the following:

Mi jas pem wan tos long stoa.
'I have just bought a torch in the shop.'

However, *jas* functions as more than just a recent tense marker, as it can also be used to indicate that an action takes place spontaneously without any outside cause. Thus:

Taem mi stap long haeskul, mi go long wan stoa mo mi jas stilim wan tos. Mi no save from wanem nao mi bin mekem rabis fasin olsem ia.
'When I was in high school I went to a shop and I stole a torch. I don't know why I did something terrible like that.'

In this example, the speaker is talking about something that happened some time ago rather than something in the recent past. The use of *jas* here indicates instead that the action took place for reasons quite beyond the speaker's control in that the speaker is claiming to have "accidentally" stolen the torch.

This is not the only way in which this can be expressed. In §4.3.2, I referred to the use of *wan* when it modifies a singular pronoun in a way that expresses a similar meaning. This construction can be used in conjunction with the form *jas* to emphasize the lack of any obvious cause for a happening. Thus:

Wud ia i jas gru hem wan.
'The tree grew by itself (without having been planted).'

5.3.5.4 *Stap*

Stap is commonly used as a verb meaning 'stay' or 'be', as in the following:

Hem i stap long haos.
'(S)he stayed at home.'

The same form is also very widely used as an auxiliary expressing two different functions in Bislama. On the one hand, it indicates that an action is a continuous one. This corresponds to the construction in English that is expressed by means of the verb *be* with the following verb carrying the suffix *-ing*. The continuous activity can take place in the present, past, or future, as in:

Tija i bin stap lanem ol pikinini.
'The teacher was teaching the children.'

Bae mifala i stap kakae long tebol ia.
'We will be eating at that table.'

The second function of *stap* is to indicate something that takes place habitually. In English, this meaning is expressed by the plain unsuffixed form of the verb with no accompanying auxiliaries. Thus:

*Ol man Vanuatu oli **stap** dring kava be ol man PNG oli **stap** kakae betel.*
'Ni-Vanuatu drink kava but Papua New Guineans chew betel nut.'

Stap is commonly pronounced in colloquial speech as *sta*. Thus:

*Hem i **stap** kakae.*
*Hem i **sta** kakae.*
'She is eating.'

5.3.5.5 Save

Save—often *sae* in colloquial speech—also behaves both as a verb and as an auxiliary. As a transitive verb, it expresses the meaning of 'know', as in:

Yu save mi no?
'Do you know me?'

As an auxiliary, it performs three different functions in Bislama. It can be used to express the related idea of permission, as in the following:

*Long saed blong kastom ol woman oli no **save** dring kava.*
'Traditionally women may not drink kava.'

*Yumi **save** raetem leta i go long niuspepa sapos yumi wantem.*
'We can write a letter to the newspaper if we want to.'

It can also be used to express an ability to do something, as in the following:

*Mi **save** toktok Franis be i no tumas.*
'I can speak French but not too much.'

*Yu **save** dring hamas sel kava?*
'How many shells of kava can you drink?'

Finally, *save* is used by some speakers to express a meaning that is not so obviously related to the meaning of *save* as a verb, i.e., the idea that an action takes place habitually. This use of *save* only seems to be common with verbs of consumption or indulgence such as *kakae* 'eat', *dring* 'drink' or *smok* 'smoke', as illustrated by the following:

*Yu **save** dring kava?*
'Do you drink kava?'

*Man Niusilan ia i **save** kakae laplap.*
'That New Zealander eats pudding.'

*Mi no **save** smok.*
'I don't smoke.'

Some speakers do not use *save* to express this habitual meaning at all, and use instead the auxiliary *stap*, as described in §5.3.5.4. The last example, for many speakers, would therefore be expressed instead as follows:

*Mi no **stap** smok.*
'I don't smoke.'

5.3.5.6 *Wantem*

Wantem is commonly used as a verb in its own right meaning 'want', as in:

Mi no wantem maniok.
'I don't want cassava.'

As an auxiliary, it is most commonly encountered expressing the meaning of 'want to' with respect to the meaning of the following verb, as in the following:[7]

Marie i wantem wok long wan ofis blong gavman.
'Marie wants to work in a government office.'

Pikinini blong mi i no wantem kakae raes.
'My child does not want to eat rice.'

There is, however, a second meaning of *wantem* that is less frequently encountered. Before an adjective, *wantem* indicates that a change of state is about to take place. This function is illustrated by the following:

Trak blong mi i wantem rosta nao.
'My car is about to rust.'

Ren i finis mo ples i wantem drae bakegen.
'The rain is over and it is about to dry out again.'

With a verb that expresses an action of some kind, *wantem* can indicate that the activity is about to happen in the immediate future, for example:

Mi luk se i wantem ren.
'I can see that it is about to rain.'

A final function of *wantem* is to indicate that a state is in some way attenuated or half-hearted. This meaning is most likely to be expressed in relation to colors, as in the following:

Set blong mi i wantem braon.
'My shirt is brownish.'

5.3.5.7 *Sud*

This auxiliary is a relatively recent addition into the grammar of Bislama, having been introduced from English. However, it is now quite well established, especially among younger speakers. Given its English source, it is worth noting that it is commonly pronounced with initial *sh* rather than *s*. *Sud* expresses the meaning of 'should' or 'ought to', for example:

Yumi no sud wokbaot long ples ia.
'We ought not to be walking here.'

---

[7] The auxiliary *wantem* is very commonly pronounced as *wandem*. This form is then frequently also reduced to *wande*.

5.3.5.8 *Kanduit*

Kanduit is a somewhat archaic form that is now falling into disuse, though some people do still use it. It expresses an inability to do something, and in particular the meaning of 'not manage to', as in the following:

Joel i kanduit klaem kasem top blong hil.
'Joel didn't manage to climb to the top of the hill.'

For those who do not use this form at all, this meaning is expressed instead by means of the auxiliary *save* with an accompanying negative marker, i.e.,

Joel i no save klaem kasem top blong hil.
'Joel couldn't climb to the top of the hill.'

Given that *kanduit* is inherently negative in meaning, it never occurs with the preceding negative marker *no* in a sentence. This is the only auxiliary that is restricted in this way. *Kanduit*—like *mas*—can also appear on its own without any accompanying verb. The following, therefore, is also possible:

Hem i traem lanem kastom danis gogo be i kanduit.
'He kept trying to learn traditional dancing but he couldn't manage it.'

5.3.5.9 *Kam* and *Go*

Kam and *go* are very commonly used as ordinary verbs of motion, for example:

Kensen i kam long haos.
'Kensen is coming home.'

Bae mi go long wok.
'I will go to work.'

However, these words can also be used as auxiliaries in what we can call inchoative predicates, expressing the meaning of 'become'. These inchoative auxiliaries only appear before adjectives or nouns and never before verbs, though they are discussed in this account of the verb phrase because their behavior otherwise fits with the behavior of the remaining auxiliaries that do appear before verbs.

While both of these words express the inchoative meaning of 'become', there is a difference in meaning depending on which form is used. With *kam*, the state that is being achieved is one that is likely to be viewed as a positive development (or is at least viewed neutrally). With *go*, on the other hand, the state that is achieved is one that is likely to be viewed negatively in some way. Compare, therefore, the following:

Hea blong mi i stap go waet.
'My hair is going grey (a fact that I regret somewhat).'

Hea blong mi i stap kam waet.
'My hair is going grey (which I either don't particularly mind, or which I might even be happy about).'

CHAPTER 5

5.3.5.10 *Stil*

In addition to all of the auxiliaries set out in the preceding sections, we should add *stil* as a word that exhibits some similarities in its behavior to these forms, though it exhibits some grammatical peculiarities of its own. *Stil* expresses the meaning of 'regardless', as in the following:

Oli blokem hem long miting be hem i stil toktok.
'They prohibited her in the meeting but she spoke regardless.'

It should be noted that *stil* does not express the meaning of 'still' in English in the sense of referring to an ongoing action. This meaning is expressed in Bislama instead by means of *yet* (§5.3.6), as in the following:

Hem i toktok yet.
'She is still speaking.'

However, *stil* differs from the other auxiliaries in a number of respects. Firstly, there is a very strong stylistic preference for *stil* not to be accompanied by another auxiliary. If it does appear in conjunction with another auxiliary, *stil* comes first, as in the following:

Hem i stil sud toktok.
'She should speak regardless.'

Hem i stil wantem kam.
'He wants to come regardless.'

Stil is further exceptional in that it commonly appears outside the verb phrase, in a similar way to what has already been described for the future marker *bae* (§5.3.3) and the negative marker *neva* (§5.3.4). This means that *stil* can also appear before the subject of the verb at the beginning of the sentence, as in:

Stil Leimara i toktok.
'Leimara spoke regardless.'

5.3.6 Post-Verbal Modifiers

Verb phrases can also include a range of modifiers that follow the verb. One set of post-verbal modifiers includes the following forms:

- *Nating*

The form *nating* can follow a verb to express several meanings. It can indicate that an action is performed free of charge, i.e., not requiring payment of money. The following shows that *nating* can appear between a verb and its object:

Bae mi givim nating samting ia.
'I will give you that thing for free.'

It can also indicate that an action takes place without any kind of accompaniment, for example:

Mi kam nating. Mi no gat janis blong karem eni kakae.
'I have come without anything. I haven't had a chance to get any food.'

The form *nating* can follow the verb *stap* 'stay' to express the idiomatic meaning of 'be unemployed' or 'have nothing to do', for example:

Plante ol yangfala oli stap nating long taon.
'Many youths are unemployed in town.'

Nating can also express the idea that an action takes place spontaneously with no outside agency being involved, for example:

Wud ia i foldaon nating.
'That tree fell down by itself.'

There are other ways of expressing the idea of spontaneous actions including the use of the pronoun construction *hem wan* (§4.3.2) or the verbal auxiliary *jas* (§5.3.5.3). Thus, the following means the same as the example just presented:

Wud ia i jas foldaon.
'The tree fell down by itself (rather than being chopped down).'

The following represents an alternative way of expressing the same meaning:

Wud ia i foldaon hem wan.
'That tree fell down by itself.'

Finally, of course, it will be remembered that *nating* co-occurs with one of the negative markers preceding the verb (§5.3.4) to express an emphatic negative, in the same way as *wanpis*, for example:

Haos blong Dudley i no strong nating.
'Dudley's house is not strong at all.'

Mi no hanggri wanpis.
'I'm not hungry at all.'

- *Finis*

In addition to functioning as an intransitive verb on its own, meaning 'finish, end', *finis* also functions as a verbal post-modifier expressing the idea that an action has been completed or that a state has come about, for example:

Yu kambak finis long Santo?
'Have you come back from Santo?'

Hem i hipimap finis ol brikis.
'He has heaped the bricks up.'

Hea blong man ia i waet finis.
'That man is already grey-haired.'

Of course, a completed action can be expressed in association with the future tense markers *bambae* or *bae* (§5.3.3), as in the following:

CHAPTER 5

Tumoro bae oli wokem finis haos blong mi.
'Tomorrow they will have built my house.'

In contrast to the form *nating*, when the verbal modifier *finis* is used in association with a transitive verb with a following object, the modifier may appear either between the verb and its object, or after the VERB + OBJECT sequence. Note, therefore, that the last example could equally well appear as:

Tumoro bae oli wokem haos blong mi finis.
'Tomorrow they will have built my house.'

- *Yet*

When *yet* is used with an affirmative verb, it expresses the idea that an action is ongoing, corresponding to the meaning of 'still'. Thus:

Hem i toktok yet.
'She is still talking.'

The combination of *no ... yet* represents the only possible negative form of a verb marked with the perfective modifier *finis*. Note, therefore, the negative of the following sentence:

Hem i toktok finis.
'She has spoken.'

Hem i no toktok yet.
'She has not spoken yet.'

The following is not a possible way to express this meaning in Bislama:

*Hem i no toktok finis.

- *Gogo*

The verb *go* can be reduplicated to give *gogo* and this form can be used as a post-verbal modifier to indicate that something happens on and on, as in examples such as the following:

Pasta i toktok gogo be mifala i sidaon kwaet nomo.
'The pastor spoke on and on but we just sat quietly.'

With this function, it is common for *gogo* to be repeated an indefinite number of times to indicate the extent to which a happening is drawn out:

Pasta i toktok gogogogogogogo.
'The pastor droned on and on and on and on and on.'

Although *gogo* is most frequently used in association with a verb expressing an action, it is sometimes also used, especially by younger speakers, as a colloquial way of indicating that a state pertains to an excessive amount. We therefore encounter examples such as the following:

Mi harem kava ia i konkon gogo.
'This kava tastes really bitter.'

Ples i hot gogo!
'It's soooo hot.'

- *Mo*

The form *mo* can be used after a verb to express the meaning of 'more', as in the following:

Hem i kakae mo.
'He ate more.'

It is very often followed by a prepositional phrase introduced by *bitim* (§6.1.5.2.2) to express a comparative meaning, for example:

Hem i kakae mo bitim mi.
'He ate more than I did.'

Mo can also follow an adjective in the same way, for example:

Hem i strong mo.
'He is stronger.'

Hem i strong mo bitim mi.
'He is stronger than I am.'

However, adjectival predicates differ from verbs with respect to the behavior of *mo* in that they can be optionally preceded by *mo* to express the same meaning. Thus:

Hem i mo strong.
'He is stronger.'

Hem i mo strong bitim mi.
'He is stronger than I am.'

But note:

Hem i kakae mo.
**Hem i mo kakae.*
'He ate more.'

5.3.7 Modifiers of Manner

In addition to the various modifiers within the verb phrase described above, there is also a set of forms that appear after the verb to express the manner in which an action is carried out. These can all function as adjectives, though when an adjective that accepts the suffix *-fala* (§4.3.3.2) occurs in this position, it appears in its unsuffixed root form. Examples of this kind of construction are set out below:

Pakoa i katem nogud kenu blong hem.
'Pakoa carved his canoe poorly.'

Yu mas stanemap stret ol pos blong haos.
'You have to stand the house posts up straight.'

CHAPTER 5

*Sapos yu holem **strong** samting ia, bae i brok wantaem.*
'If you grab that thing hard, it will break straight away.'

*Yu mas talem **klia** samting we yu minim.*
'You have to say clearly what you mean.'

*Sam woman oli stap mekem **naes** ol gato.*
'Some women make cakes nicely.'

*Oli no holem **taet** rop.*[8]
'They didn't hold the rope tightly.'

Some adjectives have specialized meanings when they function as adverbial modifiers in this way. The form *gud* 'good' can be used to mean 'well' or 'properly', as suggested by its meaning as an adjective. Thus:

Yu mas raetem gud ol ansa blong yu.
'You have to write your answers well.'

Sometimes, *gud* can also be used to indicate that an action is performed thoroughly, or that a state has been thoroughly achieved, even where the resulting state of affairs is one that might be seen as bad or unpleasant in some way. We therefore fine examples such as the following:

*Hariken Uma i spolem **gud** Vila long 1987.*
'Cyclone Uma really damaged Vila in 1987.'

*Ol klos blong mi i wetwet **gud** long ren.*
'My clothes got thoroughly wet in the rain.'

*Letrik i nogat mekem se mit i sting **gud**.*
'There was no electricity so the meat went really rotten.'

The word *krangki* as an adjective means 'crazy'. The same form can also be used as an adverbial modifier after a verb to indicate that an action is performed un-usually, awkwardly, or wrongly in some way, for example:

*Hem i putum **krangki** trak blong hem long saed blong rod.*
'He parked his car awkwardly along the road.'

*Man ia i sidaon **krangki**.*
'That man is sitting in such a way that we can see things we shouldn't be seeing.'

Krangki can also be used to indicate that an action is performed without the conscious control of the subject, as in the following:

*Johnnah i stap singsingaot **krangki** taem i stap slip.*
'Johnnah calls out uncontrollably while he's sleeping.'

---

[8] While most people write verbs and their following modifiers as separate words, some such forms are written in translated church materials as part of the preceding verb. You can therefore expect to encounter variations in spelling such as *Oli no holem taet rop* and *Oli no **holemtaet** rop* for 'They didn't hold the rope tightly'.

When used after an adjective, *krangki* can indicate that the state has been achieved in a way that is unpleasant, for example:

*Klos blong mi i wetwet **krangki** from bigfala ren ia.*
'My clothes got wet through in the heavy rain.'

6: SIMPLE SENTENCES

While the previous chapters talked about the internal make-up of words in Bislama and how these go together to make up noun phrases and verb phrases, this chapter shows how these phrases are put together with each other and with other elements to make up complete sentences.

Sentences in any language can be described as either simple or complex. Simple sentences are those that talk about a single happening, or a single situation. Any sentence that contains just a single verb will automatically represent a simple sentence, as well as any sentence that does not contain any verb at all. The following, therefore, are examples of simple sentences in Bislama:

Mi go long taon.
'I went to town.'

Hemia dog blong mi.
'That's my dog.'

Sentences such as these contrast with complex sentences in which there are two (or more) situations, or happenings, referred to. Compare the last two examples with the following, which involves a complex sentence:

Mi go long taon blong pem wan aeskrim.
'I went to town to buy an ice-cream.'

In this example, two separate events are expressed by *Mi go long taon* 'I went to town' on the one hand and *blong pem wan aeskrim* 'to buy an ice-cream' on the other. This chapter describes the make-up of the various kinds of simple sentences in Bislama, while complex sentences are described in Chapter 7.

Simple sentences can be divided into two basic types: those that make statements, and those that ask questions. These two basic sentence types are described separately below.

6.1 Statements

We can draw a distinction between statements that have the form of predicate sentences on the one hand, and non-predicate sentences on the other. The vast majority of statements in Bislama are predicate sentences. These are sentences that are made up of a subject that indicates what the sentence is about and the predicate which says something about what the subject is doing or what the subject is like. The sentence below, therefore, is a predicate sentence, with the mark (|) dividing the subject from the predicate:

Reva blong mifala | i nomo stap ron.
'Our river is no longer flowing.'

The first part of the sentence (*reva blong mifala* 'our river') is what the whole sentence is about, and the second part (*i nomo stap ron* 'is no longer flowing') is what we are saying about the subject.

A much smaller number of statements are expressed instead as non-predicate sentences. Such sentences only refer to a single noun phrase without saying anything at all about that person or thing in terms of what that person or thing is doing, or what that person or thing is like. Such sentences also consist of two parts. The following is a non-predicate sentence, with the two parts of the sentences separated again by the mark (|):

Hemia | reva blong mifala.
'That's our river.'

In this sentence, we are only talking about a single noun phrase (*reva blong mifala* 'our river'). The other part of the sentence (*hemia* 'that') does not say anything at all about what the river is like or what it is doing.

6.1.1 Predicate Sentences and Predicate Markers

Predicate sentences can be described as consisting of an initial subject with a following predicate. The predicate in such a sentence can be a verb phrase of any kind (§5.3), as in the following, with the mark (|) again indicating the boundary between the subject and the predicate:

Mi | stap singsing.
'I am singing.'

Mifala evriwan | i no save kam.
'None of us can come.'

However, a predicate can also consist of an adjective (along with any accompanying modifiers), as in the following:

Yu | krangki.
'You are crazy.'

A noun phrase can also function as a predicate, as in the following:

Hem | i wan polis.
'He is a police officer.'

Taso | i no barava dokta.
'Taso isn't a real doctor.'

Even a prepositional phrase can function as a predicate, for example:

Dog ia | blong mi.
'That dog is mine.'

Haos blong mi | long narasaed reva.
'My house is across the river.'

Regardless of whether it is a verb phrase, a noun phrase, an adjective, or a prepositional phrase that makes up a predicate, they all behave in basically the same sorts of ways. In particular, these constituents can be preceded by the "predicate markers" *i* or *oli* (§5.3.2), and they can also be preceded by negative markers (§5.3.4) and verbal auxiliaries (§5.3.5), and they can be followed by verbal modifiers (§5.3.6). The following demonstrate these features:

CHAPTER 6

Hem | i wan polis finis.
'He is already a police officer.'

Hem | i bin polis fastaem.
'He was a police officer before.'

Taso | i wantem dokta be hem i no skul naf.
'Taso wanted to be a doctor but he wasn't educated enough.'

Mifala | i no bos yet.
'We're not the bosses yet.'

In order to describe the various sentence patterns that conform to this general type, there is one aspect of the grammar of Bislama that it is necessary to describe first, and that is what have often been referred to as "predicate markers". These represent features of the grammar of Bislama that are difficult to describe simply for the reason that there are many particular patterns encountered with specific types of subjects and in a wide variety of different grammatical constructions.[1] There is also a fair amount of variation between different speakers of Bislama in the behavior of these forms. What follows is an account of the behavior of *i* and *oli* in simple predicate sentences among a broad cross-section of speakers.

In Bislama the form *i*—and less commonly *oli*—often appears between a subject and a following predicate. We therefore find examples such as the following (with the predicate markers presented in bold type in each case):

Hem | i singsing.
'(S)he is singing.'

Roro | i save lukluk.
'Roro can see.'

Whether or not a predicate is introduced by a predicate marker, and if so, whether that predicate marker will take the form *i* or *oli*, depends in part on whether the subject is a noun or a pronoun and in part on whether the subject is singular or plural.

When the subject noun phrase is made up of a singular noun rather than a pronoun, the form *i* almost always appears before the predicate. Thus:

Wan dog | i stap singsingaot long naet.
'A dog was barking in the night.'

When the subject is a plural noun phrase, the predicate can be introduced by either *i* or *oli*. Thus:

---

[1] In addition, various accounts of Bislama have treated these forms somewhat differently, and sometimes also using different terminology. In continuing to use the term "predicate marker" in this grammar, I do not wish to assert that I am opposed to any particular analysis proposed by any particular linguists, but I feel that it is important to at least present the facts of Bislama grammar in a way that allows for maximum comparability between different accounts. Readers can refer to Lynch (1975), Meyerhoff (2000), and Crowley (2000b) for a range of opinions on this topic.

Sikis woman | *i kam.*
Sikis woman | *oli kam.*
'Six women came.'

Ol pikinini | *i stap singsingaot.*
Ol pikinini | *oli stap singsingaot.*
'The children are shouting.'

There is a certain amount of variation between the use of *i* and *oli* in such cases. Some speakers may prefer to use only *i* while others may use only *oli*, while sometimes the same speaker may vary between *i* on one occasion and *oli* on another occasion. Therefore it is not possible to come up with a firm rule about what constitutes correct usage in Bislama.

Things may be even more complicated than this because it seems that the choice of *i* or *oli* may sometimes even coincide with differences in the meaning of the sentence. For some speakers, *oli* is used with plural human subjects (or human and other animate subjects), while *i* is used with all non-human or inanimate subjects, whether singular or plural. Thus:

Ol pikinini | *oli foldaon.*
'The children fell over.'

Ol haos | *i foldaon.*
'The houses collapsed.'

Yet other speakers may distinguish between plural subjects acting individually (marked by *oli*) and plural subjects acting collectively (marked by *i*). Thus:

Ol pikinini | *oli foldaon.*
'The children fell over (each considered individually).'

Ol pikinini | *i foldaon.*
'The children fell over (considered as a group).'

In addition, some speakers—particularly those well educated in English—use *oli* in association with all plural nouns and *i* in association with all singular nouns, regardless of whether they refer to things, animals, or people. Thus:

Wan haos | *i foldaon.*
'A house collapsed.'

Ol haos | *oli foldaon.*
'The houses collapsed.'

Wan pikinini | *i foldaon.*
'A child fell over.'

Ol pikinini | *oli foldaon.*
'The children fell over.'

A final feature of predicate sentences involving singular noun phrase subjects that refer to people—and occasionally to nouns with non-human reference as well—is the tendency to repeat the third person singular pronoun *hem* after the subject, with the predicate marker *i* then appearing after this. Thus, in addition to:

CHAPTER 6

Bos blong mi | i sakem fulap boe.
'My boss gave many laborers the sack.'

we often the find the same meaning expressed as follows:

Bos blong mi hem i sakem fulap boe.
'My boss gave many laborers the sack.'

Such sentences effectively have two subjects, one of which is the initial noun phrase (*bos blong mi*), while the other is the following pronoun (*hem*).

With pronoun subjects, the introduction of predicates by *i*, *oli*, or nothing at all, varies somewhat from pronoun to pronoun. The following generalizations apply:

(i) Following the third person singular pronoun (*hem* 'he, she, it'), as well as any pronoun ending in -*fala*, we generally find *i*, for example:

Hem | i no swim yet.
'He has not yet bathed.'

Tufala | i no kam yet.
'The two of them have not come yet.'

However, with pronouns ending in -*fala*, the predicate marker *i* is often dropped. The last example will therefore sometimes appear as follows:

Tufala | Ø no kam yet.
'The two of them have not come yet.'

(ii) Following the third person plural subject pronoun *olgeta*, we normally find the plural form of the predicate marker (*oli*), though this alternates occasionally with *i*. Thus:

Olgeta | oli no kam yet.
Olgeta | i no kam yet.
'They have not yet come.'

(iii) The first and second person singular pronouns *mi* 'I' and *yu* 'you' never have any predicate marker. Thus:

Mi | Ø harem wan noes long naet.
'I heard a noise in the night.'

Yu | Ø no mas giaman olsem ia.
'You shouldn't tell lies like that.'

(iv) The first person inclusive forms *yumi* 'we (plural inclusive)' and *yumitu* 'we (dual inclusive)' appear most commonly without any following predicate marker, but occasionally we also find *i*, for example:

Yumitu | Ø save kakae raes nating nomo.
'We can just eat rice on its own.'

Yumi | i glad blong talem se yumi blong Vanuatu.
'We are happy to say that we are from Vanuatu.'

When any constituent appears between a pronoun and the following predicate, we always find one of the predicate markers, even after one of the pronouns where the predicate marker is optionally or obligatorily absent. A pronoun can be followed by a variety of modifiers (§4.3.2), including numerals and adverbial forms such as *tu* 'also', *bakegen* 'again', or *nomo* 'only'. In these kinds of contexts, the following additional generalizations hold:

(v) *Yumi* and *yumitu*, as well as any of the pronouns that end in *-fala*, are invariably found with the predicate marker *i* rather than zero. Thus, contrast the following:

Yumi | Ø no nid blong wet long plen tedei.
'We don't need to wait for the plane today.'

Yumitu nomo | i no nid blong wet long plen tedei.
'Just the two of us don't need to wait for the plane today.'

Note the following additional examples:

Mifala | Ø karem faeawud.
Mifala | i karem faeawud.
'We gathered the firewood.'

Mifala evriwan | i karem faeawud.
'We all gathered the firewood.'

There is an additional option, however, by which the complete subject pronoun can be repeated after the postmodifier, and before any predicate marker that might be expressed. Thus:

Mitufala nomo mitufala i go.
'Just the two of us went.'

Yumi evriwan yumi go.
'We all went.'

(vi) The pronouns *mi* and *yu* are repeated after the postmodifier, as in:

Mi nomo | mi no kam.
'Only I did not come.'

Yu bakegen | yu no save finisim.
'You again can't finish it.'

(vii) Finally, the collective pronouns *tugeta* 'they (dual)' and *trigeta* 'they (trial)' are invariably followed by the predicate marker *i*, for example:

Tugeta | i go.
'The two of them went together.'

6.1.2 Non-Predicate Sentences

Non-predicate sentences consist of two structural elements where neither behaves like a verb in any way. There are two kinds of non-predicate sentences in Bislama, which are described in turn below.

6.1.2.1 Presentative Sentences

In a presentative sentence, there is invariably a noun phrase (§4.3) while the other element is either the demonstrative pronoun *hemia* (§4.2) or the demonstrative *ia* (§4.3.5).

When we simply wish to assert the presence of something, we can make reference to it with a noun phrase with a following *ia*, as in:

Wan bigfala haos | ia.
'There's a big house.'

Mifala | ia.
'We're here' or 'It's us.'

An alternative is for the demonstrative pronoun *hemia* rather than *ia* to appear after the noun phrase. However, when *hemia* is used in a non-predicate sentence, this indicates that attention is being drawn specifically to the thing to which the noun phrase refers by pointing (or at least that its location can be deduced from the context). Note the difference between the following:

Wan bigfala haos | ia.
'There's a big house.'

Wan bigfala haos | hemia.
'That's a big house.'

When *hemia* is used in a non-predicate construction like this, it commonly also precedes the noun phrase rather than following it. Thus:

Hemia | wan bigfala haos.
'That's a big house.'

Hemia | pikinini blong krae.
'That's a cry-baby.'

Hemia | blong mi.
'That's mine.'

Ia, however, can never precede the noun phrase in this kind of construction. Thus:

Mifala | ia.
**Ia mifala.*
'It's us.'

The initial noun phrase in such a construction can also be the demonstrative pronoun *hemia*, which can itself be followed by the demonstrative *ia*, as in:

Hemia | ia.
'That's it.'

Non-predicate sentences can also be negated, though the pattern is quite different from the pattern described for the negation of verbs where a negative marker such as *no* is inserted immediately before the verb (§5.3.4). Because there is no verb phrase into which a negative marker can be placed, these non-predicate constructions are treated as if they were a kind of predicate construction. As was shown in §6.1.1, one of the main features of predicate constructions is the frequent presence of the form *i* at the beginning of the predicate. In order to negate non-predicate constructions of the type NOUN PHRASE + *ia*, the negative marker is added before the noun phrase and this is preceded by the predicate marker *i*. Such constructions therefore take the form of some of the subjectless predicate constructions described in §6.1.3.1. Thus:

I no wan bigfala haos | ia.
'There's no big house.'

I no mifala | ia.
'It's not us.'

I no hemia | ia.
'That's not it.'

When the non-predicate construction is based instead on the pattern *hemia* + NOUN PHRASE, the sequence *i no* is placed between the two elements of the sentence, again resulting in a kind of predicate construction. Thus:

Hemia | i no pikinini blong krae.
'That's not a cry-baby.'

Hemia | i no blong mi.
'That's not mine.'

6.1.2.2 Equational Sentences

The second kind of non-predicate sentence is what we can refer to as an "equational sentence". Such sentences contain two full noun phrases that are regarded as being in some way equivalent to each other. One pattern is for the two noun phrases simply to follow each other with a change of intonation marking the two noun phrases as being separate. We therefore find examples such as the following (with | marking the intonation break between the two noun phrases):

Man ia | tija blong mi.
'That man is my teacher.'

Taem | taem.
'Time is time (i.e., one should always come at an agreed time).'

Another possibility that is frequently encountered in colloquial Bislama in such constructions is for the two noun phrases to be separated by the form *se*, as in:

Taem | se vatu.
'Time is money.'

Mifala i gat evri samting we yufala i nidim. Hemia | se pepa, pen mo sises.
'We have got everything you will need. That is, paper, pens, and scissors.'

Tumoro | se wanem dei?
'Tomorrow is what day?'

CHAPTER 6

A slightly different kind of non-predicate construction of this type is one in which the first noun phrase is said to "mean" the second. In such constructions, we also find that *se* is used to introduce the second noun phrase:

"Riou" long Bislama | se nakato.
'The word *riou* (in the Paamese language) in Bislama means hermit crab.'

Mining blong grin long flaeg | se graon blong yumi.
'The meaning of the green on the flag is our land.'

Although there is a verb *se* 'say', in this construction it does not behave in any way like a verb, as it cannot be accompanied by any of the verbal auxiliaries (§5.3.5). However, when such sentences are negated, we find that a predicate marker becomes obligatory in association with the negative marker *no*. Thus:

Taem | i no se vatu.
'Time is not money.'

Equational sentences are in fact rather more commonly expressed by means of predicate sentences than by non-predicate sentences. The pattern that is used normally involves the double-subject construction described in §6.1.1 by which an initial singular noun (or a noun with some associated modifiers in a noun phrase) is followed by the pronoun *hem*, which is itself then followed by the predicate marker *i*. Thus:

Man ia hem | i tija blong mi.
'That man is my teacher.'

In contrast to the verbal predicate construction described in §6.1.1, where such NOUN PHRASE + *hem i* sequences typically involve only human noun phrases, in equational constructions such as these, the initial noun phrase can also be non-human, as illustrated by the following:

Taem hem | i taem.
'Time is time.'

Taem hem | i vatu.
'Time is money.'

6.1.2.3 'Ought to' Constructions

Another kind of non-predicate sentence is what we can perhaps refer to as 'ought to' sentences, named after their translation equivalents in English. Although this meaning is one that we might have expected to be discussed along with the auxiliaries that appear before a verb in the verb phrase (§5.3.5), its structure is so totally different from verbal auxiliaries that it really needs to be described here, along with the other kinds of non-predicate sentences.

These are sentences in Bislama that involve a noun phrase of some kind that is followed by a sentence introduced by *blong* (§7.3.2.1.1) to express the meaning of 'ought to' or 'supposed to'. We therefore find examples such as the following:

*I no **blong** ren tedei.*
'It's not supposed to rain today.'

*Yu **blong** go long Norsup?*
'Were you supposed to go to Norsup?'

*Mi **blong** karem raes.*
'I'm the one who should get the rice.'

*Ol pikinini **blong** swim long dei finis be no.*
'The children ought to have bathed during the day but they didn't.'

6.1.3 Constituent Order

The major constituents within a simple predicate sentence are the verb and its associated predicate, which invariably follows the subject. As indicated above, a variety of types of phrases can occupy the predicate position. While most predicates have the form of verb phrases, it is possible for noun phrases and a variety of other types of constituents to appear in the predicate.

6.1.3.1 Transitive and Intransitive Constructions

There are two types of verb phrase: intransitive and transitive. In the case of a transitive verb phrase, there may be a following object noun phrase. This means that Bislama can be described as having a basic SUBECT + VERB (+ OBJECT) order, just as we find in English, along with most of the local languages of Vanuatu. The following sentences exemplify this basic pattern:

Yu wok.
'You are working.'

Mi smelem smok.
'I can smell smoke.'

Papa blong Joe i wokem wan niufala haos blong hem.
'Joe's father built a new house for him.'

Third person singular pronoun subjects and objects are often expressed by means of zero rather than the pronoun *hem*, especially—though by no means always—when they refer to things or animals rather than to people (§4.2). This means that a transitive verb is not necessarily going to be followed by an object noun phrase at all, for example:

Jenny i laekem Ø.
'Jenny likes it.'

One variation on the basic pattern SUBECT + VERB + OBJECT involves predicate sentences that have no subject. However, because these sentences still function as predicate sentences, a predicate marker is required before the predicate, which can therefore represent the first element in a sentence. The various kinds of subjectless sentences in Bislama are described in turn in the following sections.

6.1.3.1.1 Meteorological Expressions

A number of verbs and adjectives expressing meteorological conditions that must appear with the preceding predicate marker *i*, which need not be associated with any subject noun phrase. Thus:

I hot.
'It's hot.'

I bin ren long naet.
'It rained overnight.'

I no kolkol yestedei.
'It wasn't cold yesterday.'

In such cases, it makes no sense to ask questions like *Wanem i bin ren?* 'What rained?', as *ren* is a verb that does not call for a subject.

There is a similar set of verbs in English, though it can be seen from the translations above that these require a noun phrase in the subject position, i.e., the "dummy" pronoun *it*. The number of verbs that require a dummy pronoun in English is substantially larger than this set of meteorological predicates in Bislama. In Bislama, meteorological predicates are sometimes, instead, associated with *ples* 'place' as a dummy subject noun before the predicate, for example:

Ples i hot.
'It's hot.'

Ples i hevi.
'It's humid.'

Sometimes, a verb that is preceded by *ples* may not be strictly meteorological, though it does represent a part of the overall physical environment, as in:

Mi harem se ples i glis.
'It feels slippery.'

Sometimes, a meteorological expression can be expressed by means of a noun referring to the surrounding conditions with an appropriate following verb in an ordinary sentence of the SUBJECT + PREDICATE type, for example:

Tanda i faerap.
'It thundered.'

Ren i ren.
'It is raining.'

6.1.3.1.2 General States

Subjectless sentences are also encountered in examples such as the following:

I gud we yumi stap yusum Bislama.
'It's good that we use Bislama.'

This example again begins with the predicate marker *i* before the predicate, in this case *gud* 'good', and there is no preceding noun phrase occupying the subject position. A sentence like this involves an adjective as the predicate, and that adjective expresses a general state that does not apply to any particular thing. Other examples of this kind of pattern include:

I had blong wivim mat.
'It is hard to weave a mat.'

I no isi tumas blong klaem hos.
'It's not very easy to ride a horse.'

I stret we yumi dring kava evri dei.
'It's appropriate that we drink kava every day.'

I nogud we ol man oli stap smok.
'It's bad that people smoke.'

6.1.3.1.3 The Existential Verb *gat*

The verb *gat* is a transitive verb meaning 'have', as in the following:

Yumi no gat kava long ples ia.
'We don't have any kava here.'

In this case, the verb clearly has a subject, i.e., *yumi* 'we (plural inclusive)'. However, sentences containing this verb *gat* with a following object can also be used without any subject at all in order to assert the existence of something. In this construction, the predicate marker is invariably *i*. No noun phrase can be inserted as a subject before the predicate marker. Thus:

I gat kava long nakamal.
'There is kava in the kava bar.'

I gat plante man long haos.
'There were lots of people at home.'

Of course, the negative form of such a sentence indicates that something does not exist. Thus:

I no gat fulap studen long skul tedei.
'There are not many students at school today.'

Given that *gat* is a transitive verb, there is always the possibility that it can be associated with a deleted object, as mentioned toward the beginning of this section. Thus, when it is quite clear from the context exactly what is present (or not present), this can be expressed as follows:

I gat.
'There is some.'

I no gat.
'There is none.'

6.1.3.1.4 Negation of Incomplete Sentences

We often find individual words or phrases used in what we might want to call "incomplete sentences". Such forms may represent perfectly legitimate utterances in their own right, though they may only be properly understood in reference to something that has already been said, or in reference to something about the surrounding context. For example, the following could not function independently of any context as a meaningful utterance:

Naoia.
'Now.'

However, it perfectly legitimate say this in response to a question such as :

Wanem taem bae yu wokem? Naoia.
'When will you do it? (I'll do it) now.'

An utterance such as *Naoia* clearly does not represent a predicate. However, it is something that can be negated. When we want to express the negative form of such an answer, it must be expressed within a negated subjectless predicate construction introduced by *i*, as follows:

Wanem taem bae yu wokem? I no naoia.
'When will you do it? Not now.'

There is also a particular negative construction involving the verb *se* 'say' that is expressed as a subjectless predicate sentence resulting in the fixed sequence of *i no se*. This expresses the idea of 'it doesn't mean ...' or, more idiomatically, 'I don't meant to say that ...'. Thus:

I no se ples i hot tumas, be stil ples i hot.
'I don't mean to say it's too hot, but it is nevertheless hot.'

Nakamal ia. Yufala i mas salem sigaret. I no se plante, be frut nomo.
'This is a kava bar. You should sell cigarettes. Not lots, just individual ones.'

6.1.3.1.5 Actions without Causers

Look at the following sentence:

Olgeta oli stilim tep blong Roy.
'They stole Roy's cassette player.'

This is a predicate sentence that contains a subject, i.e., the pronoun *olgeta* 'they'. Because the subject indicates who caused something to happen (i.e., the theft of Roy's cassette player), we can say that this is a sentence in which the cause of the happening is clearly expressed within the sentence itself.

By way of contrast, however, look at the following sentence:

Mi wekap long moning mo mi luk tep blong mi i lus. Oli stilim long naet.
'I woke up in the morning and my cassette player was missing. It was stolen in the night.'

In this situation, when we say something like *oli stilim*, we clearly are not pointing to any particular individuals as the ones who carried out the action. It could be that just a single person stole the cassette player, or it could be many people. The use of *oli* in the predicate marker position here without any preceding subject noun phrase indicates that an action takes place without the person (or persons, or thing, or things) who carried out the action being referred to within the sentence.

In English, this kind of meaning is typically expressed by using the passive verb, but without any noun phrase indicating the cause of the action, as in:

My cassette player has been stolen.

There is no passive construction at all in the grammar of Bislama.[2] However, the function of this so-called "agentless passive" corresponds very closely to the function of the subjectless predicate construction marked with the predicate marker *oli*, i.e.,

Oli stilim tep blong mi.

Some more examples of this kind of construction in Bislama include:

Bae oli katem hem long hospital from bel blong hem i solap.
'He will be operated on in the hospital because he has a swollen stomach.'

Mit we i sting finis, oli no mas kakae.
'Rotten meat should not be eaten.'

Oli luk fes blong man ia olsem mangki stret.
'That man's face looks just like a monkey.'

Kakae ia oli smelem olsem samting we i sting finis.
'That food smells like something rotten.'

There is one significant difference between sentences that involve a verb that is preceded by *oli* in Bislama and agentless passive constructions in English. It is only possible for a transitive verb with an object to be transformed into a passive construction in English. There is no way of leaving the subject unspecified in English if the verb is intransitive. However, in Bislama, it is possible to use this unspecified agent construction even with intransitive verbs. The closest that we can get to expressing this kind of meaning in English is to use a so-called "impersonal" pronoun such as *one* (in formal speech) or *you* (in informal speech):

Sapos oli daeva mo oli no gat glas oli no save luk wan samting.
'If one dives without a diving glass, one cannot see anything.'

Another possibility in English is to turn the verb into a noun by means of the suffix *-ing*, as in the following:

Mi harem oli stap pispis afsaed long naet.
'I could hear peeing outside in the night.'

---

[2] There is nothing unusual about this. Most of the local languages of Vanuatu similarly have no passive constructions. These languages express actions without causers in a very similar way to what I have described here for Bislama.

6.1.3.2 VERB + NOUN Constructions

There is a different kind of construction in which a verb *must* be immediately followed by a noun, but where the VERB + NOUN sequence differs from ordinary VERB + OBJECT constructions in a number of respects:

- The verb in these constructions is always intransitive rather than transitive.
- The following noun phrase can only be a noun—and never a pronoun—and the noun can never be accompanied by any kind of modifiers.
- Only a restricted set of nouns—sometimes just a single noun—can be associated with any particular verb.
- The noun can never be separated from the verb by any other word.

Some such constructions involve an initial verb that can be followed by a variety of nouns, though these nouns are still restricted in that they must have very specific kinds of meanings. The following patterns can be noted:

(a) The intransitive verb *toktok* 'speak' can followed by the name of a language, for example:

Yu save toktok Franis?
'Can you speak French?'

(b) The intransitive verb *plei* 'play' can be followed by the name of a sport, a game, or a musical instrument, as in the following:

Michel i stap plei ragbi.
'Michel plays rugby.'

Bae yumi plei kad?
'Let's play cards.'

Nono i save plei kibod.
'Nono plays the keyboard.'

Note that there is a corresponding transitive verb *pleim* followed by an object noun phrase that is used when talking about any other kind of playing, as in:

Yufala i save pleim Red Red Wine?
'Can you guys play the song Red Red Wine?'

Yu wantem pleim niufala kaset blong mi?
'Do you want to play my new cassette?'

(c) The intransitive verb *smel* 'smell' can be followed by the name of something that produces the smell, for example:

Gel ia i smel senta.
'That girl smells of perfume.'

Pikinini ia i smel sitsit.
'That child smells of pooh.'

SIMPLE SENTENCES

There is again a corresponding transitive verb *smelem* that accepts a full range of noun phrase objects expressing what it is that subject is smelling rather than what causes the subject to smell. Contrast the last example with the following:

Pikinini ia i smelem sitsit.
'That child is smelling the pooh.'

(d) The intransitive verbs *danis* 'dance' and *sing* (or, more commonly, *singsing*) 'sing' can be followed by the name of the kind of dance or song, for example:

Mi no save danis kastom.
'I can't do traditional dancing.'

Taem oli danis long stringban oli danis tustep.
'When dancing to stringband music, one does the two-step.'

Ol pikinini oli stap sing kores taem ol man oli stap kam insaed long jej.
'The children sing repeated verses while people are coming into the church.'

Olgeta blong Mele oli kam singsing bonane long haos.
'The people of Mele came and sang new year songs at home.'

(e) There is a small set of intransitive verbs that behave in a similar way in that they are all followed by a noun indicating a punishment or something that is owed to someone. This includes the verbs *kaon* 'borrow money' that is followed by a statement of an amount of money, for example:

Hem i kaon 50,000 vatu long mi be i no pembak yet.
'He has borrowed 50,000 vatu from me but he hasn't repaid it yet.'

It also includes the verbs *faen* 'be fined (a specific amount of money)' and *panis* 'receive as punishment', as in the following:

Ol boe we oli drong long pablik oli faen 1,000 vatu.
'The youths who got drunk in public were fined 1,000 vatu.'

Hem i panis wan manis long kalabus.
'He was punished with a month in jail.'

(f) The intransiitve verb *wok* 'work' can be followed by a noun that indicates what kind of reward or payment one is working for, for example:

Hem i wok kontrak.
'He is working on contract.'

Mifala i wok mak olsem ia, sapos mifala i finis kwik mifala i save kambak long haos.
'When we are working according to set tasks, if we finish early we can come back home.'

Olgeta oli wok rasen.
'They are working for rations.'

Mi mi wantem wok mane nomo.
'I only want to work for wages.'

CHAPTER 6

(g) The verb *saen* 'be signed' can be followed by a noun indicating the signatory.[3] Thus:

Mesej hem i saen daerekta.
'The message is signed by the director.'

A number of additional VERB + NOUN sequences exhibit the same structure as the patterns described above, though these represent non-productive patterns that cannot become the basis for new sequences involving other verbs or nouns. Such sequences include the following:

sitsit 'defecate'	*blad* 'blood'	*sitsit blad* 'defecate with bloody feces'
	wota 'water'	*sitsit wota* 'have diarrhea'
pispis 'urinate'	*blad* 'blood'	*pispis blad* 'urinate with blood'
	kalsong 'underwear'	*pispis kalsong* 'wet one's pants'
spet 'spit'	*blad* 'blood'	*spet blad* 'cough up blood'
kale 'chock'	*wil* 'wheel'	*kale wil* 'chock wheel'
se 'say'	*gres* 'grace'	*se gres* 'say grace'
	wanem 'what'	*se wanem* 'say what'
lukluk 'look'	*ples* 'place'	*lukluk ples* 'have a look around'
skul 'study'	*Inglis* 'English'	*skul Inglis* 'go to English-medium school'
	Franis 'French'	*skul Franis* 'go to French-medium school'
traot 'vomit'	*win* 'wind'	*traot win* 'burp'
fat 'fart'	*win* 'wind'	*fat win* 'fart inaudibly'

One of the characteristic features of this construction by which it is distinguished from sequences of transitive verbs with following objects is the fact that with genuine verbal objects, the noun phrase can be shifted to the head of the sentence (§6.3). We can therefore find corresponding pairs of sentences such as the following:

Pikinini ia i smelem sitsit.
'That child is smelling the pooh.'

Sitsit (nao), pikinini ia i smelem.
'As for the pooh, the child smelt it.'

In the case of these VERB + NOUN constructions, however, the verb and the following noun cannot be separated from each other. Thus, with the following, it is not possible to move the nouns to the beginning of the sentences:

Netor i save toktok Franis.
'Netor can speak French.'

*Franis, Netor i save toktok.

Pikinini ia i smel sitsit.
'The child smells of pooh.'

*Sitsit, pikinini ia i smel.

---

[3] Note the existence of the corresponding transitive verb *saenem* 'sign', e.g., *Daerekta i saenem mesej* 'The director signed the message.'

6.1.4 Double Object Constructions

In addition to the subject and object of a sentence, there is a third basic element within a sentence that is encountered in a relatively small range of sentence types in Bislama. Such constructions involve transitive verbs that accept two object noun phrases.

One verb that enters into a construction of this type is the verb *givim* 'give'. If the recipient of the act of giving is a pronoun, this can be expressed as an object immediately after the verb, with the thing that is given expressed by another noun phrase following this. Thus:

Bae mi no save givim yu mane.
'I can't give you the money.'

This meaning can be expressed alternatively by means of a single-object construction in which the recipient is marked by means of the preposition *long* (§6.1.5.1.6), i.e.,

Bae mi no save givim mane long yu.
'I can't give you the money.'

If the recipient is a noun rather than a pronoun, the double-object construction is not permitted and the prepositional phrase must be used instead. Thus:

*Bae mi no save givim mane long **brata blong yu**.*
Bae mi no save givim **brata blong yu mane.*
'I can't give your brother the money.'

Another verb that enters into this construction in Bislama is *wisim*, as in the following example, in which the recipient is again expressed immediately after the verb, and the content of the wish is expressed as the second object:

Mi wisim yufala evriwan wan hapi niuyia.
'I wish you all a happy new year.'

These appear to be the only verbs of transfer in Bislama that enter into this construction. This means that the double-object construction is much more restricted than a similar construction in English, where verbs such as *send* and *tell* also allow double objects. In Bislama, however, the recipient of verbs such as *sanem* 'send' and *talem* 'tell' can only be marked by means of a prepositional construction. Thus:

Bae mi talem wan stori long yu.
*Bae mi talem yu wan stori.
'I will tell you a story.'

Simon i postem wan leta long mi.
*Simon i postem mi wan leta.
'Simon posted me a letter.'

However, there are other patterns of double-object constructions in Bislama, one of which involves a verb that expresses buying or selling, in which the thing that is bought or sold is expressed as an object immediately after the verb, while the price follows this as the second object, for example:

CHAPTER 6

Hem i salem haos blong hem bigfala mane.
'He sold his house for a lot of money.'

Mi pem niufala tep blong mi 15,000 vatu.
'I bought my new cassette player for 15,000 vatu.'

It is again possible for one object to be expressed by means of a prepositional phrase. In this case, the second object can be introduced by *long*, as in:

Hem i salem haos blong hem long bigfala mane.
'He sold his house for a lot of money.'

The final such construction involves verbs that express some kind of naming activity. The first object is a noun phrase referring to someone or something that is named, while the second object expresses the name that is bestowed. Thus:

Mi singaot hem tawi.
'I call him brother-in-law.'

Oli putum nem blong bebe ia Mary.
'They bestowed the name of the baby as Mary.'

It is common, however, for the second of these objects in such a construction to be introduced by *se* (§7.3.2.1.2). Thus:

Oli kolem bebe ia se Mary.
'They called the baby Mary.'

Mi singaot hem se tawi.
'I call him brother-in-law.'

An alternative to this use of *se* is for either the title or the person being addressed to be introduced instead by means of the preposition *long* (§6.1.5.1.6), with the other noun phrase expressed as an object to the verb *singaot*. Thus:

Mi singaot hem long tawi.
Mi singaot tawi long hem.
'I call him brother-in-law.'

It is not necessarily only when people are named that this construction is used, as things that are named can also be referred to in this way, for example:

Ol man Paama oli singaotem nakato se riou.
'The Paamese call hermit crabs *riou*.'

This construction is not limited strictly to verbs of naming. The following examples indicate that any verb that expresses an action that results in somebody or something coming to occupy a particular position or to perform a particular function can also participate in this pattern:

Oli fomem wan komiti se disasta komiti.
'A committee was formed as a disaster committee.'

Komiti ia i putum Harry se jeaman.
'The committee appointed Harry as chairman.'

SIMPLE SENTENCES

6.1.5 Prepositional Phrases

A prepositional phrase is one that consists of an initial preposition with a following noun phrase. Prepositions in Bislama can be grouped into one of two subsets. The first—which I have termed "basic" prepositions—are words that function only as prepositions. The second subset comprises forms that function both as prepositions and as transitive verbs.

6.1.5.1 Basic Prepositions

Bislama has a set of six basic prepositions: *blong, from, wetem wetaot(em), olsem,* and *long.* The various functions of each of these are described and illustrated below.

6.1.5.1.1 *Blong*

Although this preposition is written as *blong,* it is generally pronounced in casual speech as *blo,* which often reduces further to the just *bl-* when the following word begins with a vowel. We therefore encounter alternations between *blong papa* 'for dad' and *blo papa,* as well as *blong olfala* 'for the old man', *blo olfala,* and even *bl-olfala.*

When *blong* introduces a noun phrase following a verb phrase, it expresses the beneficiary, i.e., the individual 'for' whom (or which) an action is carried out, for example:

Mi stap kuk blong woman we i sik.
'I am cooking for the woman who is sick.'

Bae mi pem wan gato blong yu.
'I will buy a cake for you.'

As indicated in §4.4, *blong* is also used to link two noun phrases together to form a complex noun phrase. In such constructions, it expresses the following meanings:

- *Possessive*

Blong marks the possessor in a possessive construction, for example *mama blong mi* 'my mother', *leg blong dog* 'dog's leg', *niufala haos blong ol man Tongoa* 'the Tongoan people's new house'. Given that both beneficiary and possessor are marked in the same way, it is possible for a sentence containing *blong* such as the following to be interpreted in more than one way in Bislama.

Bae mi pem wan gato blong yu.
'I will buy a cake for you.'
'I will buy one of your cakes.'

- *Purpose*

Blong can also mark the purpose to which something is put, for example *ki blong trak* 'car key', *spia blong fis* 'fish spear'. The purpose for which something is intended can also be expressed by means of a complete verb phrase rather than another noun phrase, as in the following:

*Bae mi karem kaoju **blong** fulumap bensin.*
'I will get the hose for filling up the petrol.'

- *Characteristic*

A noun phrase introduced by *blong* can also express something that in some way specially characterizes the preceding noun phrase, for example *ples blong sofmad* 'muddy place', *man blong giaman* 'liar'. With this characterizing function, *blong* can also be followed by a verb phrase rather than just a noun phrase. Thus:

*Vila hem i wan ples **blong** drong long kava evri dei.*
'Vila is a place to get drunk on kava every day.'

- *Part of a whole*

Finally, *blong* can indicate the whole that is made up of a particular part, as in *laet blong trak* 'lights of a car', *leg blong jea* 'chair leg'.

6.1.5.1.2 *From*

The preposition *from* expresses the reason for which something happens, as in:

Mi stap kof from sigaret.
'I cough because of cigarettes.'

Because the purpose behind something is very similar to the reason for something, we also find *from* being used to introduce noun phrases of purpose, for example:

Hem i kam from masket blong sutum flaenfoks.
'He came for a rifle to shoot the flying fox.'

Mi stap wok from vatu.
'I work for money.'

When *from* is followed by a noun phrase, it is often reduced in rapid colloquial speech to *fro*, as in the following:

Yu kam fro wanem?
'What have you come for?'

6.1.5.1.3 *Wetem*

This is an accompanitive preposition, expressing the meaning of 'with', as in:

Bae mi toktok wetem yu.
'I will speak with you.'

The same form can also be used to express the instrumental function. This corresponds to constructions expressed by 'with' or 'by means of' in English. Thus:

Mi katem bred wetem naef.
'I am cutting bread with the knife.'

SIMPLE SENTENCES

This latter function can also be expressed by means of the preposition *long* (§6.1.5.1.6), for example:

Mi katem bred long naef.
'I am cutting bread with the knife.'

It was also noted in §4.4 that *wetem* can be used to join two noun phrases to form a coordinate noun phrase. Thus:

John wetem Taso tufala i stap dring kava long haos.
'John and Taso are drinking kava at home.'

As with the other prepositions discussed above, *wetem* sometimes undergoes reduction in rapid colloquial speech when there is a following noun phrase, losing its final consonant to become *wete*. Thus:

Bae mi kam wete yu.
'I will come with you.'

6.1.5.1.4 *Wetaot(em)*

Some—though by no means all—speakers of Bislama use the preposition *wetaot* or *wetaotem* to express the meaning of 'without',[4] as in the following:

Hem i kam wetaotem basket blong hem.
'He came without his basket.'

Wetaot(em) tends to be used by those who have been more highly educated in English. For those people who do not use this preposition, this meaning is expressed by joining two separate sentences into a single complex sentence, as follows:

Hem i kam i no gat basket blong hem.
'He came without his basket.'

This literally means 'He came (but) he didn't have his basket'.

6.1.5.1.5 *Olsem*

This form has a number of functions though as a preposition it expresses similarity, as in the following:

Mi no stap wokem olsem yu.
'I don't do it like you.'

It can also be used in association with an adjective a following noun phrase to express the meaning of 'as much as', for example:

Natora i strong olsem aean.
'Java cedar is as strong as iron.'

---

[4] *Wetaot* is sometimes used on its own with the specific meaning of 'not wearing any underwear', as *Mi luk se yu yu stap wokbaot wetaot* 'It looks to me as though you are going knickerless.'

This preposition also undergoes optional reduction in rapid speech to *olse* when there is a following noun phrase, as in the following:

Hem i singaot olse pikinini.
'He is yelling like a child.'

6.1.5.1.6 *Long*

This preposition behaves similarly to *blong* in that it is written as *long*, but it is generally pronounced in casual speech as *lo*, which often reduces further to the just *l-* when the following word begins with a vowel. We therefore encounter alternations between *long trak* 'in the car' and *lo trak*, as well as *long ofis* 'in the office', *lo ofis*, and even *l-ofis*.

Long has been described last in this section because it is in a sense the "default" preposition, covering a wide range of functions about which it is probably impossible to offer any single generalization. It therefore expresses the following specific meanings:

- Location

It can indicate the location ('at, in, on'), as in the following:

Mi wok long Vila.
'I work in Vila.'

Hem i katem gras long yad blong hem.
'He is cutting the lawn in his yard.'

- Goal

It can also indicate the place towards which an action is moving, corresponding to the forms 'to' and 'toward' in English. Thus:

Dog i stap wokbaot i go long pubel.
'The dog is walking to the rubbish bin.'

Similar to this is the use of *long* to indicate the receiver of a verb of giving or transfer, for example:

Hem i no bin givim long mi.
'She did not give it to me.'

Bae yu sanem leta i go long Santo?
'Are you sending the letter to Santo?'

In addition, *long* can be used to mark the addressee of an utterance. Thus:

Bae mi talem wan stori long yu.
'I will tell you a story.'

- Source

Along with location and goal, *long* can also indicate the place away from which an action is moving. This corresponds to English 'from' or 'out of'. Thus:

Maki i jas kam long Paama.
'Maki has just arrived from Paama.'

Hem i karemaot mani long bang.
'She took money out of the bank.'

Because *long* is potentially three-ways ambiguous between the meanings of 'to', 'from', and 'at', the directional serial verb construction described in §7.1.1 can be used to eliminate this ambiguity when the context does not make it clear which specific meaning is intended.

- *Time or duration*

The preposition *long* can also be used to indicate a particular point in time or a duration over a period of time. Thus:

Long Sande bae mi kam.
'I will come on Sunday.'

Bae mi kam stap wetem yu long wan manis.
'I will stay with you for a month.'

However, many expressions of time or duration are expressed by means of a simple noun phrase in Bislama with no prepositional marking at all. Thus:

Sande bae mi kam.
'I will come on Sunday.'

Mi stap spel tri manis.
'I am on holiday for three months.'

Bae mi kambak nekis manis.
'I will return next month.'

- *Comparison*

Related to the locative meaning described above is the use of *long* to indicate the point of comparison between two noun phrases with respect to a quality expressed by an adjective, for example:

Mi longfala long Noel.
'I am taller than Noel.'

More commonly, however, this meaning is expressed by the verbal preposition *bitim* (§6.1.5.2.2) or by means of *mo* (with a following *long*-phrase), which is described in §5.3.6 as a post-verbal modifier. Thus:

Mi longfala bitim Noel.
Mi longfala mo long Noel.
'I am taller than Noel.'

- *Instrument*

As indicated in §6.1.5.1.3, *long*, in alternation with *wetem*, can be used to express the instrument by means of which an action is carried out. Thus:

CHAPTER 6

Bae yumi ramem kopra long wud ia.
'Let's ram down the copra with this piece of wood.'

There are other functions of *long* for which it is difficult to offer generalizations about the meaning. In a very real sense, *long* is a default preposition that is used when the descriptions presented above call for no other particular preposition. We therefore find *long* used in some very specific constructions such as the following:

Mi fraet long dog ia.
'I'm afraid of that dog.'

Mi les long ol man blong smok.
'I'm sick of smokers.'

Mi ded long yu.
'I'm dying for you.'[5]

Hem i drong long kava.
'He's drunk with kava.'

Many transitive verbs are related to corresponding intransitive verbs by means of the suffix *-Vm* (§5.1.3.1), for example *foget* and *fogetem* 'forget', *boel* and *boelem* 'boil', *draon* and *draonem* 'sink', *rid* and *ridim* 'read'. In these cases, when something is affected by the action of the verb—the book that is read, the water that is boiled and so on—this is expressed as the object of the suffixed transitive verb, i.e.,

Mi ridim buk.
'I read the book.'

Hem i boelem wota.
'She boiled the water.'

However, many intransitive verbs have no transitive equivalent carrying the suffix *-Vm*. For instance, *debi* 'charge goods to account' does not have a corresponding transitive form **debim*. Such verbs can, of course, be expected to be associated with a noun phrase referring to something affected by the action expressed in the verb. In cases like these, the affected noun phrase can be placed after an intransitive verb with the preceding preposition *long*, allowing it to function as a kind of object, as in the following:

Mi debi long mit mo raes.
*Mi debim mit mo raes.
'I charged the meat and rice to my account.'

This use of *long* to mark "pseudo-objects" in this way is widespread in Bislama. In fact, there are many intransitive verbs with both a genuine transitive form that is

---

[5] This is a very widely used idiomatic expression that really means something like 'I am dying to have you'. To indicate that one is more literally dying for somebody, one would be far more likely to use the preposition *from* (§6.1.5.1.2) instead, as in *Jisas i ded from yumi* 'Jesus died for us'.

marked by -*Vm* alongside a pseudo-transitive construction involving the preposition *long*, with both expressing the same meaning. Thus:

Bae mi odarem jips.
Bae mi oda long jips.
'I will order chips.'

The preposition *long* also appears in the prepositional construction *long saed blong* with a number of specialized functions. Literally, this means 'on the side of' or 'beside', and *long saed blong* can certainly be used with this meaning in Bislama, as in the following:

Wan bigfala wud i stap gro long saed blong haos.
'A big tree is growing beside the house.'

However, this construction is very frequently used to express the specific meaning of 'about' when referring to the content of an utterance. Thus:

Hemia stori long saed blong ol man blong kastom bifo.
'That is a story about the traditional people of before.'

It is also commonly used in a broader sense to mean 'in relation to', 'with regard to', 'in terms of', or 'concerning', as in the following:

Long saed blong yumi ol man ples, i no gat tumas man yet we oli skul long samting ia.
'In relation to us local people, there are not yet very many people who have studied that.'

Man ia hem i rij long saed blong vatu be i no long saed blong fasin blong hem.
'That man is rich in relation to money but not in relation to his behavior.'

Finally, this prepositional construction can also be used to express one's language of instruction or the subject of one's educational specialization, as in:

Mi skul long saed blong Inglis.
'I studied in English.'

Bae mi go skul long saed blong bisnis.
'I will go to study about business.'

6.1.5.2 Verbal Prepositions

In addition to the prepositions described in §6.1.5.1 are a number of words that function both as transitive verbs and as prepositions. Some of these represent relatively recently developed prepositions in Bislama that are still becoming established in the grammar alongside the prepositions described above.

6.1.5.2.1 *Kasem*

The first of these verbal prepositions is *kasem*, which, as a transitive verb, means 'reach, arrive at'. Thus:

Bae mi kasem Vila tumoro moning.
'I will arrive in Vila tomorrow morning.'

As a preposition, it expresses the related meanings of 'as far as' (when used in relation to a noun referring to a place) and 'until' (when used in relation to a noun referring to a time), for example:

*Bae yumitu wokbaot **kasem** en blong taon.*
'Let's walk as far as the end of town.'

*Olgeta oli praktis **kasem** medelnaet wantaem.*
'They practised right until midnight.'

6.1.5.2.2 *Bitim*

As a transitive verb, *bitim* means 'defeat', as in:

*Niusilan i nomo stap **bitim** Ostrelia long ragbi evri taem.*
'New Zealand no longer always beats Australia at rugby.'

Used as a preposition, this has come to express the meaning of 'past, beyond' when used in relation to a noun phrase referring to a place or a time. Thus:

*Bae yumitu no wokbaot **bitim** en blong taon.*
'Let's not walk past the end of town.'

*Olgeta oli praktis **bitim** tri klok.*
'They practised past three o'clock.'[6]

Bitim is also used as a preposition in comparative constructions to indicate the point of comparison between one thing and another, for example:

*Mi longfala **bitim** yu.*
'I am taller than you.'

*Olgeta oli save plei **bitim** mifala.*
'They can play better than we can.'

It was mentioned in §6.1.5.1.6 that this comparative function can also be expressed by means of the basic preposition *long*.

6.1.5.2.3 *Ronem*

The transitive verb *ronem* means 'chase' or 'hunt for', as in the following:

*Bae yumi go **ronem** waelpig.*
'Let's go hunting for wild pigs.'

---

[6] When telling the time in terms of minutes past the hour, the functionally highly restricted preposition *pas* is normally used instead of *bitim*, as in *ten pas fo* 'ten past four', *kwota pas ten* 'quarter past ten'. When *haf* 'half' appears with *pas* in this way, the sequence is normally reduced to *hapas*, as in *hapas faef* 'half past five'.

Ronem can also be used as a preposition in expressions of clock time meaning 'to', as in:

Naoia hem i ten minit ronem faef klok.
'Now it is ten minutes to five.'[7]

6.1.5.2.4 *Agensem*

The verb *agensem* means 'oppose', for example:

Bae mi no agensem yufala be bae mi no sapotem yufala tu.
'I won't oppose you but I won't support you either.'

When used as a preposition, this expresses the meaning of 'against' in the sense of 'in opposition to', as in the following:

Bae mi toktok agensem yu.
'I will speak against you.'

6.1.5.2.5 *Raonem*

Raonem can be used as a verb meaning 'surround' or 'go around', as in:

Bae yumi raonem aelan long rentaka.
'Let's go around the island in a hire-car.'

As a preposition, it expresses the meaning 'around', as in:

Mi pulum fanis raonem yad blong buluk.
'I made a fence around the cattle yard.'

6.1.5.2.6 *Folem*

The verb *folem* means 'follow' or 'accompany, come along with', for example:

Bae mi folem yu from se yu yu save rod.
'I will follow you because you know the way.'

I oraet sapos yu wantem folem mifala.
'It's OK if you want to come along with us.'

When *folem* is used as a preposition it expresses a number of related meanings. It sometimes expresses the idea of 'according to' or 'in accordance with'. Thus:

Mi wokem kek folem buk blong kuk.
'I made a cake according to the cookbook.'

---

[7] When a time is expressed in terms of minutes to the hour, the functionally restricted preposition *tu* is normally used in ways that parallel *pas*. Thus: *ten tu seven* 'ten to seven', *kwota tu sikis* 'quarter to six'. Occasionally, however, people may say *ten minit ronem seven klok* 'ten to seven.'

Hem i wokem folem ol rul blong komiti.
'She did it in accordance with the committee's rules.'

Folem tingting blong yu, bae yumi stap long haos nomo.
'In accordance with your ideas, we will just stay at home.'

The same form can also be used to express the spatial meaning of 'along'. Thus:

Mi wokbaot folem rod nomo.
'I just walked along the road.'

Finally, it can also be used to express 'after (in time)' or 'since', as in:

Folem miting we oli holem yestedei, bae yumi nomo wokem olsem.
'After yesterday's meeting, we will no longer do things like that.'

6.1.5.2.7 *Tokbaot*

The verb *tokbaot* as a transitive verb means 'discuss' or 'talk about', as illustrated by the following:

Bae yumi tokbaot problem ia.
'Let's discuss this problem.'

This can also be used as a preposition expressing the idea of 'in relation to', for example:

Tokbaot niufala kaen kokonas ia, yumi save talem se hem i mo gud.
'In relation to this new coconut variety, we can say that it is better.'

This prepositional use of *tokbaot* corresponds closely to the use of fronted noun phrases as discussed in §6.3 to indicate what it is that a sentence is talking about.

6.1.5.2.8 *Yusum*

The verb *yusum* means 'use', as illustrated by the following:

Kompiuta oli save yusum blong mekem plante difren wok.
'Computers can be used to do all sorts of thing.'

However, this word is occasionally used also as a preposition with the meaning 'by means of', particularly when used in reference to tools or implements, for example:

Bae yu no drilim yusum skrudraeva.
'Don't drill it with the screwdriver.'

It is much more common, however, for the instrumental meaning to be expressed by means of the prepositions *long* (§6.1.5.1.6) or *wetem* (§6.1.5.1.3), as in the following:

Bae yu no drilim wetem skrudraeva.
Bae yu no drilim long skrudraeva.
'Don't drill it with the screwdriver.'

6.1.5.3 Position of Prepositional Phrases

The prepositional phrases in §6.1.5.1 and §6.1.5.2 show that there is no single position in a sentence that is designated as the place where all prepositional phrases must appear. Such phrases are therefore somewhat free in that they can appear at the beginning of a sentence or elsewhere in the sentence. Thus:

Long Sande bae mi kam stori wetem yufala.
Bae mi kam stori wetem yufala long Sande.
Bae mi kam stori long Sande wetem yufala.
Mi long Sande bae mi kam stori wetem yufala.
'I will come and chat with you all on Sunday.'

Although there is considerable freedom in the placement of some prepositional phrases, there are nevertheless some restrictions. For one thing, a prepositional phrase can never be placed within another phrase such as a noun phrase or a verb phrase. Prepositional phrases may also not be placed between a transitive verb and a following object. Thus:

Ol pikinini oli stap lanem Inglis long skul.
Long skul ol pikinini oli stap lanem Inglis.
*Ol pikinini oli stap lanem long skul Inglis.
'The children are learning English at school.'

Some prepositional phrases are freer than others in the extent to which they can be moved within a sentence. Prepositional phrases introduced by *long* referring to location, time, and duration are free to appear at the beginning of a sentence whereas phrases introduced by *long* expressing other meanings cannot move around in the same way. Compare the behavior of the following in which *long* expresses first location and then goal:

Mi lanem Inglis long skul.
Long skul mi lanem Inglis.
'I learned English at school.'

Bae mi go long skul.
*Long skul bae mi go.
'I will go to school.'

Prepositional phrases introduced by *folem* and *tokbaot* are also free to appear at the beginning of a sentence, while all other prepositional phrases normally appear after the verb (or an accompanying object).

6.1.5.4 Complex Prepositions

In addition to the prepositions described in §6.1.5.1 and §6.1.5.2, there is a set of forms that can be used in conjunction with the preposition *long* to express a range of more specific meanings. Forms such as the following can be used on their own to express some kind of meaning relating to place or time without any associated noun phrases:

CHAPTER 6

antap	'above'
ananit	'below'
ova	'over'
klosap	'nearby, nearly'
longwe [8]	'far off, a long time in the future'
farawe	'far off'
insaed	'inside'
aotsaed [9]	'outside'
afta	'after (in time)'
bihaen	'after (in time or space)'
bifo, fastaem	'before (in time)'
raon	'around'
narasaed [10]	'across'

Klosap 'nearby' and *longwe* 'far off' are the only members of this set that undergo reduplication. Given that *klosap* is also often pronounced as *kolosap*, this results in the alternating reduplicated forms *klo-klosap*, *ko-kolosap*, and *kol-kolosap*, all meaning 'near each other'. Compare, therefore, the following forms:

Haos blong mi i stap klosap.
'My house is nearby.'

Tufala i sevet i go kokolosap.
'The two of them moved close to each other.'

The form *longwe* 'far off' reduplicates as *long-longwe*, meaning 'far from each other', for example:

Haos blong mi i stap longwe.
'My house is far off.'

Tufala i sevet i go longlongwe.
'The two of them moved far apart from each other.'

While all of these forms can appear without any associated noun phrases, effectively functioning as a kind of adverbial (§6.1.6), they can also be associated with a following noun phrase that expresses some kind of information about location or time. In such cases, the preposition *long* must appear between these adverbial forms and the accompanying noun phrase. Thus:

Wan bredfrut i foldaon antap long kapa.
'A breadfruit fell on top of the roof.'

Torres i stap longwe long Tanna.
'The Torres Islands are a long way from Tanna.'

Sip i angka aotsaed long pasis.
'The ship is anchored outside the anchorage.'

---

[8] Commonly pronounced as *lowe*.

[9] Often also pronounced as *aosaed* or *afsaed*.

[10] Often also pronounced as *narsaed*.

Bae mi kam fastaem long yu.
'I will come before you.'

Haos blong mi i stap klosap long haos blong yu.
'My house is near yours.'

While *kasem* 'as far as, until' is very frequently used as a verbal preposition (§6.1.5.2.1), it is sometimes treated instead as if it belongs in this set of forms in that when there is a following noun phrase, it may be introduced by the preposition *long*. Thus:

Hem i wokbaot kasem reva.
Hem i wokbaot kasem long reva.
'She walked as far as the river.'

Kasem differs from all of the other location or time markers in this set, however, in that it can never be used on its own without an accompanying noun phrase. This means that we must always say either *kasem* + NOUN PHRASE or *kasem* + *long* + NOUN PHRASE, but never just *kasem* on its own.

6.1.6 Adverbs

In addition to prepositional phrases, simple predicate sentences can also contain an array of adverbial markers. It is difficult to characterize these by means of any single set of generalizations in terms of how they behave. They can be grouped together partly on the basis of the kinds of meanings that they express, though this is no guarantee that members of each set all necessarily behave in exactly the same sorts of ways.

6.1.6.1 Adverbs of Place

These are words that indicate something about the place in which something happens. This set includes words such *daon* 'below', *samples* 'somewhere', *saedsaed* 'on both sides', *soa* 'ashore', *hom* 'home', *raonwol* 'around the world', and *olbaot* 'everywhere, anywhere'. They normally follow a verb phrase, as illustrated by the following:

Klos blong mi i stap daon longwe.
'My clothes are down there.'

Mi stap luk yu olbaot.
'I see you everywhere.'

I nomo gat batri olbaot long Vila.
'There are no batteries anywhere in Vila any more.'

Hem i stap lukluk saedsaed.
'He was looking on both sides.'

Olgeta oli stap swim i kam soa.
'They are swimming back to shore.'

CHAPTER 6

*Bae mi go **hom** long Krismas.*
'I will go home at Christmas.'

There is also a collection of phrasal items that function as adverbial markers of place in a similar way, including *wan saed* 'to one side' and *wan ples* 'together'. Thus:

*Haos blong olgeta i lei **wan saed** afta long hariken.*
'Their house leaned to one side after the cyclone.'

*Bae yumi kam selebret **wan ples** long taem blong lafet.*
'Let's come to celebrate together at the time of the party.'

Also included in this set are the pronoun phrases *mi wan* 'alone, by myself', *yu wan* 'alone, by yourself', and *hem wan* 'alone, by itself, by himself, by herself' (§4.3.2). Thus:

*Hem i stap toktok **hem wan**.*
'He was talking to himself.'

6.1.6.2 Adverbs of Time

There is also a substantial group of adverbs that express time. These tend to be rather more free in where they can appear in a sentence, sometimes appearing at the beginning of a sentence, sometimes at the end, and sometimes between a variety of other constituents. Forms of this type include the following:

afta	'afterwards, later'
bifo	'beforehand, earlier'
fastaem	'beforehand, earlier'
oltaem	'always'
olbaot	'any time'
wantaem	'together, at the same time'
samtaem	'sometimes'
tumora	'tomorrow'
yestedei	'yesterday'
longtaem	'for a long time'
laeftaem	'for life'
fogud	'forever'

The following illustrate the behavior of such words:

***Afta** bae yumitu go long taon.*
'Afterwards let's go to town.'

*Hem i stap toktok olsem ia **oltaem**.*
'She always talks like that.'

*Bae yumi karem raes **tumora**.*
'Let's get the rice tomorrow.'

***Yestedei** oli bin kam long haos.*
'They came to the house yesterday.'

*Mi no luk yu **longtaem**.*
'I haven't seen you for a long time.'

The phrasal items *afta tumora* 'day after tomorrow' and *bifo yestedei* 'day before yesterday' also behave in the same way. Thus:

Bifo yestedei i no gat fulap man long hia.
'The day before yesterday there were not many people here.'

The noun *delaet* 'daybreak' is very frequently used as an adverbial to express the meaning of 'all night' or 'until daylight'. Thus:

*Hem i wekap **delaet**.*
'He was awake all night.'

*Olgeta oli singsing **delaet**.*
'They were singing until daybreak.'

This can be followed by a prepositional phrase introduced by *long* to provide further specification of the time. Thus:

*Olgeta oli singsing Satede **delaet** long Sande.*
'They were singing all Saturday night (i.e., until daybreak on Sunday).'

6.1.6.3 Adverbs of Manner

There is a set of forms that we can refer to as adverbs of manner in that they indicate something about how an action is carried out. This set includes the adverbs *spid*, *kwik*, and *hariap*, all meaning 'quickly', *sloslo* 'slowly', *let* 'late', and *eli* 'early', as well as forms such as *olwe*, *evriwan*, and *olgeta*. The adverbs that indicate the speed of an action are illustrated by the following:

*Hem i ron **hariap** i go long nakamal.*
'She ran quickly to the meeting house.'

*Bae mi wokbaot **sloslo** folem rod.*
'I will walk slowly along the road.'

*Yu no mas kam **let** long miting.*
'You mustn't come late to the meeting.'

*Yestedei mi slip **eli** long naet.*
'Last night I went to bed early.'

The adverbs *kwik*, *spid*, and *hariap* are unusual in that they are the only adverbs that can be reduplicated to indicate intensity, as in the following:

*Hem i ron **spidspid**.*
'She ran very quickly.'

*Trak ia i stap ron **harhariap** tumas.*
'That car is traveling much too fast.'

The adverb *olwe* expresses the idea that an action is performed to its spatial or temporal conclusion without interruption. Thus:

CHAPTER 6

*Masing i go long Paris, hem i go **olwe** nomo.*
'When Masing went to Paris, he went non-stop.'

*Bae yumitu go **olwe** long Mele.*
'Let's go all the way to Mele.'

*Ol mobael oli stanap stret **olwe** kasem en blong toktok blong ol bigbigman.*
'The mobile force stood to attention right till the end of the speeches of the dignitaries.'

Olwe can also be used in association with adjectives, in which case it indicates that the state expressed in the adjective holds completely, as in the following:

*Santo hem i hot krangki **olwe** nomo.*
'Santo is really really hot.'

A verb phrase can also be followed by *evriwan* or *olgeta*. These both express the idea that an action or a state is fully achieved. Thus:

*Haos ia, faea i bonem **evriwan**.*
'The house was completely burnt by the fire.'

*Matres blong mi i wetwet **olgeta** long hariken.*
'My mattress got drenched in the cyclone.'

However, *evriwan* (but not *olgeta*) can appear after an intransitive verb to indicate not just that the action is completely performed, but also to indicate that all of the referents of the subject noun phrase are involved. Thus:

*Yufala i welkam **evriwan**.*
'You are all welcome.'

An alternative way of expressing this meaning would be for the forms *evriwan* or *olgeta* to directly follow a pronoun subject (§4.3.2) or for *evri* or *olgeta* to precede a noun subject (§4.3.1), as in the following:

*Yufala **evriwan** i welkam.*
'You are all welcome.'

***Evri** studen i welkam.*
'Every student is welcome.'

Under this general heading, we can also include a number of nouns that are used in conjunction with verbs to express adverbial meanings. A common pattern involves the verb *wokbaot* 'walk' followed by a noun, such as *dabolbut* 'two pairs of boots' and *tustori* 'two storeys' which gives *wokbaot dabolbut* and *wokbaot tustori*, both meaning 'walk with mud sticking to the soles of one's shoes'. We also encounter *dakdak* 'duck' in this construction as *wokbaot dakdak* 'waddle, stagger', *draeleg* 'barefoot' as *wokbaot draeleg* 'go barefoot', and *foleg* 'four legs' as *wokbaot foleg* 'crawl'.

6.1.6.4 Miscellaneous Adverbs

Finally, there is a set of words performing a diverse range of functions that can also be included within the overall class of adverbs:

bakegen	'again'
maet	'perhaps'
mebi	'perhaps'
ating	'perhaps'
nomo	'only'
tumas	'too, very'
tu	'too, either, also, as well, in addition'
mestem	'if things go well/badly'
sua	'certainly'
mobeta	'preferably'
mogud	'preferably'

These adverbs often have distributions that are specific to that individual word, so the behavior of each form is described separately below.

- *Maet, mebi,* and *ating* 'perhaps'

Maet and *mebi* express the meaning of 'perhaps' and appear always at the beginning of the sentence. Neither is used nearly as commonly as the synonymous form *ating*, which is free to occur in a variety of positions in the sentence in addition to the beginning of the sentence. Thus:

Maet hem i kam.
Mebi hem i kam.
'Perhaps he will come.'

Ating hem i kam.
Hem ating i kam.
Hem i kam ating.
'Perhaps he will come.'

- *Bakegen* 'again'

This word is often used as a postmodifier with a verb phrase to express repetition of an action, for example:

Hem i toktok bakegen.
'He spoke again.'

Man ia ronem dog bakegen.
'That man chased the dog again.'

In addition to the meaning of 'again', it can also express the idea of 'extra', as in the following:

Samting ia bae yumi mas pem bakegen.
'We'll have to pay extra for that.'

However, it can also be used as a postmodifier in a noun phrase with the meaning of 'other' or 'another', as illustrated by the following:

I gat tu haos bakegen i stap long ples ia.
'There are two other houses there.'

CHAPTER 6

Wan man bakegen i kam.
'Another man came.'

As a modifier of a pronoun, it can also express the meaning of 'own', as in the following:

Man ia i karem gel blong hem bakegen.
'That man took his own daughter.'

Finally, it can also be used on its own as a modifier at the beginning of a sentence to mean 'once again', as in the following:

Bakegen, bae yumi no save wokem olsem.
'Once again, we cannot do it like that.'

- *Tu* 'too, either'

The word *tu* is used as a verb phrase modifier to express the meaning of 'too' or 'either', as in the following:

Jif bae i mas toktok tu.
'The chief will also have to speak.'

Mi no save tu.
'I don't know either.'

This form can also be used within a noun phrase to express the meaning of 'also', as in the following:

Adela tu i go stap long aelan.
'Also Adela went and stayed on the island.'

Finally, *tu* can be used on its own as a clause-initial modifer in the expression *mo tu* meaning 'also' or 'in addition', as in the following:

Mo tu bae olgeta oli tok long yumi.
'In addition they will tell us off.'

- *Nomo* 'only, just'

Nomo is very widely used with the basic function of 'only' or 'just', where it is commonly used in conjunction with either a verbal or a nominal predicate, as illustrated by the following:

Mi stap wokem ol haos nomo.
'I just build houses.'

Mi wan wokman nomo.
'I am just a laborer.'

However, it can be used as a postmodifier in association with any kind of constituent, as illustrated by the following:

Bae mi kam naoia nomo.
'I will come right now.'

Andrew nomo i wokem.[11]
'Just Andrew did it.'

- *Tumas* 'too, very'

The word *tumas* can be used as a verb phrase postmodifier to express the idea of 'too much', 'a lot', or 'very much', for example:

Hem i stap toktok tumas.
'He talks too much.'

Mi no stap wokem tumas ol samting olsem ia.
'I don't do such things a lot.'

However, this word also functions as a postmodifier to any non-verbal predicate. Thus:

Ples i hot tumas.
'It is very hot.'

Haos ia i no ofis tumas.
'This building is not much of an office.'

- *Mestem* 'according to circumstances'

The word *mestem* is a verb meaning 'miss', though it is commonly also used these days as an adverb at the beginning of a sentence. It is sometimes used to express the meaning of 'in unfortunate circumstances, in case of accident', as in:

Mestem masin ia bae i nogud mo bae yumi no save fiksim long Vila.
'In case of accident, the machine might break down and we won't be able to repair it in Vila.'

It can also be used to mean just the opposite, i.e., 'if all goes well', for example:

Mestem bae mifala i kam long haos long aftenun.
'If all goes well we will come to see you at home in the evening.'

- *Gudsab, gudlak,* and *laki* 'fortunately'

As adverbs at the beginning of a sentence, these words all express the meaning of 'fortunately'. Thus:

Gudsab faea i no kasem haos blong mi.
'Fortunately the fire did not reach my house.'

Laki nomo yumi kam long ples ia.
'Fortunately we came here.'

- *Sua* 'certainly'

This is used as an adverb at the beginning of a sentence to express the meaning of 'certainly', for example:

---

[11] *Nomo* can also be used with the quite separate meaning of 'no longer' (§5.3.4). Thus: *Andrew i nomo wokem* 'Andrew no longer does it.'

Sua bae i gat problem long saed blong graon long ples ia.
'There will certainly be a land problem here.'

- *Mobeta* and *mogud* 'preferably'

These both express the meaning of 'preferably' or 'ought to' at the beginning of a sentence, as in the following:

Mobeta yumi lukluk long samting ia bakegen.
'We ought to look at that again.'

6.1.6.5 Placement of Adverbs and Post-Verbal Modifiers

A set of post-verbal modifiers was described in §5.3.6, including the forms that appear as the second element of an emphatic negative construction (for example *no ... nating, no ... wanpis* 'not at all') and the forms *yet* 'still, yet' and *finis* 'completive'. These modifiers, along with many of the adverbs described above, can be associated with a transitive verb that is accompanied by an object noun phrase. In such cases, these adverbs and modifiers can appear in two rather different positions in a sentence. On the one hand, they can appear immediately after the verb and before the object, while on the other hand they can appear after the object of the verb. We therefore find alternations such as the following:

Oli no katem yet boe blong mi.
Oli no katem boe blong mi yet.
'My son has not yet been circumcized.'

The forms *nating* and *yet*, along with the modifier *finis*, behave in the same way when they are used in association with verbs in the affirmative. Thus:

Oli wokem finis haos blong mi.
Oli wokem haos blong mi finis.
'They have built my house.'

*Bae mi givim **nating** pig ia long yu.*
*Bae mi givim pig ia **nating** long yu.*
'I will give you this pig for nothing.'

The appearance of these modifiers after the object becomes obligatory rather than optional when the object is instead a pronoun. Compare, therefore, the following examples:

Oli no katem yet boe blong mi.
Oli no katem boe blong mi yet.
'My son has not yet been circumcized.'

Oli no katem yu yet.
'You have not yet been circumcized.'

Note, therefore, the ungrammaticality of the following to express the same meaning:

*Oli no katem yet yu.

6.2 Questions

There are many different kinds of questions, but the ways of forming all kinds of questions in Bislama are described here under this single heading. We can distinguish between what we can call yes-no questions on the one hand and content questions on the other. A yes-no question is one in which the appropriate answer is either "yes" or "no" (or, obviously, "I don't know"). An example of such a question in Bislama would therefore be the following, as the answer could be *yes* 'yes', *no* 'no', or *mi no save* 'I don't know':

Bae yu kam tumoro no?
'Will you come tomorrow?'

A content question, on the other hand, is one that cannot be answered by *yes* or *no*, but which calls for some kind of information to be provided. An example of a content question in Bislama would therefore be the following:

Wanem taem bae yu kam?
'When will you come?'

Clearly, a cooperative answer would have to either provide some kind of statement about when you are planning on coming such as the following:

Bae mi kam long moning.
'I will come in the morning.'

Long sikis klok.
'At six o'clock.'

Bae mi wet long ol pikinini blong mi oli go long skul fastaem.
'I'll wait for my children to go to school first.'

Bae mi kam taem oli hangem laet long nakamal.
'I will come when they hang the light out at the kava bar.'

Alternatively, of course, the reply could indicate that you do not intend to come at all, for example:

Bae mi no save kam.
'I won't be able to come.'

6.2.1 Yes-No Questions

Yes-no questions in Bislama are very frequently distinguished from statements only by means of a change in intonation. The only way that we can signal this in writing is to place a question mark at the end of an ordinary statement. Thus, the following will be pronounced with a falling intonation at the end:

Yu luk boe ia yestedei.
'You saw that boy yesterday.'

In the following, by way of contrast, the intonation rises towards the end as a signal that this is a question rather than a statement:

CHAPTER 6

Yu luk boe ia yestedei? [12]
'Did you see that boy yesterday?'

Another way to form this kind of question is to add the word *no* (or *o*) at the end of the sentence. The intonation in this case is quite different from the ordinary statement intonation, as well as being different from the intonation used for yes-no questions when there is no such question tag present at the end. There is a rise toward the end of the main part of the question but not as much as when intonation alone marks the question. There is then a sudden drop in intonation with the question tag itself. Yes-no questions of this type therefore have this form:

Yu luk boe ia yestedei o?
Yu luk boe ia yestedei no?
'Did you see that boy yesterday?'

The tags *no* and *o* are alternative ways in Bislama of expressing the meaning of 'or' (§7.2.3). This type of tag question can actually be regarded as a shortened form of a longer type of yes-no question in which the opposite possibility is presented after the form *no* or *o*. The questions just presented could therefore also be expressed as follows:

Yu luk boe ia yestedei o yu no luk hem?
Yu luk boe ia yestedei no yu no luk hem?
'Did you see that boy yesterday or did you not see him?'

Another tag that is often used to change a statement into a yes-no question is *a*. The intonation is once again quite different from the other kinds of yes-no questions that we have just examined. In this case, the main part of the sentence carries more or less the same intonation that we find with a statement, while the tag *a* is pronounced with a sharp rise and sudden fall in intonation. When this tag is added to the end of the statement, the resulting question usually indicates that there is an assumption that the answer will be in the affirmative. Thus:

Bae yu kam long aftenun a?
'You'll be coming in the evening won't you?'

Yet another way to express yes-no questions is to preface a statement with the question words *olsem wanem*. This phrase is commonly used in forming content questions to mean 'how' (§6.2.2.14), but in an example such as the following the answer that is required is simply *yes* or *no*, so this clearly represents another strategy for expressing yes-no questions:

Olsem wanem bae yu kam tumoro? Yes, bae mi kam.
'Will you come tomorrow? Yes, I will come.'

The word *se* has a wide range of functions in Bislama (§7.3.2.1.2). In one of its functions, it occurs as a minimal utterance with no preceding or following material, effectively functioning as a questioning interjection meaning 'what' or 'beg your

---

[12] In translated biblical materials, yes-no questions are often written with a question mark at both the beginning and the end of the question, as in *?Yu luk boe ia yestedei?* 'Did you see that boy yesterday?'

pardon' (§6.2.2.2). This same form *se* is also sometimes used at the beginning of a sentence in colloquial Bislama to change that sentence from a statement into a yes-no question. Thus:

Se bae yu kam tumoro?
'Will you come tomorrow?'

While on the topic of yes-no questions, we should also talk about the kinds of answers that can be given to such questions. The form *yes*—sometimes *yo* in colloquial speech—is used in response to any question where the person answering the question agrees with whatever is asserted in the the question. If the question is asked in the affirmative, then *yes* indicates that the person answering agrees with the corresponding statement form of that question. Thus:

Bae yu kam long haos blong mifala? Yes (bae mi kam long haos blong yufala).
'Will you come to our place? Yes (I will come to your place).'

If a question is asked in the negative, then the answer *yes* agrees with the negative statement that underlies the question. Note that this represents quite a different pattern to the use of *yes* and *no* in English. Thus:

Bae yu no kam long lafet? Yes (bae mi no kam long lafet).
'Won't you come to the party? No (I won't come to the party).'

If the person wants to disagree with the negative statement that underlies such a question, the form *si* must be used instead. Thus:

Bae yu no kam long lafet? Si (bae mi kam long lafet).
'Won't you come to the party? Yes (I will come to the party).'

Si in an answer does not depend entirely on the presence of the negative marker *no* in the question itself. Even if there is just a hint of some kind of negative meaning in the statement that underlies a question, *si* can be used to turn this negative meaning into a positive answer. In the following, for example, there is an assumption in the question that the man in question no longer drinks kava even though the word *no* does not appear in the question itself. For this reason, it is possible to use *si* to overturn this negative assumption in the answer:

Man ia i lego kava finis? Si, hem i stap dring yet.
'Has that man given up kava? No, he still drinks.'

A negative answer to a question that is asked in the affirmative is normally answered with *no*, as illustrated by the following:

Bae yu kam long lafet? No (bae mi no kam long lafet).
'Will you come to the party? No (I won't come to the party).'

A particularly emphatic negative answer, however, can be expressed instead by *nogat*, as in the following:

Bae yu kam long lafet? Nogat (bae mi no kam long lafet).
'Will you come to the party? No way (I won't come to the party)!'

CHAPTER 6

It is also possible to answer a question that contains the verbal modifier *finis* 'completive' such as the following with *yes* or *no*:

Yu luk man ia finis? Yes (mi luk hem finis). No (mi no luk hem yet).
'Have you seen that man? Yes (I've seen him). No (I haven't seen him).'

However, with this kind of questions there are some additional options available as responses. Such questions can also be answered in the affirmative with *saye*, while in the negative they can be answered with *no yet*. Thus:

Yu luk man ia finis? Saye (mi luk hem finis). No yet (mi no luk hem yet).
'Have you seen that man? Yes (I've seen him). No (I haven't seen him).'

6.2.2 Content Questions

There is a variety of simple question words used in the formation of content questions. These question words belong to a number of different parts of speech, as described below.

6.2.2.1 *Wanem*

Wanem—occasionally pronounced *wenem*—functions as a noun phrase and asks about an inanimate or non-human animate noun phrase with the meaning of 'what'. Thus:

Wanem i bin kakae yu?
'What bit you?'

Because *wanem* is a kind of noun, it appears in the body of a sentence in exactly the same place as the noun phrase that it is asking about. Thus, if *wanem* is asking about an object to a verb, it appears after the verb. This represents a significant point of contrast with English where question words like *what* normally appear at the beginning of the sentence. Thus, compare the Bislama and English sentences below, where the question words in both languages are highlighted in bold:

*Olgeta oli planem **wanem** long garen blong yu?*
'**What** did they plant in your garden?'

Also, when *wanem* is asking about a noun phrase that is found within a prepositional phrase, the question word normally appears after the preposition, as in the following:

*Yu stap sidaon long **wanem**?*
'**What** are you sitting on?'

*Bae mi katem wetem **wanem**?*
'**What** will I cut it with?'

Wanem can also precede a noun to express the meaning of 'which'. When used as a modifier before a noun in this way, *wanem* expresses the same function as *wijwan* when used in association with a non-human noun (§6.2.2.6) and *hu* when used in association with a human noun (§6.2.2.3). Thus:

Bae yu tekem wanem kos long USP?
Bae yu tekem wijwan kos long USP?
'Which course will you take at USP?'

Wanem man nao i stil?
Hu man nao i stil?
'Which man stole?'

When used as a modifier within a noun phrase like this, *wanem* can be reduplicated to give *wanem-wanem* when the noun phrase is marked as plural with the plural marker *ol* or *olgeta* (§4.3.1). Thus:

Wanemwanem ol samting bae yumi karem i kam long haos?
'Which things will we bring to the house?'

Wanem also appears in set question phrases such as *wanem taem* 'what time' and *wanem kaen* 'what kind (of)', as illustrated by the following:

Wanem taem bae oli finis wok?
'What time will they finish work?'

Yufala i gat wanem kaen buk?
'What kind of books do you have?'

6.2.2.2 *Se*

The use of *se* in forming yes-no questions was described in §6.2.1. The same word can also be used to form a fairly restricted kind of content question corresponding to the function of 'what' in English in the sense of 'beg your pardon'. This use of *se* in Bislama functions as an interjection, so it typically does not appear with any other words along with it in a sentence. It is pronounced with the rising intonation of a question meaning 'what (did you say)' or 'what (do you want)' when a statement or an instruction has not been clearly heard. The following, therefore, is a possible exchange:

Jeffrey! Jeffrey o! Se?
'Jeffrey!' 'Hey, Jeffrey!' 'What?'

6.2.2.3 *Huia*

Huia 'who' also functions as a noun phrase, in this case to ask about humans, as in the following:

Huia i stap stadi long klasrum?
'Who is studying in the classroom?'

Like *wanem*, *huia* appears in the position of the sentence of the noun phrase that it is seeking information about. Thus:

Yu stap slip wetem huia?
'Who are you living with?'

Huia is also often used by people to ask about a person's name, as in:

CHAPTER 6

Huia nem blong yu?
'What is your name?'

When asking about the name of something that is not human, however, the question word *wanem* is used instead:

Wanem nem blong muvi we yumi luk yestedei?
'What is the name of the movie that we saw yesterday?'

However, some people use the question word *wanem* to ask about all names, whether human or non-human. Thus, you can expect to hear some people say:

Wanem nem blong yu?
'What is your name?'

The question word *huia* also has the shorter form *hu* expressing the same meaning. Some people prefer to use *huia* while others prefer *hu*, and yet other speakers tend to alternate freely between the two. For most people, there is probably no difference in meaning between *hu* and *huia*, though the shorter form can sometimes seem a little abrupt in comparison to the longer form. Thus:

Nem blong yu huia?
Nem blong yu hu?
'What's your name?'

Huia (or *hu*) is used when a singular noun phrase is being asked about, or where a plural answer is possible but this is not an important consideration for the person asking the question. However, when a specifically plural answer is being sought, the question word must be followed by the number marker *olgeta* (§4.3.1). In such constructions, the pronoun always appears as *hu* and never as *huia*, as in:

Bae yumi fesem hu olgeta long maj nekis wiken?
'Who will we be playing against in the match next weekend?'

Hu and *huia* can also be used with a following noun within a noun phrase to ask 'which' person. Thus:

Yu stap toktok wetem hu man?
'Which person were you talking with?'

Huia VMF ia i stap wok long get blong presiden?
'Which VMF member is on duty at the president's gate?'

Note that while *wanem* can be used to mean 'which' with respect to any noun, *hu(ia)* can only be used with respect to people. This means that you can expect to find variation such as the following involving nouns referring to people:

Yu stap toktok wetem hu man?
Yu stap toktok wetem wanem man?
'Which person were you talking with?'

Hu(ia) can also be used as a modifier with a preceding first or second person pronoun to ask who the unknown individuals are. Thus:

152

Yufala huia i stap aotsaed?
'Who are you outside?'

Yu ting se mifala hu?
'Who do you think we are?'

Yu hu i stap toktok?
'Who are you who is speaking?'

With a third person pronoun, however, the form *hu(ia)* comes before the pronoun rather than after it, for example:

Huia olgeta oli stap singsingaot bigwan long rod?
'Who are they who are yelling in the street?'

6.2.2.4 *Hamas*

This form can function as a modifier before a noun within a noun phrase (§4.3.1). With count nouns it calls for a specific number as an answer, i.e., 'how many', while with mass nouns it calls for some kind of statement of quantity, i.e., 'how much'. This question word directly precedes the noun phrase that it is asking about in any position in the sentence. Thus:

Hamas man i bin kam long lafet?
'How many people came to the celebration?'

Yu save kakae hamas raes?
'How much rice do you eat?'

Hamas can also function by itself as a noun phrase with no accompanying noun when the context makes it clear what is being asked about. Thus:

Yu stap winim hamas long wan manis?
'How much do you earn in a month?'

Hamas appears in the phrase *hamas klok* to express the meaning of 'what time'. However, the same meaning is more commonly expressed by means of the phrase *wanem taem* (§6.2.2.1). The following are therefore synonymous:

Hamas klok blong yu?
Wanem taem blong yu?
'What time do you have?'

6.2.2.5 *Hameni*

While most speakers of Bislama use *hamas* to express the meaning of both 'how much' and 'how many', *hamas* is used by a minority only to ask about amounts in general. The separate form *hameni* is used to ask about amounts which call for a number as part of the answer. Thus, the following can be used to express the same meaning:

CHAPTER 6

Hamas man i bin kam long lafet?
Hameni man i bin kam long lafet?
'How many people came to the celebration?'

6.2.2.6 *Wijwan*

This is another question word that can precede a noun within a noun phrase, in this case to ask 'which'.[13] Thus:

Wijwan mobael i stap wok long get blong presiden?
'Which mobile force member is on duty at the president's gate?'

Bae yu tekem wijwan kos long USP?
'Which course will you take at USP?'

From what has already been said in §6.2.2.1 and §6.2.2.3, it is clear that the meaning of 'which' can therefore be expressed in Bislama in a variety of ways. For nouns referring to humans, *wijwan* can alternate with *hu(ia)* or *wanem* as a modifier to a following noun, while for nouns referring to non-humans, *wijwan* can alternate with *wanem*. However, only *wijwan* can be used on its own as a noun phrase to express the meaning of 'which', as in the following:

Yu ting se wijwan i mo gud?
'Which one do you think is better?'

6.2.2.7 *Waswe*

The form *waswe*—sometimes also *wiswe*—can be used at the beginning of a sentence to ask about the reason for whatever is expressed in the following sentence. Thus:

Waswe yu no kam luk mi?
'Why didn't you come to see me?'

This is not the most common way of expressing the meaning of 'why', however. This meaning would normally be expressed as *from wanem* (§6.2.2.12), as in the following:

From wanem yu no kam luk mi?
Yu no kam luk me from wanem?
'Why didn't you come to see me?'

---

[13] For some speakers, the shorter form *wij* is used instead of *wijwan* before a noun phrase, though *wijwan* is used when there is no following noun phrase. Thus:

Wij kos bae yu tekem?
'Which course will you take?'

Wijwan bae yu tekem?
'Which will you take?'

SIMPLE SENTENCES

However, *waswe* expresses a degree of impatience or annoyance that is not implied with *from wanem*, rather similar to the effect of asking a question in English with 'how come' instead of 'why'.

6.2.2.8 *Watfo*

Another question word that is used to ask the reason for something is the form *watfo*. This is used like *waswe* in that it always appears at the beginning of the sentence. Thus:

Watfo yu stap luk mi?
'Why are you looking at me?'

Like *waswe*, there is a strong hint of impatience or annoyance associated with a question that is asked in this way. Not only this, but *watfo* seems to be disappearing from use altogether, and many people no longer use this word at all.

6.2.2.9 *Wataem*

The word *wataem*—alternating sometimes with *wetaem*—asks a question that calls for a statement of time in the answer. It was mentioned in §6.2.2.1 that *wanem taem* is also used to ask questions about time, and for some speakers of Bislama, *wataem* and *wanem taem* mean more or less the same thing, as illustrated below:

Bae kava i redi wataem?
Bae kava i redi wanem taem?
'When will the kava be ready?'

However, for some speakers there is a difference in meaning between questions involving *wataem* and *wanem taem*, with a question involving *wataem* calling only for a general statement of time while *wanem taem* calls for a specific clock time in response. Thus:

Bae kava i redi wataem? Bae i redi i no longtaem.
'When will the kava be ready? It'll be ready soon.'

Bae kava i redi wanem taem? Bae i redi long hapas faef.
'When will the kava be ready? It'll be ready at 5.30.'

6.2.2.10 *We*

The question word *we*—along with its common variant *wea*—asks about location, expressing the meaning of 'where'. It appears in a sentence in the position where the prepositional phrase or locational phrase that is called for in the answer would appear. It should be noted that *we* can ask about location ('where at'), direction to ('where to'), and direction from ('where from'). Thus:

Yu stap wok we? Mi wok long Tour Vanuatu.
'Where do you work? I work at Tour Vanuatu.'

CHAPTER 6

Lised ia i klaem i go we? I klaem i go antap long siling.
'Where did the lizard climb to? It climbed up to the ceiling.'

Yu kambak we? Mi kambak long Eromango.
'Where have you returned from? I have returned from Erromango.'

Because this question word is asking about location, it commonly appears after the preposition *long* (§6.1.5.1.6), as in the following:

Yu stap wok long we? Mi wok long Tour Vanuatu.
'Where do you work? I work at Tour Vanuatu.'

Yu kambak long we? Mi kambak long Eromango.
'Where have you returned from? I have returned from Erromango.'

As with many other question words, *we* can also be used before a noun, though only used before the noun *ples* 'place', as in *we ples* 'which place'. Thus:

We ples *nao yu go skul long hem?*
'Which place did you go to school at?'

Bae yu mufi go long **we ples***?*
'Which place will you move to?'

Although *we* asks 'which' regarding a place, *we* cannot be used before any other noun, and forms such as *wanem* or *wijwan* must be used instead. Thus, note the following:

Yu blong wanem aelan?
Yu blong wijwan aelan?
**Yu blong we aelan?*
'Which island are you from?'

When *we* is used to ask about location after a transitive verb that has an object noun phrase, the question word normally appears after the object, as in:

Yu lukaotem sop we?
'Where did you look for the soap?'

However, it is also possible sometimes for the question word *we* to appear between the verb and its object, as in the following:

Yu lukaotem we sop?
'Where did you look for the soap?'

Yu karem we ol samting ia?
'Where did you get those things?'

6.2.2.11 Wehem

Another question word is *wehem*, which is more commonly encountered in the shorter form *wem*. This also asks about place, though it differs from *we* in a number of respects. Firstly, whereas *we* asks about location as well as direction to and from, *wehem* asks only about the location of something. Secondly, whereas *we* appears in sentences that contain verbs, *wehem* only ever appears in non-predicate sentences (§6.1.2). Thus:

***Wehem** olgeta buk blong mi?*
'Where are my books?'

***Wem** ol man?*
'Where are the people?'

The following example shows how a question is asked when the sentence contains a verb where we must use *we* rather than *wehem*. Thus:

*Olgeta buk blong mi i stap **we**?*
Olgeta buk blong mi i stap **wehem?*
'Where are my books?'

Although *wehem* normally appears at the beginning of a sentence, it is occasionally found as the final element of the sentence. This is more likely to be interpreted as a rather brusque—and even accusing—kind of question, as indicated by the translation of the following example:

*Buk blong mi **wehem**?*
'Where on earth is my book?'

6.2.2.12 From

The preposition *from* marks, among other things, something that causes something to happen (§6.1.5.1.2). This can also be used as a question word to ask 'why', as in the following:

*Yu kam **from**?*
'Why did you come?'

This particular question word differs in its behavior from any of the other content question words discussed in this section in that it is pronounced with a final rising intonation instead of the normal falling intonation associated with the other question words. *From* also differs from other question words in that it cannot be moved to the beginning of the sentence as described in §6.3. Thus:

*From yu kam?

6.2.2.13 From wanem

The meaning of 'why' is, in fact, more frequently expressed by means of the preposition *from* followed by the question word *wanem* 'what', which is pronounced with the ordinary downward-falling intonation of a content question. Thus:

*Yu kam **from wanem**?*
'Why did you come?'

CHAPTER 6

This is the most widely used expression for expressing this meaning, with the shorter question word *from* being restricted to more colloquial speech.

Olsem wanem can also be used to express the meaning of 'why', and the earlier discussion above also indicated that *waswe* could also be used to ask about reason. This means that there is a variety of different ways of asking 'why':

Yu kam from wanem?
Yu kam olsem wanem?
Waswe yu kam?
Watfo yu kam?
Yu kam from?
'Why did you come?'

6.2.2.14 *Olsem wanem*

The preposition *olsem* 'like' (§6.1.5.1.5) can be followed by the question word *wanem* 'what' to produce the complex question marker *olsem wanem*. This can, of course, have a literal meaning, as in the following:

Lif blong namariu i olsem wanem?
'What is the leaf of the acacia tree like?'

However, *olsem wanem* is much more commonly encountered with meanings other than this literal meaning. Very closely related to this literal meaning of *olsem wanem* is its behavior in the following example:

Man ia i olsem wanem?

While this literally means 'What is that man like?', this construction is used colloquially in Bislama to mean something like 'What's up with that man?' or 'What's wrong with that man?' This is usually not intended to elicit a response, so it is more of a rhetorical question that is intended to criticize or make fun of somebody.

In §6.2.1 I indicated that *olsem wanem* can be placed at the beginning of a statement to make the statement into a yes-no question, as in the following:

Olsem wanem bae yu kam?
'Will you come?'

However, *olsem wanem* can also be used to form content questions asking about the manner in which an action is performed, thus translating into English as 'how', as in the following:

Mi no gat naef, bae mi katem bred olsem wanem?
'Without a knife, how will I cut the bread?'

Yu kam olsem wanem?
'How did you come?'

The form *hao*, appearing at the beginning of a clause and followed obligatorily by the focus marker *nao* (§6.3), represents an alternative way of asking a manner question, particularly among speakers who are more familiar with English. Thus:

Hao nao yu kam?
'How did you come?'

When used after an adjective, *olsem wanem* can ask about the extent to which the state expressed in the adjective has been achieved. This is something that we do in English also by means of the question word 'how', as in the following:

Wota i hot olsem wanem?
'How hot is the water?'

However, *hao nao* cannot be used to form questions of this type. Thus:

Hao nao wota i hot?

can only mean something like 'How did the water get hot?' and not 'How hot is the water?'

Olsem wanem is sometimes also used to ask about reason, translating as 'why', as in the following:

Yu kam olsem wanem?
'Why did you come?'

Finally, *olsem wanem* is commonly used by itself as a friendly greeting, as follows:

Olsem wanem?
'How's things?', 'Wassup?'

6.3 Fronted Noun Phrases

A very important feature of the grammar of Bislama is the fact that noun phrases can be freely moved from the positions in a sentence that have been described so far in this chapter to the beginning of the sentence. This is true of sentences that express statements, and it is perhaps especially common in questions. Noun phrases can be moved in this way to express contrast. A noun phrase is very often—but not always—followed by the marker *nao*,[14] or sometimes by the demonstrative *ia* (§4.3.5). There will typically also be a downward shift in intonation at the end of a fronted noun phrase with the rest of the sentence having the normal intonation of a completely new sentence.

It is not easy to find a direct translation equivalent of such sentences in English. It is possible to shift a noun phrase to the front of a sentence in English as well, but this happens much less frequently in English than in Bislama. It is therefore perhaps not a good idea to translate a sentence with a fronted noun phrase with the same kind of construction in English. Another way to express this kind of meaning in English is to place the fronted noun phrase in a sentence in the frame *it is NOUN PHRASE* with the rest of the sentence following the noun phrase as a relative clause introduced by a relative pronoun such as *who, which,* or *that.*

Noun phrases can be fronted in Bislama from anywhere in a simple sentence. Depending on what kind of noun phrase has been shifted and what kind of structural position it has been shifted from, some kind of pronoun may or may not be

---

[14] This is often shortened to *na.*

CHAPTER 6

left behind to indicate where the noun phrase originated from. Here is an example where an object noun phrase has been shifted and the pronoun *hem* is left behind:

Mi stap folem Antoine → *Antoine (nao) mi stap folem **hem**.*
'I am accompanying *Antoine*.'

The following, by way of contrast, shows a fronted object noun phrase in which no pronoun is left behind:

Antoine i katem faeawud → *Faeawud (nao) Antoine i katem.*
'It is firewood that Antoine chopped.'

A pronoun will generally be left behind when a noun phrase that expresses a singular noun is fronted and that noun refers to a human or an animate being. However, when the shifted noun refers to a singular thing (or maybe an animal) rather than a human, there is often no pronoun left behind at all (§4.2). This is why we see a different kind of behavior in the examples just presented, as the human noun *Antoine* is shifted in one case while the inanimate noun *faeawud* 'firewood' is fronted in the other. However, when a plural noun is fronted—regardless of whether it refers to humans, animals, or things—there will normally be a plural pronoun left behind. Thus:

*Mi laekem ol taro ia. Ol taro ia (nao) mi laekem **olgeta**.*
'It is those taros that I like.'

When the fronted noun phrase is itself a pronoun, there will always be a pronoun left behind. This means that the same pronoun will effectively appear twice in the sentence, as in the following:

Mi laekem yu. Yu (nao) mi laekem yu.
'I like *you*.'

As mentioned in §6.1.1, there is no passive construction in Bislama. However, the meaning of an agentless passive in English can often be expressed in Bislama by means of a subjectless verb introduced by the plural predicate marker *oli*, as in the following:

Oli stilim tep blong mi.
'My cassette player has been stolen.'

Given that agentless passive constructions in English and subjectless verbs introduced by *oli* in Bislama are both effectively shifting attention away from the performer of an action to the noun phrase that is affected by the action, it is quite common for the object noun phrase in Bislama to be fronted to the beginning of the sentence. Thus, the meaning of the example just presented is very commonly expressed instead as follows:

Tep blong mi oli stilim.
'My cassette player has been stolen.'

Although the examples presented above involve movement from the position of the object of a transitive verb, noun phrases can be moved from any non-subject position of the clause. This means that noun phrases appearing in prepositional phrases can also readily be fronted. Thus:

Mi wokbaot wetem papa → *Papa (nao) mi wokbaot wetem hem.*
'I walked with *Father*.'

Even the complex prepositional constructions described in §6.1.5.4 can have a noun phrase moved to the front of the sentence. Thus:

Bae mi wokem fenis raon long yad blong mi → *Yad blong mi (nao) bae mi wokem fenis raon long hem.*
'It is my yard that I will make a fence around.'

Another consideration that must be kept in mind in determining whether or not a pronoun will be left at the point from which the noun phrase is fronted is the nature of the preceding preposition. If the preposition before the fronted noun is one of the basic prepositions *long* (§6.1.5.1.6) or *blong* (§6.1.5.1.1), there must always be a pronoun left behind, regardless of whether the fronted noun phrase refers to a human, an animal, or a thing. Thus:

Mi mestem ki blong trak → *Trak (nao) mi mestem ki blong hem.*
'It is the car that I have misplaced the key of.'

Leimara i stap slip long haos blong Jaylene → *Haos blong Jaylene (nao) Leimara i stap slip long hem.*
'It is Jaylene's house that Leimara lives in.'

However, with any of the other prepositions, whether or not there is a pronoun left at the original site of the fronted noun phrase depends on whether the noun refers to a human or a thing (with animals sometimes being treated as humans and sometimes treated as things), in the same way that we find when objects of verbs are fronted. Thus, compare the examples of noun phrases fronted from behind *long* and *blong* in the examples above with the behavior of noun phrases fronted from after the prepositions *wetem* and *from*:

Mi katem bred wetem naef → *Naef (nao) mi katem bred wetem.*
'It is a knife that I cut the bread with.'

Mi wokbaot wetem abu → *Abu (nao) mi wokbaot wetem hem.*
'I walked with *Grandfather*.'

Mi kam from samting ia → *Samting ia (nao) mi kam from.*
'That's the thing that I have come for.'

Mi kam from man ia → *Man ia (nao) mi kam from hem.*
'I have come for *that man*.'

There is, however, one restriction against the movement of noun phrases and this involves nouns that appear in the special VERB + NOUN construction described in §6.1.3.2. Thus, while it is possible to shift the object of the transitive verb *lanem* 'learn' in the following example, it is not possible to shift the same noun phrase when it appears after the intransitive verb *toktok* 'speak':

CHAPTER 6

Mi lanem Franis → *Franis (nao) mi lanem.*
'It is French that I am learning.'

Mi toktok Franis → **Franis (nao) mi toktok.*
'I speak French.'

If we wanted to focus attention on *Franis* 'French' in *toktok Franis* 'speak French', the only way that we could do this is to reorganize the sentence such that *Franis* appears as the object of a transitive verb, or so that it appears after a preposition. The preposition *long* can be used to express more or less the same meaning (§6.1.5.1.6), so the noun phrase could then be fronted, as follows:

Mi toktok long Franis → *Franis (nao) mi toktok long hem.*
'It is French that I speak.'

It was mentioned in §6.2.2 that the question words in Bislama frequently appear in the same position of the sentence as the word expressing the idea that they are asking about. Thus:

Hem i karem wanem long kartong?
'What did he take from the box?'

Hem i karem suga long wanem?
'What did he take the sugar from?'

In the corresponding English sentences, however, the question word *what* normally appears at the beginning of the sentence. Because question words usually focus our attention on whatever it is that we are asking about, it is quite common for question words in Bislama to be shifted to the front of the sentence. When this happens, these forms behave just like any other fronted noun phrase. Thus:

Wanem nao hem i karem long kartong?
'What did he take from the box?'

Wanem nao hem i karem suga long hem?
'What did he take the sugar from?'

When the fronted question word is *hu(ia)*, this is often associated with a pronoun being left in the original location, as this word refers to humans. Thus:

Hu nao yu karem hem long trak blong yu?
'Who did you bring in your car?'

While verbal objects and noun phrases from within prepositional phrases can be fronted, it is also possible to focus attention on the subject of a verb. Because the subject is already at the beginning of the sentence, the noun phrase cannot literally be "fronted" as such. However, what happens is still similar to what happens when other noun phrases are shifted to the beginning of the sentence in that the subject may be followed in the same way by the focus markers *nao* or *ia*, and the noun phrase is then followed by an appropriate pronoun. Thus:

Antoine i katem faeawud → *Antoine (nao) hem i katem faeawud.*
'It was Antoine who cut the firewood.'

Antoine mo James i laetem faea → *Antoine mo James (nao) tufala i laetem faea.*
'It was Antoine and James who lit the fire.'

Ol tija (nao) olgeta oli kam long miting.
'It was the teachers who came to the meeting.'

Consider now the following sentence:

Reva i bin karemaot haos blong mifala.
'The river took away our house.'

The subject here is *reva* 'river', which is an inanimate noun phrase. Such noun phrases do not usually get replaced with the pronoun *hem* when they are shifted. When our attention is focused on the subject, this is indicated simply by using one of the focus markers *nao* or *ia*, without a following pronoun. Thus:

Reva nao i bin karemaot haos blong mifala.
'It was the river that took away our house.'

When the subject of the sentence upon which attention is focused involves a pronoun rather than a noun, what happens is the following:

(i) With first and second person singular subjects, the fronted pronoun appears first and there is a copy of that pronoun immediately following it, with an optional focus marker (*nao* or *ia*) appearing after the focused first pronoun. Thus:

Mi wokbaot → *Mi (nao) mi wokbaot.*
'It is I who is walking.'

Yu singsing → *Yu (nao) yu singsing.*
'It is you who is singing.'

(ii) With the third person singular subject *hem*, it is possible to do exactly the same thing except that in this case one of the focus markers obligatorily separates the two occurrences of the pronoun. Thus:

Hem i singaot → *Hem nao hem i singaot.*
'It was he who was shouting.'

With this type of subject, it is also possible to delete the second instance of the pronoun *hem* (but retaining the obligatory predicate marker). The same thing is not possible with the pronouns *mi* and *yu*. Thus:

Hem nao i singaot.
'It was he who was shouting.'

Yu nao yu singaot.
**Yu nao singaot.*
'It was you who was shouting.'

(iii) With remaining pronoun subjects, what happens is essentially the same as we find with *hem*. This means that there are two possibilities. Firstly, the pronoun may be obligatorily followed by a focus marker (*nao* or *ia*) with the full pronoun along with any following predicate marker; Thus:

CHAPTER 6

Mifala i wok → *Mifala nao mifala i wok.*
'It is us who are working.'

Secondly, the fronted pronoun must again be followed by a focus marker but the subject position may be left empty, though with the original predicate marker retained, for example:

Mifala i wok → *Mifala nao i wok.*
'It is we who are working.'

Although focused noun phrases are fronted from elsewhere in the sentence, it is possible for an initial noun phrase not to have originated from within the sentence if the context makes it quite clear how this noun phrase relates to the content of the sentence. Examine the following example:

Mifala (nao) ol jif oli strong.

The noun phrase that appears at the beginning of this sentence is *mifala* 'we (plural exclusive)' and what comes next is the following sentence:

Ol jif oli strong.
'The chiefs are tough.'

However, from the context it will be clear that the speaker is contrasting the situation regarding chiefs in his or her society with the situation regarding chiefs in other parts of Vanuatu. Even though there is no mention of *mifala* 'us (plural exclusive)' in the original sentence, this is very clearly implied. No direct translation of this example into English is possible, though the following represents a good approximation:

Mifala (nao) ol jif oli strong.
'With regards to us, our chiefs are tough.'

The following are additional examples of the same kind of pattern which I have heard people using recently:

Malakula ples i hot lelebet.
'It is quite hot on Malakula.'

Futbol ol boe Vanuatu oli karem nambatri praes.
'The Vanuatu guys received third prize in the football.'

Numan Setan i gud lelebet.
'Satan is quite good in comparison to Numan.'

Mi solwota i drae naoia.
'I am broke.'[15]

Things are actually a bit more complicated than this because it is not just a question of a single noun phrase being focused by being shifted to the front of a

---

[15] *Solwota i drae*, literally 'the sea is dry' but usually meaning 'the tide is out', can also be used idiomatically to mean 'to be broke'.

sentence. Sometimes we actually find two noun phrases appearing at the beginning of the sentence in the same kind of construction. Thus:

David pig ia bae hem i karem i go long narasaed?
'Will David take this pig across the island?'

In this example, *David* represents a focused subject, while *pig ia* 'this pig' represents a focused object.

7: COMPLEX SENTENCES

This chapter describes the various ways in which the simple sentences described in Chapter 6 can be combined to form complex sentences.

7.1 Serial Verbs

It is very common in Bislama for verbs to be linked together in what can be referred to as "serial verb" constructions. These are like complex sentences in that they involve several verbs, each with their own predicate marking. However, they are at the same time more like simple sentences in that the two verbs really only refer to a single situation. The following is an example of this type:

Avok i lukluk i go long olfala blong hem.
'Avok looked away to his father.'

Although there are two verbs involved here, *lukluk* 'look' and *go* 'go', Avok did not look and then go somewhere. Rather, the looking and the going happen at the same time as parts of a single overall happening involving a single action, i.e., looking away.

The complex verbs described in §5.2 represent another kind of serial verb construction, though that pattern differs from this one in a number of respects. Firstly, the construction described in §5.2 involves only a single predicate marker for the verb series (*i katem spletem* 'chop along the middle'), whereas the construction in this chapter has a predicate marker for each verb (*i lukluk i go* 'look away'). Secondly, elements of the discontinuous emphatic negative construction *no ... nating* 'not at all' (§5.3.4) are placed around the entire sequence with complex verbs (*i no katem spletem nating* 'not chop along the middle at all') whereas they are placed around only the first verb with this kind of construction (*i no lukluk nating i go* 'not look away at all'). Thirdly, with complex verbs, there can only be an object to the series as a whole, whereas with this serial verb construction, there can be an object expressed independently in relation to the first verb. Thus:

Bae mi no putum kaliko i stap long ples ia.
'I won't put the cloth here.'

Hem i holem rop i taet.
'(S)he held the rope tightly.'

Finally, unlike complex verbs, it is also possible with serial verbs of this type to introduce adverbial modifiers or prepositional phrases after the initial verb, as in the following:

Avok i lukluk oltaem i go long olfala blong hem.
'Avok always looked to his father.'

Avok i lukluk long spaeglas i go long olfala blong hem.
'Avok looked through the binoculars to his father.'

Avok i lukluk yestedei i go long olfala blong hem.
'Avok look to his father yesterday.'

7.1.1 Directional Verbs

Perhaps the most widely encountered serial verb construction of this type in Bislama is that in which an initial verb involving some kind of inherent directionality in the action is followed by one of the basic motion verbs *go* 'go', *kam* 'come', *gobak* 'go back', and *kambak* 'come back'. When verbs appear after another verb in a serial verb construction, they specify the direction in which the action takes place. Contrast, therefore, the following:

Hem i lukluk i kam long mi.
'(S)he looked toward me.'

Olgeta oli lukluk i go long yu.
'They looked toward you.'

In exactly the same way, these basic motion verbs can also follow a transitive verb, including its object, as illustrated by the following:

Bae yu sakem manggo i kam.
'Throw the mango over here.'

Bae yu sakem manggo i go.
'Throw the mango over there.'

The difference in meaning between the English verbs 'bring' and 'take' can be expressed in Bislama by means of this serial verb construction in association with the verb *karem*, which can be used to refer to an action that takes place in either direction. Thus:

Hem i karem buk i kam.
'(S)he brought the book.'

Hem i karem buk i go.
'(S)he took the book.'

In addition to these basic motion verbs, the non-motion verb *stap* 'stay; exist' can also appear in this construction where there is no direction specified for the action. Thus, if an action takes place within a particular location without moving either toward or away from that location, then *stap* can be used after the initial verb. Thus:

Hem i ronron i stap long yad.
'(S)e is running about in the yard (without actually going anywhere).'

Stap can also be used in association with a transitive verb where an action results in something being at rest somewhere, as in the following:

Hem i putum buk i stap long tebol.
'(S)he put the book down on the table.'

This construction is obviously very different from anything in the grammar of English. Forms such as *away* or *over here* can be used to provide information about the direction of a verb, while in formal (and even archaic) English, we can use *hither* and *thither* in this way as well. However, in English the direction of an

CHAPTER 7

action does not normally need to be spelled out at all. In Bislama, by way of contrast, it is very common for this extra directional information to be provided.

In all of the examples presented so far, the predicate marker on the first verb is determined by the rules set out in §6.1.1, while the predicate marker on the second verb has invariably been *i*. However, there are other possibilities for the predicate marker on the second verb. Where the first verb is intransitive, the predicate marker on the second verb is invariably *i*, regardless of the form of the predicate marker associated with the initial verb. Thus:

Yu lukluk i go.
'You looked away.'

Yu nomo yu lukluk i go.
'Just you looked away.'

Olgeta oli lukluk i go.
'They looked away.'

Where the first verb is transitive, the predicate marker on the second verb takes its shape from the object of the initial verb. Where the first verb has a singular noun phrase as its object, then the predicate marker is also going to be *i*. Thus:

Bae olgeta oli sendem leta i kam long mi.
'They will send the letter to me.'

If the object is a plural noun—as well as the plural pronoun *olgeta* 'they'—the predicate marker can be either *i* or *oli*, with the choice depending on the same kinds of considerations described in §6.1.1 for the choice of *i* or *oli* after plural noun subjects. Thus:

Wilfred i karem ol bag kopra i go long bed blong kopra.
'Wilfred took the bags of copra to the drying rack.'

Agrikalja So i pulum plante man oli kam.
'The Agricultural Show attracted many people.'

Ol drong man oli ronem olgeta oli go.
'The drunk men chased them away.'

Where the object of the initial verb is a pronoun, the predicate marker is *i* when the pronoun is one of those described in §6.1.1 as being followed by *i* in the subject position, for example:

Olgeta oli singaotem mifala i kam.
'They called us over.'

Where the object of the initial verb is one of those pronouns that appears with no predicate marker at all, it is more difficult to describe what happens in serial verb constructions, as there are sometimes competing patterns between different speakers. The particular pronouns involved are *mi* 'I', *yu* 'you (singular)', and *yumi* 'we (plural inclusive)'. Some people will use the predicate marker *i* after such objects, as in:

Bae mi livim yu i stap long haos.
'I will leave you at home.'

Hem i karem mi i kam.
'(S)he brought me.'

However, other people will use a form that is identical with the pronoun itself as the second predicate marker, as in the following:

Bae mi livim yu yu stap long haos.
'I will leave you at home.'

Hem i karem mi mi kam.
'(S)he brought me.'

Finally, some people do not use a predicate marker with the second verb. Thus:

Bae mi livim yu stap long haos.
'I will leave you at home.'

Hem i karem mi kam.
'(S)he brought me.'

As mentioned above, the use of the basic motion verbs *go* 'go', *kam* 'come', *gobak* 'go back', and *kambak* 'come back' in this kind of directional construction is very common in Bislama. The preposition *long* in Bislama has many meanings (§6.1.5.1.6) and this serial verb construction is one way in which the specific meaning of the preposition can be established. With some verbs, this preposition may be ambiguous between a location ('in', 'at', 'on'), a goal ('to', 'toward') or a source ('from'). If a motion reading is specifically intended over a locative reading, this can be unambiguously expressed by incorporating the directional verbs *kam* 'come' or *go* 'go' respectively. Thus, while the following example has three different possible meanings:

Maki i bin wokbaot long bus.
'Maki walked in the bush.'
'Maki walked to the bush.'
'Maki walked from the bush.'

it is possible to distinguish between the two quite distinct motion meanings using the serial verb constructions below:

Maki i bin wokbaot i go long bus.
'Maki walked to the bush.'

Maki i bin wokbaot i kam long bus.
'Maki walked from the bush.'

A verb phrase that has not been further specified as to direction by means of a serial verb construction in this way would normally be given a location interpretation. Thus, in the absence of any information from the context, the sentence *Maki i bin wokbaot long bus* would probably end up being interpreted as meanng 'Maki walked *in* the bush'. However, this locative meaning can also be unambiguously expressed with *stap* in the same serial verb construction. Thus:

CHAPTER 7

Maki i bin wokbaot i stap long bus.
'Maki walked in the bush.'

An imperative initial verb of transfer or placement, such as *givim* 'give', *putum* 'put', or *livim* 'leave', can be deleted altogether. This results in the object of the deleted initial verb appearing immediately before the verb of direction or posture and its associated predicate marker. We therefore encounter alternatives such as the following:

Givim raes i kam!
Raes i kam!
'Give (me) the rice.'

Livim raes i stap!
Raes i stap!
'Leave the rice alone.' 'Don't bother with the rice.'

While the shorter expressions here look like ordinary statements, they are pronounced with imperative intonations, indicated here by means of exclamation marks. There is therefore a difference in intonation between the following:

Raes i stap.
'There is rice.'

Raes i stap!
'Leave the rice alone.'

Although the basic motion verbs and the verb *stap* 'stay, exist' are very commonly used in directional serial verb constructions, these are not the only motion and posture verbs that can be used in this way. Verbs such as *hang* 'be suspended', *slip* 'be in a prone position', *stanap* 'be in an upright position', and *lei* 'be at an angle' can also enter into serial constructions of this kind. Thus:

Hem i putum pos i slip long graon.
'(S)he lay the post on the ground.'

Hem i putum pos i stanap long hol.
'(S)he stood the post up in the hole.'

Oli putum ol pos i lei long wol blong jios.
'The posts were leaned against the wall of the church.'

Mama blong mi i pinim klos blong mi i hang long laen.
'My mother hung my clothes up on the line.'

7.1.2 Manner Constructions

The second major type of serial verb construction in Bislama expresses manner. In such constructions, the second predicate is not a motion or posture verb but is instead an intransitive verb that expresses a state. We therefore find examples such as the following:

Maki i holem rop i slak.
'Maki held the rope loosely.'

Manner constructions such as this differ from the directional serial constructions described above in that the preceding predicate marker is always *i* regardless of the nature of the preceding object. Thus:

Hem i faetem ol man i strong.
**Hem i faetem ol man oli strong.*
'He punched the men hard.'

Hem i faetem mi i strong.
**Hem i faetem mi mi strong.*
'He punched me hard.'

With some adjectives, there are two possible constructions in which they can appear when they are being used to express manner. They can on the one hand appear in this kind of serial verb construction, while on the other hand they can function as adverbial modifiers within the verb phrase (§5.3.2). Thus, such meanings can be expressed alternately as follows:

Maki i holem rop i taet.
Maki i holem taet rop.
'Maki held the rope tightly.'

However, this kind of variation is only possible with a restricted set of intransitive verbs, as most only have the option of appearing in this serial verb construction. The form *slak* 'loose', for example, cannot behave like *taet* 'tight':

Maki i holem rop i slak.
**Maki i holem slak rop.*
'Maki held the rope loosely.'

For some speakers, the adverbial modifier may also appear after the object of the verb. This results in the following as alternative ways of expressing the same meaning:

Hem i faetem mi strong.
Hem i faetem mi i strong.
Hem i faetem strong mi.
'He punched me hard.'

7.1.3 Causative Constructions

Causative constructions indicate that some agent makes something or somebody else do something (or become something). The verbs *mekem* 'make' and *letem* 'let, permit' are both causative verbs which appear as the first verb in a serial verb construction, with the verb expressing the resulting action or state appearing after it. These are both transitive and followed by an object. The predicate marker that appears before the second verb is determined by the same set of rules that determine the shape of the predicate marker associated with the construction involving directional verbs described in §7.1.1. Thus:

CHAPTER 7

San i mekem hed blong mi i soa.
'The sun made my head sore.'

Jif i letem mifala i huk long rif.
'The chief let us go fishing on the reef.'

Kava i mekem yu drong.
Kava i mekem yu yu drong.
Kava i mekem yu i drong.
'The kava made you drunk.'

7.1.4 Sequential Actions

A final type of serial verb involves *kirap*. As an ordinary verb, this meaning 'get up' or 'wake up', as in the following:

Yu kirap long stul, mi bae mi skrasem kokonas.
'Get up from the stool, I will grate the coconut.'

Boe blong mi i no stap kirap eli long moning.
'My son doesn't wake up early in the mornings.'

Kirap—often in the shortened forms *kira*, or even *kra*—is increasingly used in colloquial Bislama to indicate that an action happens after something else in a sequence of happenings, especially when somebody is telling a story. Thus:

Olfala we i stanap long stoa i kirap i tok long ol pikinini we oli mekem noes.
'The old man standing at the shop told off the noisy children.'

In this case, since the old man was already standing up, it makes no sense to interpret *kirap* as 'get up', so the serial verb *i kirap i tok* indicates that he had been standing for some time, the old man then told the children off.

7.2 Coordination

The term "coordination" is used to describe the process whereby two simple sentences are "added" to each other to produce a single complex sentence.

7.2.1 *Mo*

Coordination in Bislama can be marked by linking two simple sentences together by means of the coordinator *mo* 'and',[1] as in:

Tom i go long stoa mo Joseph i go long maket.
'Tom went to the shop and Joseph went to the market.'

If the same noun phrase appears in both sentences that have been coordinated, the second instance of the noun phrase can be replaced by a pronoun (or it can be

---

[1] *Mo* is also used to link noun phrases in coordinate noun phrase constructions (§4.5).

deleted altogether) according to conditions for the deletion and retention of pronouns described in §4.2. Thus:

Tom i go long maket mo hem i pem tu manggo.
'Tom went to the market and bought two mangoes.'

Wan ston i rol long hil mo i brekem haos blong mifala.
'A rock rolled down the hill and smashed our house.'

The second simple sentence in a coordinate construction in Bislama—and all subsequent simple sentences—must represent complete sentences containing verbs. Thus, Bislama differs from English in that we cannot have "reduced" coordinate constructions with deleted verbs such as we find in the English translation of the following example:

Tom i go long stoa mo Joseph i go long maket mo Harry i go long nakamal.
*Tom i go long stoa mo Joseph long maket mo Harry long nakamal.
'Tom went to the shop and Joseph to the market and Harry to the kava bar.'

Another coordinate construction involves the placing of two simple sentences one after the other with no *mo* separating the two. Such sentences give the superficial appearance of being like the directional serial verbs described in §7.1.1 in that they contain two verbs in sequence, each of which is introduced by a predicate marker:

Kali i katem tri i foldaon.
'Kali cut the tree and it fell down.'

Such constructions differ from serial verb constructions, however, in that:

- The two verbs refer to things that happen one after the other rather than as different aspects of a single overall happening.

- The verbs in these sequential constructions can still optionally be separated by the coordinator *mo*, which is not possible with genuine directional serial verb constructions.

Compare, therefore the following sequential example with the optional deleted coordinator, and a serial construction where the coordinator cannot be used:

Kali i katem tri i foldaon.
Kali i katem tri mo i foldaon.
'Kali cut the tree and it fell down.'

Kali i sakem bol i kam.
*Kali i sakem bol mo i kam.
'Kali threw the ball over here.'

Kali i putum kakae i stap.
*Kali i putum kakae mo i stap.
'Kali put the food there.'

Thus, these kinds of sentences are regarded as being another type of coordinate sentence rather than being treated as a kind of serial verb construction.

7.2.2 Be

Another kind of coordinate sentence involves the linking of two simple sentences with *be* 'but',[2] as in the following:

Tom i go long stoa be Joseph i go long maket.
'Tom went to the shop but Joseph went to the market.'

Again, noun phrases common to the two coordinated sentences can be deleted or replaced by pronouns under the appropriate conditions:

Tom i go long stoa be hem i no pem wan samting.
'Tom went to the shop but he didn't buy anything.'

Hariken i blu strong be i no karemaot haos blong mifala.
'The cyclone blew hard but it didn't knock down our house.'

It is possible for a considerable amount of material in the second of two sentences linked by *be* to be deleted if it can be deduced from the context. Thus:

Dog blong mi i wael. I no jam long leg blong man be nek wantaem.
'My dog is savage. It doesn't just go for people's legs but right for their throats.'

Sometimes, an understanding of the nature of the deleted material may be dependent on the context in which an utterance takes place. Consider the following example:

Yu ron be wetem potmenta blong yu.

The initial element here is:

Yu ron.
'You ran.'

This is followed by the prepositional phrase *wetem potmenta blong yu* 'with your suitcase', which is separated from the initial sentence by means of *be* 'but'. Literally, then, this means:

'You ran but with your suitcase.'

Without any appreciation of the context in which this utterance is produced, this is almost meaningless, and the English translation that I have just given is probably ungrammatical in any situation. However, a complex sentence like this can be used in Bislama in a context that can be captured by the following fuller translation into English:

'You ran but you did so with your suitcase when one would have expected you not to be holding a suitcase.'

Given that *be* marks something that happens contrary to expectation, it also appears in a number of different subordinate clause constructions where there is an expression of the idea that something happens contrary to expectation (§7.3.1,

---

[2] Some people use English-derived *bat* while others use the hybrid *bet*.

§7.3.2.2.4, §7.3.2.2.6, §7.3.2.2.7). In such cases, *be* introduces what we can call a contrafactual main clause preceded by a subordinate clause. Thus:

Nomata we hem i go long stoa be hem i no pem wan samting.
'Even though he went to the shop, he didn't buy anything.'

Sapos se man i stil be bae i go long kalabus.
'If one steals, one will go to jail.'

7.2.3 (N)o

Finally, there are so-called "disjunctive" sentences where the form *o* (or *no*) links two simple sentences to indicate that there are two options being presented, as in:

Bae yu kam no bae yu stap long haos?
'Will you come or will you stay at home?'

Again, when two sentences contain identical material, this will often be deleted when the two are linked by *(n)o*. Thus, when combining *Bae yu kam tedei?* 'Will you come today?' and *Bae yu kam tumora?* 'Will you come tomorrow?', we frequently encounter reductions to the second sentence of the following kind:

Bae yu kam tedei o tumora?
'Will you come today or tomorrow?'

There is a second disjunctive construction involving the form *sapos no*, literally 'if not'. This sequence is used specifically when there is an assumption that the option mentioned first represents the preferred option on the part of the speaker. Thus:

Bae mifala i go wok long garen sapos no bae mifala i go huk.
'We will either go to work in the garden (by first choice) or (as second choice) we will go fishing.'

Just as *o* (or *no*) can be used to link noun phrases or other kinds of constituents, we also find the same with *sapos no*. The following illustrates a pair of noun phrases linked in this way:

Bae mifala i kakae raes sapos no maniok.
'We will eat rice (if we can) or cassava (if we have to).'

The following indicates that other kinds of constituents—in this case prepositional phrases—can also be linked by means of this disjunctive device:

Bae hem i skul long Malapoa sapos no long Matevulu.
'She will go to school either at Malapoa (as I suspect) or Matevulu (which is less likely).'

7.3 Subordination

Subordinate constructions are those in which there is a complex sentence with a main element that can stand on its own referring to a primary event, along with an accompanying element that is often—though by no means always—structurally

CHAPTER 7

reduced in some way such that it cannot stand on its own. The subordinate element typically expresses a situation that is in some way dependent on whatever situation is described in the main part of the complex sentence. Examine, therefore, the following example:

Mi kam long ofis blong harem nius.
'I came to the office to hear the news.'

This consists of two separate elements. The first is the main part that can stand on its own, i.e.,

Mi kam long ofis.
'I came to the office.'

The sequence *blong harem nius* 'to hear the news' expresses another happening altogether, but this clearly cannot stand on its own. It constitutes, therefore, the subordinate element in this complex sentence.

The subordinate element of a complex sentence can be related to the main element in one of two ways:

- The two can simply be placed one after each other, though there may be some kind of change of intonation to indicate that there are two separate elements within the sentence. In such cases, we can speak of the two unmarked clauses being "juxtaposed".

- There may be some kind of grammatical marker, which we can call a "subordinator", on the subordinate element, usually at the beginning. The subordinate element may also be structurally reduced in some way in comparison to the main element.

7.3.1 Juxtaposition

The juxtaposition of simple sentences in Bislama to make up complex sentences is commonly used to express conditional relationships between two sentences, corresponding to constructions that are marked in English by means of *if*. In such constructions, it is always the hypothetical situation that is stated first, with the conditional situation that follows from this being mentioned second. Thus:

Dog ia i ron i kam, mi bae mi resis i go.
'If that dog runs over here, I will hurry away.'

However, while it is very common for juxtaposed simple sentences to express the conditional in this way, it will be shown separately in §7.3.2.2.6 that it is possible also for the subordinator *sapos* 'if' to introduce the hypothetical situation, as in the following:

Sapos dog ia i ron i kam, mi bae mi resis i go.
'If that dog runs over here, I will hurry away.'

In addition to conditional constructions, juxtaposition can also be used to express a time relationship between two events. Thus:

Mi klaem hil, win blong mi i finis.
'When I climbed up the hill, I ran out of breath.'

In such cases, it is normally possible for the subordinate element to be introduced instead by means of the form *taem* (§7.3.2.2.4), as in the following:

***Taem** mi klaem hil, win blong mi i finis.*
'When I climbed up the hill, I ran out of breath.'

The main element that is juxtaposed after a conditional sentence or a time sentence can also be introduced by *be* (§7.2.2) just as we find when the subordinate elements are introduced by the subordinators *sapos* or *taem*. Thus:

*Yu ronewe **be** yu go wetem potmenta blong yu.*
'If you escaped, you would go with your suitcase.'

*Taem mi klaem hil **be** win blong mi i finis.*
'When I climbed up the hill, I ran out of breath.'

Juxtaposition can also be used when the subject of the predicate of the main element is itself a complete simple sentence. Look at the following example:

Malon i mekem olsem ia i nogud.
'It is bad that Malon did that.'

Here, the predicate is *i nogud* 'it is bad'. If this were part of an ordinary simple sentence, the subject would be a noun phrase, such as:

Fasin ia i nogud.
'That behavior is bad.'

What occupies the subject position is in fact an entire simple sentence, i.e.,

Malon i mekem olsem ia.
'Malon did that.'

7.3.2 Subordinator Constructions

The second way in which elements can be linked within a complex sentence is by means of a subordinator, i.e., a form that is placed at the beginning of the subordinate element. In an example such as the following, the form *blong* is being used as a subordinator:

*Mi go long stoa **blong** pem raes.*
'I went to the shop to buy some rice.'

Many subordinators have double functions, performing other tasks in the grammar of Bislama. The subordinator *blong*, for example, can also be used as a preposition expressing possession along with a wide range of other functions (§4.4, §6.1.5.1.1). Contrast, therefore, the prepositional function of *blong* in the example below with the subordinating function in the preceding example:

*Bae mi kuk **blong** ol pikinini.*
'I will cook for the children.'

CHAPTER 7

There are two types of subordinators in Bislama: simple subordinators and complex subordinators. A simple subordinator is a form that only ever introduces a subordinate element within the complex sentence by itself, i.e., there is no possibility of an additional subordinator being used in conjunction with it. There are five simple subordinators in Bislama: *blong*, *long*, *we*, *se*, and *nogud*. A complex subordinator, however, is one that can optionally be followed by either *se* or *we* with no change of meaning.

7.3.2.1 Simple Subordinators

7.3.2.1.1 *Blong* and *Long*

The possessive preposition *blong* (along with its alternative shapes *blo* and *bl-*) (§4.4) is very commonly used to introduce a purpose clause, expressing therefore the meaning of '(in order) to' or 'for (to)'. Where the subjects of the main clause and the subordinate clause are identical, this will normally be deleted in the subordinate clause. Thus:

Mi kam blong harem nius.
'I came to hear the news.'

We can say that the subject of the subordinate clasue has been deleted here because we would not normally say:

*Mi kam blong mi harem nius.

However, the subject of the main clause and the subordinate clause can be different, in which case the two clauses remain structurally intact when linked by the subordinator *blong*, and the subjects of both verbs will be present. Thus:

Mi kam blong ol man oli askem kwestin long mi.
'I came for people to ask me questions.'

The purposive subordinator *blong* is very commonly deleted between the basic motion verbs *kam* 'come' and *go* 'go' in the main clause and a following verb in a subordinate clause, as in the following:

Hem i kam blong luk mi.
Hem i kam luk mi.
'She came to see me.'

Bae yu go blong pem raes long stoa.
Bae yu go pem raes long stoa.
'Go and buy some rice in the shop.'

However, with other verbs of motion, this kind of deletion of the subordinator is not possible. Thus:

Manu i daeva blong karem troka.
*Manu i daeva karem troka.
'Manu dived to get the trochus.'

178

*Tom i spid **blong** harem nius.*
*Tom i spid harem nius.
'Tom hurried to hear the news.'

The subordinator *blong* is also not deleted after *kam* and *go* when material such as an adverb or a prepositional phrase follows the verb. Thus:

*Hem i kam long haos **blong** luk mi.*
*Hem i kam long haos luk mi.
'She came to the house to see me.'

*Bae yu go long sapa **blong** pem raes long stoa.*
*Bae yu go long sapa pem raes long stoa.
'Go in the evening to buy the rice in the shop.'

Blong can also be used to introduce other kinds of relationships within complex sentences. Any of the following verbs (and many others) can be followed by a subordinate element introduced by *blong*, though in these constructions, *blong* alternates freely with the preposition *long* as a subordinator:

tingting	'think'
traem	'try'
wantem	'want'
laekem	'like'
stat	'start'
hop	'hope'
promis	'promise'
askem	'ask'
intres	'interested'
sapos	'supposed (to)'
agri	'agree'
naf	'sufficient, up to'

We therefore encounter alternations between *blong* and *long* in the following:

*Mi tingting **long** kam be mi no gat taem.*
*Mi tingting **blong** kam be mi no gat taem.*
'I thought about coming but I had no time.'

*Joel i no laekem **long** dring waen.*
*Joel i no laekem **blong** dring waen.*
'Joel doesn't like to drink wine.'

*Yu bin promis **long** kam.*
*Yu bin promis **blong** kam.*
'You promised to come.'

*Mi intres **long** pem trak.*
*Mi intres **blong** pem trak.*
'I'm interested in buying the car.'

CHAPTER 7

*Oli sapos **long** go long hospital.*
*Oli sapos **blong** go long hospital.*
'They were supposed to go to the hospital.'

*Gel ia i naf **long** mared naoia.*
*Gel ia i naf **blong** mared naoia.*
'That girl is up to marrying now.'

*Mi no save agri **long** wok wetem yufala yet.*
*Mi no save agri **blong** wok wetem yufala yet.*
'I can't agree to work with you all yet.'

The subordinators *blong* and *long* can be deleted altogether after the initial verbs *traem* 'try', *finis* 'finish', *stat* 'start', *giaman* 'pretend', and *wantem* 'want'. We therefore find alternations such as the following:

Hem i traem wokem.
*Hem i traem **long** wokem*
*Hem i traem **blong** wokem.*
'(S)he tried to do it.'

Hem i finis wokem haos blong hem.
*Hem i finis **long** wokem haos blong hem.*
*Hem i finis **blong** wokem haos blong hem.*
'(S)he finished building his/her house.'

Bae hem i stat wokem bakegen tumora.
*Bae hem i stat **long** wokem bakegen tumora.*
*Bae hem i stat **blong** wokem bakegen tumora.*
'He'll start building it again tomorrow.'

Hem i giaman karem foto.
*Hem i giaman **long** karem foto.*
*Hem i giaman **blong** karem foto.*
'He pretended to take a photo.'

Hem i wantem kakae sam yam.
*Hem i wantem **long** kakae sam yam.*
*Hem i wantem **blong** kakae sam yam.*
'(S)he wants to eat some yams.'

In such cases, the resulting patterns may look like sequences of auxiliaries followed by verbs (§5.3.5) or complex verbs (§5.2). However, these should simply be treated as subordinate constructions with deleted subordinators for the following reasons:

- The subordinators *blong* or *long* can always be inserted between the two verbs with no appreciable change of meaning, as indicated by the preceding examples.

- If some kind of post-verbal modifier appears after the initial verb, the second verb is obligatorily preceded by one of the subordinators. Thus:

*Hem i traem oltaem **long** wokem.*
*Hem i traem oltaem **blong** wokem.*
*Hem i traem oltaem wokem.
'(S)he always tries to do it.'

*Hem i finis naoia nomo **long** wokem haos blong hem.*
*Hem i finis naoia nomo **blong** wokem haos blong hem.*
*Hem i finis naoia nomo wokem haos blong hem.
'(S)he has only just finished building his/her house.'

*Bae hem i stat bakegen **long** wokem tumora.*
*Bae hem i stat bakegen **blong** wokem tumora.*
*Bae hem i stat bakegen wokem tumora.
'(S)he will start building it again tomorrow.'

*Hem i wantem tumas **long** kakae sam yam.*
*Hem i wantem tumas **blong** kakae sam yam.*
*Hem i wantem tumas kakae sam yam.
'(S)he really wants to eat some yams.'

A subordinate element can also be optionally introduced by *blong* or *long* to produce sentences such as the following:

Malon i mekem olsem ia i nogud
'It is bad that Malon did that.'

When a simple sentence appears as subject (*Malon i mekem olsem ia* 'Malon did that'), this can be shifted to a position after the predicate (*i nogud* 'it is bad'), in which case a subordinator is optionally inserted between the two ele-ments. Thus:

*I nogud **long** Malon i mekem olsem ia.*
*I nogud **blong** Malon i mekem olsem ia.*
I nogud Malon i mekem olsem ia.
'It is bad that Malon did that.'

Note also the following additional examples:

*I no stret **long** ol man oli dring bia long pablik rod.*
*I no stret **blong** ol man oli dring bia long pablik rod.*
I no stret ol man oli dring bia long pablik rod.
'It's not right for people to drink beer along a public road.'

Note that the same function can also be expressed by means of the subordinators *se* (§7.3.2.1.2) and *we* (§7.3.2.1.3). This means that the following represent additional possibilities for expressing these meanings:

*I nogud **se** Malon i mekem olsem ia.*
*I nogud **we** Malon i mekem olsem ia.*
'It is bad that Malon did that.'

*I no stret **se** ol man oli dring bia long pablik rod.*
*I no stret **we** ol man oli dring bia long pablik rod.*
'It's not right for people to drink beer along a public road.'

7.3.2.1.2 Se

Se is sometimes used as a transitive verb (§5.1.3.1), as in the following:

Hem i se wanem?
'What did he say?'

However, it is much more frequently used to mark a range of different types of subordinate clauses. The function by which it most closely resembles its meaning as a verb meaning 'say' is when it is used as a subordinator after a verb of saying. The initial verb in such constructions can be intransitive, as in:

Joseph i giaman long mi se hem i stap wok.
'Joseph lied to me that he has a job.'

Mi ges nomo se i gat samting olsem fifti man oli kam.
'I just guessed that about fifty people came.'

Yumi evriwan i mas agri fastaem se gavman i save yusum pis graon ia.
'We all have to agree first that the government can use this plot of land.'

Alternatively, the initial verb can be a transitive verb of saying, as in:

Peter i talem long mi se hem i gat sam vatu.
'Peter told me that he had some money.'

Mi bin askem yu se bae yu kam o no.
'I asked you whether you were coming or not.'

While the subordinate element that is introduced by *se* can be a complete sentence that can stand on its own (as in the examples just presented), it can also be an incomplete sentence or even just a word or a phrase, as long as it can be used as an answer to a question. Thus:

Mi no talem se mi.
'I didn't say it was me.'

Hem i promes se tumora.
'She promised that it will be tomorrow.'

The material preceding a subordinate element marked by *se* can contain a verb that is not a saying verb as long as the overall meaning of the clause involves some kind of speaking. This means that there must at least be a noun phrase that refers to an utterance somewhere in the main clause. Thus:

Nius i stap go olbaot se bae oli jenisim taem blong eleksen.
'There are reports all over that the election date will be changed.'

Mi harem wan stori se yu no kam long haos long wiken.
'I heard a story that you didn't come home over the weekend.'

I stap long Tabu Buk se yumi mas harem toktok blong God.
'It's in the Holy Book that we must obey God.'

Any sentence containing a verb that expresses an intellectual activity or an emotion in Bislama can also be followed by a subordinate element that is introduced by the subordinator *se*. We therefore find sentences such as the following:

Mi hop se bae i no gat hariken bakegen.
'I hope that there will not be another cyclone.'

Oli no save se sip ia bae i kam tedei.
'They didn't know that the ship would come today.'

Yumi mas bilif se praes blong kopra bae i go antap bakegen.
'We have to believe that the price of copra will go up again.'

Mi harem se Kaonsel blong Olgeta Jif i agri long samting ia finis.
'I heard that the Council of Chiefs has agreed to that.'

Olgeta oli wantem se gavman i mas halpem olgeta.
'They want the government to help them.'

Mi fraet se bae oli faenemaot yumitu.
'I'm worried that they might found out about the two of us.'

Once again, the main element of the sentence does not have to contain an explicit verb of intellectual activity or emotion, as long as there is some reference to an act of thinking or feeling, as in:

Tingting i stap se bae mi kam long lafet.
'There is an idea that I'll come to the party (i.e., I'm thinking about coming to the party).'

The subordinator *se* can also be used to indicate that an action happens as a result of something that is expressed in the first part of the complete sentence. Given that purpose can also be expressed by means of *blong* (§7.3.2.1.1), we find alternations between *se* and *blong* such as the following:

Mahit i haedem ki se bae mi no faenem.
Mahit i haedem ki blong bae mi no faenem.
'Mahit hid the key so I would not find it.'

Fenis ia i blokem yumi se bae yumi no pas long ples ia.
Fenis ia i blokem yumi blong bae yumi no pas long ples ia.
'That fence prevents us from going through there.'

Yu no save fosem man se bae hem i vot long pati ia.
Yu no save fosem man blong bae i vot long pati ia.
'You can't force somebody to vote for that party.'

Se can also indicate that the event described in the second part of the sentence represents the result of the action that is brought about by the event that is expressed in the first part. This function of *se* is illustrated by the following:

Ol boe oli mekem se mi dring, be mi no wantem.
'The guys made me drink, but I didn't want to.'

CHAPTER 7

Oli stap maj long Independens Pak tedei se bae mifala i plei long Tuste.
'They are marching at Independence Park today, so we will play on Tuesday.'

Se can also be used where a simple sentence has been moved out of the subject position of an intransitive verb to a position after the verb. Thus, corresponding to:

Yumi stap lukaotem dog long haos i gud.
'It is good that we keep a dog at home (literally, We keep a dog at home is good).'

we can derive the following:

I gud se yumi stap lukaotem dog long haos.
'It's good to keep a dog at home.'

Note the following additional example of the same kind of pattern:

I tru se mi no pem takis blong mi yet.
'It's true that I haven't paid my tax yet.'

It is possible to bring an entire sentence into focus by shifting it to the front, with this then linked to the rest of the sentence by means of *se*. Thus:

Samting we i hapen se mifala i no sendem kwik.
'What happened is we didn't send it quickly.'

Wanem mi faenem se taem mi dring kava be tumora long hem mi stap kakae bigwan.
'What I find is when I drink kava I eat a lot the next day.'

Wanem mi stap talem se mi no finisim wok blong mi yet.
'What I am saying is I haven't finished my work yet.'

It should be noted, however, that such a use of *se* is not universal, and sentences like these could be equally well expressed without the *se*, but with an accompanying intonation break, as in the following:

Samting we i hapen, mifala i no sendem kwik.
'What happened is we didn't send it quickly.'

This construction can be seen as a variant of the optional use of *se* in equational sentences (§6.1.2.2) to link the topic and the comment. With the last example, *samting we i hapen* could be seen as the topic while *mifala i no sendem kwik* could be seen as the comment, with the two being optionally separated by *se*.

7.3.2.1.3 *We*

In §4.3.6, it was indicated that *we* is used to introduce a relative clause following a noun phrase. Thus:

Bos i bin singaotem ol wokman we oli no kam long wok long moning.
'The boss called the workers who had not come to work in the morning.'

The subordinator *we* can also be used on its own to introduce a relative clause that does not modify a preceding noun phrase, as in the following:

Pikinini ia i krae long naet we mi no wantem nating.
'The baby cries at night, which I don't want at all.'

Ol drong man ia oli stap singsingaot plante we i no gud tumas.
'The drunk men were shouting a lot, which wasn't very good.'

This form can also be used to introduce a complement that provides further detail to the information that is provided in the first part of the sentence. Thus:

Ol boe ia oli stap stil we i bitim mak.
'Those youths steal more than can be imagined.'

Bos i pem mifala we mifala i no kasem bigfala mane nating.
'The boss paid us without paying us very much at all.'

A very common construction based on *we* involves the repetition of a predicate to express emphasis, as in the following:

Mi harem mi kros we mi kros.
'I was absolutely livid.'

Ples i hot we i hot.
'It is incredibly hot.'

Mi hanggre we mi hanggre.
'I'm absolutely starving.'

Where a predicate consists of a transitive verb followed by an object, then both the verb and the object are repeated in this construction, as in:

Mi luk yu yu kakae laplap we yu kakae laplap.
'I saw you eating a huge amount of pudding.'

Long nakamal i gat man we i gat man.
'There were heaps of people at the kava bar.'

The repeated predicate in such constructions is often deleted leaving only the stranded subordinator *we* to express the emphasis, as in the following:

Mi harem mi kros we.
'I was absolutely livid.'

Long nakamal i gat man we.
'There were heaps of people at the kava bar.'

Long maket ol man oli fulap we.
'There were lots of people at the market.'

Mi hanggre we.
'I'm absolutely starving.'

This kind of deletion of the predicate, however, is only possible when the predicate appears at the end of a sentence. As soon as anything else is added after the predicate, the deletion of material cannot take place. Thus:

CHAPTER 7

Long naet i ren we i ren.
Long naet i ren we.
'In the night it poured.'

I ren we i ren long naet.
**I ren we long naet.*
'It poured in the night.'

For many of its remaining functions, *we* very frequently represents an alternative for the functions of *se* described in §7.3.2.1.2. It can therefore mark a complement to a clause expressing locution, thinking, or feeling:

*Joseph i giaman long mi **we** hem i stap wok.*
'Joseph lied to me that he has a job.'

*I stap long Tabu Buk **we** yumi mas harem toktok blong God.*
'It's in the Holy Book that we must obey God.'

It can also be used to introduce an extraposed clausal subject to a stative predicate:

*I gud **we** yumi stap lukaotem dog long haos.*
'It's good to keep a dog at home.'

Finally, it can be used along with *se* to introduce a clause of result, as in:

*Mahit i haedem ki **we** bae mi no faenem.*
'Mahit hid the key so I would not find it.'

Although *se* and *we* appear to be fairly interchangeable (except in relative clauses, where only *we* is found), it seems that some particular types of subordinate clauses more strongly favor the use of *se* while other clause types favor the use of *we*. In particular, complements of saying, thinking, and feeling are far more frequently introduced by *se* than by *we*.

7.3.2.1.4 *Nogud*

Nogud functions as an adjective meaning 'bad', and it can also be used as an adverb expressing a warning with the meaning of 'what if' or 'I hope not'. Thus:

***Nogud** oli faenemaot yumitu.*
'What if the two of us are discovered?'

***Nogud** mi stap westem yu long wok ia.*
'I hope I'm not wasting your time with this task.'

However, *nogud* can also be used as a subordinator to introduce an adversative clause that expresses the idea of 'in case', as in the following:

*Bae yumi karem ambrela **nogud** bae i ren.*
'We will take an umbrella in case it rains.'

*Mi bin haed aotsaed **nogud** ol man oli stap toktok long nakamal.*
'I hid outside in case the people were speaking in the meeting house.'

7.3.2.2 Complex Subordinators

Complex subordinators are forms that introduce subordinate clauses with the option of being followed by either *we* or *se* with no change of meaning. The function of each of these complex subordinators is described in turn below.

7.3.2.2.1 *From*

From functions as a preposition expressing cause or reason (§6.1.5.1.2). When introducing a subordinate clause, it expresses reason and translates as 'because':

Bae yumi go long piknik from san i saen.
'We will go on a picnic because the sun is shining.'

Hem i karemaot vatu from we i gat wan mared long wiken.
'He withdrew some money because there is a wedding on the weekend.

Olgeta oli kam luk mi from se mi no pembak vatu blong olgeta yet.
'They came to see me because I haven't repaid their money yet.'

The clause marked by means of *from* normally appears after the main part of the sentence, as shown by the examples just presented. However, it can also precede the main part of the sentence, as in the following:

From san i saen, bae yumi go long piknik.
'Because the sun is shining, we will go on a picnic.'

7.3.2.2.2 *Kasem*

Used as a preposition, *kasem* expresses the idea of 'until' or 'as far as' (§6.1.5.2.1). *Kasem* is sometimes also used as a subordinator, optionally followed by *we* (but not, it seems, *se*) with the meaning of 'until'. Thus:

Bae mi no go kasem oli stretem samting ia.
Bae mi no go kasem we oli stretem samting ia.
'I will not go until that matter has been settled.'

However, for many—if not most—people, *kasem* cannot be used as a subordinator in this way. To express 'until', such people use *kasem* in a prepositional phrase in conjunction with the noun *taem*, as in the following:

Bae mi no go kasem taem we oli stretem samting ia.
'I will not go until that matter has been settled.'

7.3.2.2.3 *Olsem*

The preposition *olsem* 'like, as' can also be used as a subordinator to express the meaning of 'as' or 'like' (§6.1.5.1.5). Used in this way, it can also optionally be followed by either *we* or *se*. Thus:

CHAPTER 7

Bae yumi go long Rentabao olsem oli talem.
Bae yumi go long Rentabao olsem we oli talem.
Bae yumi go long Rentabao olsem se oli talem.
'We will go to Rentabao like they said.'

7.3.2.2.4 *Taem*

In addition to functioning as a noun meaning 'time', *taem* can also be used as a subordinator to introduce a time clause, expressing, therefore, the meaning of 'when' or 'while'. Used in this way, it can appear on its own or it can be optionally followed by *we* or *se* without any change of meaning. Material introduced by *taem* can appear after the main element of the sentence, as in:

Bae yumi go long Rentabao taem i gat san.
'We will go to Rentabao when there is sun.'

Oli singaotem hem taem se ol pikinini oli kamaot long skul.
'They called her when the children came out of school.'

Alternatively, it can appear before the main element, as in the following:

Taem we oli kam mifala i stap dring kava finis.
'When they came we were already drinking kava.'

When *taem* is used as a subordinator with no following *we* or *se*, it is sometimes reduced to just *tae* in rapid colloquial speech. Thus:

Tae yu kam, bae yumi dring kava.
*Tae we yu kam, bae yumi dring kava.
*Tae se yu kam, bae yumi dring kava.
'When you come we will drink kava.'

When the *taem* element appears first in the sentence, the following main element is sometimes introduced by contrafactual *be* (§7.2.2), as in the following:

Taem mifala i pas aotsaed be si i nogud we i nogud.
'When we sailed through the open sea, the sea was really rough.'

7.3.2.2.5 *Tetaem*

Tetaem can be used as a noun meaning 'that time', usually with the following demonstrative *ia* (§4.3.5). Thus:

Tetaem ia mi no pulum resa yet.
'At that time I was not yet shaving.'

It can also be used to introduce a subordinate clause of time (optionally followed by *we* or *se*) when the particular time is known rather than when it is non-specific. Thus:

Yumi go piknik long Rentabao tetaem we san i stap saen.
'We went for a picnic at Rentabao at that time when the sun was shining.'

COMPLEX SENTENCES

The subordinator *taem* can be used to express any tense. The form *tetaem*, by way of contrast, can only be used to refer to events in the past. Thus:

Bae yumi go long Rentabao taem san i saen.
*Bae yumi go long Rentabao tetaem san i saen.
'We will go to Rentabao when the sun shines.'

7.3.2.2.6 *Sapos*

Unlike the subordinators described so far, *sapos* does not have a common non-subordinating use. It expresses the meaning of 'if' in conditional constructions. While *sapos* commonly appears on its own, it does also appear in conjunction with following *we* or *se*. Thus:

Bae yumi gobak long haos sapos i no gat man.
Bae yumi gobak long haos sapos we i no gat man.
Bae yumi gobak long haos sapos se i no gat man.
'We will return home if there is nobody there.'

Material introduced by *sapos* can appear either after the main element of the complex sentence, as just illustrated, or before it, as in the following:

Sapos yu no harem nius, bae yu stap long haos nomo.
Sapos we yu no harem nius, bae yu stap long haos nomo.
Sapos se yu no harem nius, bae yu stap long haos nomo.
'If you don't hear any news, just stay at home.'

Where the conditional element appears before the main clause, *be* (§7.2.2) is sometimes added before the following main clause. Thus:

Sapos i no gat kava be yumi no nid blong go.
'If there is no kava, we don't need to go.'

Sapos exhibits a fair amount of variation in its shape in more rapid colloquial speech, where it is commonly pronounced as *spos*, and even *sos* or *pos*. Thus:

Bae yumi go sapos oli no kam.
Bae yumi go spos oli no kam.
Bae yumi go sos oli no kam.
Bae yumi go pos oli no kam.
'We will go if they don't come.'

7.3.2.2.7 *Nomata, Nevamaen, Nating,* and *Iven*

These four words all mean more or less the same thing when they introduce a subordinate clause in Bislama, expressing the idea of 'even though' or 'even if'. They can all be followed either by *we* or *se* or they can appear on their own at the beginning of a subordinate clause. Thus:

Bae yumi go long Rentabao nomata we i stap ren.
'We will go to Rentabao even if it is raining.'

CHAPTER 7

Bae yumi go long Rentabao nevamaen se i stap ren.
'We will go to Rentabao even if it is raining.'

The subordinate clause can appear either following the main clause (as just illustrated) or before it. When the main clause appears second, the form *be* is commonly used at the beginning in association with any of these subordinators. We therefore find complex sentences such as the following:

Nating i stap ren bae yumi go long Rentabao.
'Even if it is raining we will go to Rentabao.'

Nevamaen we i bin ren be piknik i gud.
'Even though it rained, the picnic was still good.'

Although *iven* is used with the same function as *nomata, nevamaen,* and *nating,* it tends to be restricted to the speech of better-educated people who have been taught in English-medium schools. We therefore also find examples such as:

Iven man ia i kam long haos blong mi be mi no wantem luk hem.
'Even if that man comes to my house, I don't want to see him.'

7.3.2.2.8 *Afta* and *Bifo*

The word *afta* is used as an adverbial to express the meaning of 'afterwards', and as a preposition meaning 'after'. It can also be used as a subordinator expressing time, optionally followed by *we* or *se*, as in the following:

Afta hem i go long stoa, hem i go lukaot taksi.
'After he went to the shop, he went in search of a taxi.'

Bifo (optionally followed by *we* or *se*) can also be used as a subordinator, as illustrated by the following:

Bifo we waetman i no kam yet ol vilej i stap long bus antap.
'Before the Europeans arrived, the villages were up in the bush.'

Subordinate clauses introduced by *afta* and *bifo* can appear before the main clause, as in the examples just presented, or they can appear after the main clause, as in the following example:

Kalorongo i foldaon afta we hem i dring kava.
'Kalorongo fell over after he drank kava.'

Johnnah i go long bang bifo hem i go long miting.
'Johnnah went to the bank before he went to the meeting.'

Afta and *bifo* as subordinators are more common in the speech of people who are better educated in English. Some people tend to avoid these forms and express these meanings using the time subordinate *taem* in conjunction with the verbal modifiers *finis* 'already' and *no ... yet* 'not yet', as follows:

Taem hem i go long stoa finis, hem i go lukaot taksi.
'After he went to the shop, he went in search of a taxi.'

Taem we waetman i no kam yet, ol vilej i stap long bus antap.
'Before the Europeans arrived, the villages were up in the bush.'

7.3.2.2.9 Question Words as Subordinators

While question words (§6.2.2) are normally used to seek information, there is one construction in which they are not used to seek information at all. Rather, there is a subset of question words that are used before nouns to express a particular kind of subordinate construction. Forms of this type, and the meanings that they express, are *hu man* 'whoever', *wanem samting* 'whatever', *we ples* 'wherever', and *wanem taem* 'whenever, whatever time'. These appear in an appropriate structural position within an initial subordinate clause that is then followed by the main clause. The following main clause may be unmarked or it may be preceded by *be* 'but'. These forms are illustrated below:

Hu man *i wokem fasin nogud olsem ia i mas go long han blong polis.*
'Whoever does anything bad like that must go to the police.'

Wanem samting *i rong be yumi save stretem long nakamal.*
'Whatever is wrong we can settle it in the meeting house.'

We ples *yumi stap long hem stil yumi save toktok Bislama.*
'Wherever we are we can still speak Bislama.'

Yumi wekap long ***wanem taem*** *long moning bae yumi mas laetem faea.*
'Whenever we wake up in the morning we have to light a fire.'

Sometimes the subordinate clause containing these noun phrases with question markers may also be preceded by the subordinator *nomata*, as in the following:

Nomata wanem samting *i rong be yumi save stretem long nakamal.*
Wanem samting *i rong be yumi save stretem long nakamal.*
'Whatever is wrong we can settle it in the meeting house.'

The form *hamas* 'how much, how many' is also used in this kind of construction, though its behavior is slightly different. For one thing, it is not associated with a single following noun resulting in fixed expressions as noted above. Rather, it can be followed by any noun at all that refers to something that has been quantified, for example:

Hamas *navara i go long bel bae yumi no save fulap long hem.*
'However much sprouting coconut goes into your stomach, you can't get full on it.'

Yumi winim ***hamas*** *vatu be stil bae yumi no save pem wan haos olsem.*
'However much we earn we will not be able to buy a house like that.'

This meaning with *hamas* can also be expressed by separating *hamas* from the following noun and placing it at the end of the subordinate clause, as in:

Navara i go long bel ***hamas*** *bae yumi no save fulap long hem.*
'However much sprouting coconut goes into your stomach you can't get full on it.'

CHAPTER 7

*Yumi winim vatu **hamas** be stil bae yumi no save pem wan haos olsem.*
'However much we earn we will not be able to buy a house like that.'

Hamas can also be used in association with an adjective or a verb in a similar way. In this construction, the question word always appears at the end of the clause. Another feature of this construction with adjectives is that *hamas* can be replaced by *olsem wanem* to express the same meaning. Thus:

*Ples i hot **hamas** bae yumi no save swim long reva.*
*Ples i hot **olsem wanem** bae yumi no save swim long reva.*
'However hot it is we will not be able to swim in the river.'

*Yumi wok **hamas** stil bae yumi no save winim vatu olsem ia.*
*Yumi wok **olsem wanem** stil bae yumi no save winim vatu olsem ia.*
'However much we work we will still not be able to earn that much money.'

7.4 Sentences in Discourse

This grammar has shown how words are constructed out of their smallest meaningful elements, and how these make up noun phrases, verb phrases, prepositional phrases, and so on. It also shows how these make up simple sentences, and how simple sentences make up a variety of different kinds of complex sentences.

The grammars of many languages stop at that point and do not attempt to explain how sentences are linked together in longer narratives or conversations (or paragraphs, in the case of written language). The study of longer stretches of speech is referred to as discourse structure, and this is an aspect of the structure of Bislama that nobody has yet studied in any detail. However, I would not want readers to think that sentences can be put together in just any kind of way in Bislama. In this final section, therefore, I propose to offer some brief comments on ways in which sentences can be linked together to make up longer stretches of natural-sounding speech in Bislama.

There are, in fact, some elements of the grammar that have already been presented which, in one way or another, involve linkages between different sentences, as well as relationships between the forms that sentences take and different aspects of the non-linguistic context in which people happen to be speaking. For instance, the discussion of the fronting of noun phrases in §6.3 depends very much on these kinds of considerations, as does the discussion of the replacement of nouns by third person pronouns (§4.2), the use of demonstratives (§4.3.5), and the use of the demonstrative pronoun in so-called presentative constructions (§6.1.2.1). In this final section of this grammar, I want to draw attention to a variety of additional points that govern the way that we can link one sentence with another, or which can even be used by one speaker to link a sentence to a sentence that was uttered by a previous speaker.

7.4.1 The Sequencing of Events

One of the things that speakers of a language must be able to do is to clearly—and elegantly if they want—indicate the sequence in which events take place. One way to indicate the sequencing of events, of course, is to express each event in the form of a sentence, and for each of those sentences to be simply juxtaposed one after the other in the same sequence of the events being described. It is possible to do this in Bislama, but it would be stylistically highly unusual for anybody to do this more than occasionally. It would sound just as odd—as well as boring—in Bislama to say something like this as it would be to express the same meaning by means of the direct English translation:

Mi go long taon. Mi pem wan aeskrim. Mi kakae aeskrim blong mi. Aeskrim i ron long han blong mi. Mi waepem han blong mi. Mi gobak long haos.
'I went to town. I bought an ice-cream. I ate my ice-cream. The ice-cream melted on my hand. I wiped my hand. I went back home.'

Speakers would be much more likely to make use of a variety of discourse strategies to indicate the sequence in which these various events took place, and to link these sentences in a variety of different ways.

One commonly encountered strategy is for clauses to be simply juxtaposed with no overt marking of a sequential relationship between events. Thus:

Mifala i godaon long solwota. Trak i putum mifala.
'We went down to the sea. The vehicle dropped us off.'

Where sequentially related clauses share the same subject, it is not uncommon in conversational Bislama for the subject of the second clause to be deleted, along with the predicate marker that is associated with the verb that remains. Thus:

Mifala i go stap long bluhol. Swim long hol aftenun.
'We went to the saltwater inlet. And we swam the whole afternoon.'

It is possible in conversational Bislama, in fact, for several sentences in a row to appear with no subjects and predicate marking in this way. Thus:

Mifala i swim finis. Aot. Wokbaot bakegen long ples we trak i putum mifala.
'We swam. Then we left. Then we walked back to where the vehicle had dropped us off.'

One common pattern in narrative style to indicate a sequential relationship between events involves the repetition of the verb from a sentence that expresses the initial event at the beginning of the following sentence. The repeated verb is commonly followed by the modifier *finis* (§5.3.6), as in the following:

Kalo i swim long solwota. **Swim** *i gobak long haos.*
Kalo i swim long solwota. **Swim finis** *i gobak long haos.*
'Kalo swam in the sea. Then he went back home.'

Where the initial sentence contains a transitive verb with an object, the object is not normally repeated along with the verb in such constructions. Thus:

Kalo i hukum sam fis long solwota. **Hukum finis** *i laetem faea.*
'Kalo caught some fish in the sea. Then he lit a fire.'

Sometimes, however, the second occurrence of the verb may be associated with additional adverbial or directional information that is not provided with the first mention of the verb. Thus:

CHAPTER 7

*Mifala i go karem faeawud. **Karem i kam** mifala i rusum faol.*
'We gathered the firewood. Then we cooked the chicken.'

This kind of pattern is sometimes referred to as head-to-tail linkage because what we are doing is linking the head (or beginning) of the second sentence to the tail (or the end) of the preceding sentence.

The word *ale* 'and then' is ubiquitous in spoken Bislama. Its basic function is to introduce a sentence that expresses something that happens in direct sequence after a preceding event. A story told in Bislama will often involve a whole series of sentences introduced by *ale* if the events referred to happen one after the other. Thus, it would be possible to link two events by introducing the second event with *ale* as follows:

*Mi go long taon. **Ale**, mi pem wan aeskrim.*
'I went to town. Then I bought an icecream.'

Essentially the same in meaning is also expressed by the form *afta* 'afterwards', though this is probably less commonly used. It would therefore be possible to say the following:

*Aeskrim i ron long han blong mi. **Afta** mi waepem han blong mi.*
'The icecream melted on my hand. Then I wiped my hand.'

Some speakers even use *afta* and *ale* together, in that order, for the same function. Thus:

*Trak i putum mifala. **Afta ale** mifala i putum evri samting i stap.*
'The vehicle dropped us off. Then we put everything down.'

The words *oraet* and *nao*, and sometimes *oraet nao* together, can also be used to perform the same kind of function. Thus:

*Mi waepem han blong mi. **Oraet** mi gobak long haos.*
'I wiped my hand. Then I went home.'

*Mi go long taon. **Nao** mi pem wan aeskrim.*
'I went to town. Then I bought an icecream.'

*Mi pem wan aeskrim. **Oraet nao** mi kakae aeskrim blong mi.*
'I bought an icecream. Then I ate my icecream.'

In addition to the use of these sentence-initial discourse markers as ways of linking sentences in sequence, there are some other grammatical devices described elsewhere in this grammar as part of the sentence-internal structure that can be used to express sequence in discourse. The word *finis*, for example, is used as a verbal postmodifier to express the idea that an action is completed (§5.3.6), but it is also often used in discourse to indicate that an event has been completed and that the speaker is moving on to the next happening. *Finis* can occasionally be used as a sentence-initial marker in a similar way to forms such as *ale* described above, giving patterns such as the following:

*Mi waepem han blong mi. **Finis** mi gobak long haos.*
'I wiped my hands. Then I went home.'

7.4.2 Cause and Effect

There is a variety of ways to indicate that two events are not only linked sequentially but that the second takes place as a direct result of the first. This kind of cause-and-effect relationship can be expressed firstly by introducing the second sentence by *mekem* 'make, cause', optionally followed also by *se* or *we* (§7.3.2.1.2, §7.3.2.1.3). This translates as 'so' or 'therefore'. Although *mekem* ordinarily functions as a verb meaning 'make' or 'do', when used in this way it has no subject and no associated predicate marker. We therefore find examples such as the following:

Mael i kam long haos. Mekem se mi no nid blong go lukaotem hem.
'Mael came to the house. Therefore I did not need to go in search of him.'

Very often, there is no intonation break between two sentences that are linked by means of *mekem* in this way, so this discourse marker now appears to have become yet one more complex subordinator of the types described in §7.3.2.2, i.e.,

Mael i kam long haos mekem se mi no nid blong go lukaotem hem.
'Mael came to the house so I did not need to go in search of him.'

The form *olsem* 'thus' (or *olsem nao*) can also be used to link two sentences where there is a relationship of consequence between the two:

Ples hot tumas. Olsem aeskrim i ron long han blong mi.
'It was very hot. Therefore the icecream melted on my hand.'

Mael i kam long haos. Olsem nao mi no nid blong go lukaotem hem.
'Mael came to the house so I did not need to go in search of him.'

The form *taswe* can also introduce a clause that expresses an event that follows as a direct consequence of the previously mentioned event, translating again as 'thus', 'therefore', or 'so'. Thus:

Hem i swe long bos blong hem. Taswe hem i no kam long wok tedei.
'He swore at his boss. Therefore he hasn't come to work today.'

Finally, *hemia nomo*, literally meaning 'that's just it', can also be used to introduce a sentence that expresses something that is a consequence of a previous event, especially where the result would be something undesirable. Thus:

Mi stap dring kava evri dei. Hemia nomo mi stap slak long hem long moning.
'I drink kava every day. Unfortunately, I feel very down in the mornings.'

The transitive verb *minim* 'mean' can be used as an ordinary verb, as in:

Man ia i minim wanem?
'What did that man mean?'

The corresponding intransitive form is *min*, and this can be used as a discourse marker at the beginning of a sentence followed by *se*, to express a cause-and-effect relationship between the events described in the two sentences. We therefore find examples such as the following:

CHAPTER 7

Man ia i stap long haos. Min se mi no nid blong go luk hem long ofis.
'That guy is at home. Therefore I don't need to go to see him at the office.'

7.4.3 Contrary to Expectation

The final discourse marker that will be described here is the form *mowas*, which is optionally followed by *we* to give *mowas we*. This introduces a second sentence in discourse where the relationship between the two events involves the idea that the second event takes place in a way that is contrary to the expectation of the speaker, at least on the basis of the information that has just been expressed in the first sentence. This therefore corresponds to the meaning of 'even then' in English. Thus:

Hem i no stap mekem gud wok blong hem. Mowas we hem i stap let oltaem.
'He doesn't do his job well. Even then he always comes late.'

7.4.4 The Pragmatic Particle *ia*

There is a widely used demonstrative of the form *ia* that appears as part of the noun phrase in Bislama (§4.3.5). The form *ia* also functions widely as a discourse particle that is not part of the noun phrase at all. The fact that *ia* has two quite distinct functions is indicated firstly by the fact that it can appear after words that clearly do not belong in a noun phrase, as in:

Mi no wantem swim ia.
'I don't want to bathe.'

It is also possible for two instances of *ia* to appear in sequence, where the first *ia* is part of a noun phrase and the second *ia* is not. Thus:

Mi no save man ia ia.
'I don't know that man.'

Another indication that there are two different kinds of *ia* is the fact that in the local variety of Bislama spoken in Matanvat on Malakula, the pragmatic particle is often expressed instead by means of *wor* whereas the demonstrative function is expressed invariably as *ia*. Thus:

Mi no save man ia wor.
'I don't know that man.'

Most of the patterns described so far in this volume represent clearly definable grammatical constructions. The behavior of *ia*, however, appears to be rather different. It will probably never result in an ungrammatical sentence if instances of *ia* in its non-demonstrative functions are left out. While a sentence very often "sounds" better if *ia* is kept in, there are clearly some kinds of rules governing its use, as it also sounds bad if *ia* is used too frequently.

Ia is perhaps best described as a "pragmatic" particle. This means that its use is closely related to how the speaker relates to the people that he or she is speaking to, as well as what the speaker feels about what he or she is speaking about, as well as considerations of what information the speaker and the hearer already share regarding what the sentence is talking about. Because the use of *ia* is based very much on such pragmatic considerations, it should not be surprising to find that there is considerable variability in whether it appears in particular contexts or is absent. In a grammar such as this one, perhaps the best advice that can be given is for people to listen carefully to how different people use this form and to learn from them.

APPENDIX: PREVIOUS STUDIES OF BISLAMA GRAMMAR

From the outset, my intention has been to avoid loading the text of this volume with what might be seen as distracting references to other published sources to the non-specialist audience that it is hoped this volume succeeds in attracting. Although this is the first attempt towards a comprehensive published grammatical description of Bislama, my work has not proceeded in a vacuum. This volume represents not only a development out of previously published work of my own, but also derives less directly from the published work of others.

As an appendix to this grammar, I propose to provide the specialist reader who wishes to seek out alternative points of view on certain issues and, in some cases more detailed discussions of analytical problems, with a brief signposted guide to major published sources. Lynch and Crowley (2001: 139-47) provide a detailed compilation of all published materials relating to Bislama, as well as a listing of the major substantial publications of material written *in* Bislama. I do not propose to repeat that material, as the dedicated reader will seek out that source independently. Rather, I will draw attention here specifically to some of the more significant sources of information about the grammar of Bislama.

The earliest attempt by a trained linguist to describe the grammar of Bislama is Guy (1974). This contains a short grammatical description of Bislama in English, along with a French version of the same account. Although of some value at the time because it was all that was available, the inadequacies of this work were immediately apparent to anybody with any background in Bislama (Lynch 1975) and this volume has long been superseded.

Tryon (1987) represents the only other published attempt towards an account of the grammar of Bislama as a whole. This volume is much more successful than Guy (1974), as well as containing grammatical information that is somewhat more comprehensive. However, this volume was written primarily as language lessons for newly arrived expatriates in Vanuatu—and it comes with an accompanying set of recordings—so it was not designed as a comprehensive grammatical reference volume. Given that it was intended to cater for complete beginners, there are many widely used grammatical patterns that are simply not mentioned, and it adopts a somewhat prescriptive approach in that it does not mention the phonologically reduced variants of many grammatical markers.

A number of graduate research scholars have subjected various aspects of Bislama to more detailed scrutiny. Zhuang (1985) described the internal structure of the verb phrase in Bislama largely on the basis of written sources that were available at the time, though supplemented with some original material from Bislama speakers. Miriam Meyerhoff's spoken corpus became the basis of a quantitative variationist study of pronominal marking, with her primary findings appearing in print in Meyerhoff (2000). Paviour-Smith (2000) examined the issue of "predicate marking" in Melanesian Pidgin making use of some original data from Bislama.

Apart from these sources, however, much of what has been published about Bislama grammar involves discussions primarily from a historical viewpoint. Camden (1979) represents one of the earliest of these "incidental" sources of information about Bislama grammar in his discussion of the origin of Bislama grammatical patterns. He carried out a detailed comparison of a wide variety of grammatical features between Bislama and the otherwise undescribed South Santo

APPENDIX

language. Crowley (1990b) also looks at the historical development of Bislama grammar, though adopting a documentary approach to examine the evolution of a number of modern grammatical features between the mid-1800s and the present. Other more or less incidental grammatical information about Bislama comes in brief statements in the introductory sections of published dictionaries such as Camden (1977) and Crowley (1995, 2003).

There is now a growing accumulation of published materials that represent detailed discussions of fairly specific points of Bislama grammar. Because these sources are listed in full in Lynch and Crowley (2001), I do not propose to repeat the bibliographical details that are presented there, though some of the more substantial article-length discussions relate to the following grammatical topics: serial verbs (Crowley 1990c), complementation (Crowley 1989a), transitive marking (Camden 1996), and "predicate marking" (Crowley 2000b).

Although this volume does not aim to discuss the historical development of Bislama in any detail, scholars who are interested in this side of things will find a wealth of relevant published material, of which the more substantial and significant sources are Clark (1979–80), Charpentier (1979), Keesing (1988), Crowley (1990b), and Baker (1993). Finally, although this volume does not purport to treat the socio-political status of Bislama in Vanuatu society today, a range of relevant matters are discussed in Charpentier (1979), Crowley (1989b), Crowley (2000a), Lynch (1996), and Siegel (1998).

REFERENCES

Baker, Philip. 1993. Australian influence on Melanesian Pidgin English. *Te Reo* 36: 3–67.

Camden, Pastor Bill. 1977. *A descriptive dictionary: Bislama to English*. Port Vila: Maropa Bookshop.

___. 1979. Parallels in structure of lexicon and syntax between New Hebrides Bislama and the South Santo language as spoken at Tangoa. In P. Mühlhäusler (ed.) *Papers in pidgin and creole linguistics*, No. 2, pp. 51–117. Canberra: Pacific Linguistics.

___.1996. Transitive verbs using *long* in Bislama. In John Lynch and Fa'afo Pat (eds.) *Oceanic studies: proceedings of the First International Conference on Oceanic Linguistics*, pp. 319–351. Canberra: Pacific Linguistics.

Charpentier, Jean-Michel. 1979. *Le pidgin bislama(n) et le mutlilinguisme aux Nouvelles-Hébrides*. Langues et civilisations à tradition orale 34. Paris: Société d'Études Linquistiques et Anthropologiques de France (SELAF).

Clark, Ross. 1979–80. In search of Beach-la-Mar: towards a history of Pacific pidgin English. *Te Reo* 22/23: 3–63.

Crowley, Terry. 1989a. 'Say', 'c'est' and subordinate constructions in Melanesian Pidgin. *Journal of Pidgin and Creole Languages* 4(2): 185–210.

___. 1989b. Language issues and national development in Vanuatu. In István Fodor and Claude Hagège (eds.) *Language reform: history and future*, vol. 4, pp. 111–139. Hamburg: Helmut Buske Verlag.

___. 1990a. *An illustrated Bislama-English and English-Bislama dictionary*. Port Vila: Pacific Languages Unit (University of the South Pacific).

___. 1990b. *Beach-la-Mar to Bislama: the emergence of a national language in Vanuatu*. Oxford Studies in Language Contact. Oxford: Clarendon Press.

___. 1990c. Serial verbs and prepositions in Bislama. In John W.M. Verhaar (ed.) *Melanesian Pidgin and Tok Pisin*, pp. 57–89. Studies in Language Companion Series 20. Amsterdam: John Benjamins.

___. 1995. *A new Bislama dictionary*. Port Vila and Suva: Pacific Languages Unit and Institute of Pacific Studies (University of the South Pacific).

___. 2000a. The language situation in Vanuatu. *Current Issues in Language Planning* 1(1): 47–132.

___. 2000b. "Predicate marking" in Bislama. In Jeff Siegel (ed.) *Processes of language contact: case studies from Australia and the Pacific*, pp. 47–74. Montréal: Fides.

___. 2003. *A new Bislama dictionary (2nd edition)*. Port Vila and Suva: Pacific Languages Unit and Institute of Pacific Studies (University of the South Pacific).

Guy, J.B.M. 1974. *Handbook of Bichelamar/Manuel de bichelamar*. Canberra: Pacific Linguistics.

Keesing, Roger. 1988. *Melanesian Pidgin and the Oceanic substrate*. Stanford: Stanford University Press.

Lynch, John. 1975. Bislama phonology and grammar: a review article. *Kivung: Journal of the Linguistic Society of Papua New Guinea* 8(2): 18–27.

REFERENCES

———. 1996. The banned national language: Bislama and formal education in Vanuatu. In France Mugler and John Lynch (eds.) *Pacific languages in education*, pp. 245–57. Suva: Institute of Pacific Studies (University of the South Pacific).

Lynch, John, and Terry Crowley. 2001. *Languages of Vanuatu: a new survey and bibliography*. Canberra: Pacific Linguistics.

Meyerhoff, Miriam. 2000. *Constraints on null subjects in Bislama (Vanuatu): social and linguistic factors*. Canberra: Pacific Linguistics.

Paviour-Smith, Martin. 2000. *Tok Pisin and i: Subject and verb agreement in Melanesian Pidgin English and two other unrelated creoles of Melanesia*. Unpublished PhD thesis, Victoria University of Wellington.

Siegel, Jeff. 1998. Literacy in Melanesian and Australian pidgins and creoles. *English World-Wide* 19(1): 104–133.

Tryon, D.T. 1987. *Bislama: an introduction to the national language of Vanuatu*. Canberra: Pacific Linguistics.

Zhuang, Dejun. 1985. *The grammar of the verb in Bislama*. Unpublished MA thesis, University of Auckland.

INDEX

Items which are clearly signaled by headings in the table of contents are not always entered in this index, which is geared specifically toward guiding readers to material within individual sections of this grammar.

a- (on numerals), 55
ability, 99
about, 133
accompaniment, 128
according to, 136
adjective, 38–39
adversative, 186
again, 144–144
against, 135
agent noun, 44–45
agentless passive, 120–121
ale, 194
along, 136
anglophone, 13
archaic forms, 40
around, 135
as far as, 134
attributive adjective, 30
auxiliary, 31, 96–102

-bak, 58, 83–84
bakegen, 58
Beach-la-Mar 5
because, 187
Beche-de-Mer English, 5
become, 101
beneficiary, 127
bin, 35, 93, 97
blong, 68–70, 127–128, 178–182
broken English, 1, 2

cause, 128, 157–58
certainly, 146
characteristic, 69–70, 128
cognate object, 122–124, 162–163
collective pronoun, 48
comparative, 105, 131–32, 134
compound, 3, 7, 20–21, 37, 38–41, 42–43, 55, 63–64, 76–77, 86
condominium government, 5
constitutional status of Bislama, 3

continuous, 30, 75, 98–99
countable noun, 52–53
creole, 2, 4
culture, Melanesian, 6

default preposition, 130–134
demonstrative, 64–66, 114;
    pronoun, 49
desiderative, 100
diglossia, 4
diphthongs, 19
disjunctive sentence, 175
dual pronoun, 46–47, 48, 57
duration, 131

education, 4
Efate, 11
emphasis, 185–186
even though, 189–190
exclusive pronoun, 47
expansion of vocabulary, 3

-fala 29, 31, 43, 54–55, 57, 59, 60–63, 105, 112
finis, 35, 103–104, 194–195
fortunately, 146
francophone, 13
fronting, 124, 159–165, 184
future tense, 89, 92–95, 103–104

geographical spread of Bislama, 5
givenness, 61–62
goal, 130–131, 169
gogo, 104–105
grammatical terminology, 24

habitual, 30, 35, 75, 98–99
hamas, 52, 53, 153–154
hameni, 52, 53, 154
head-to-tail linkage, 194
hemia, 49, 65, 114–115
Hiri Motu, 2

INDEX

history of Bislama, 1, 4–5
hortative, 91–92
how, 158–159; many, 153–144; much, 153–154
however much, 191–192

i, 92, 109–113, 168
immediate future, 100
imperative, 89–91, 170
impersonal pronoun, 47, 121
inchoative, 101
inclusive pronoun, 47
incomplete sentence, 120
informal speech, 13
instrument, 129, 132, 136–137
intensity, 60, 76
interrogative, 147–160, 163
intransitive verb, 28, 30, 36, 74–75, 88, 117
-*ish*, 100

jas, 93, 98

kirap, 172

linguistic demography, 3
local languages, 3; influence on Bislama pronunciation, 1, 11, 15; influence on Bislama vocabulary, 1, 7
location, 130, 170
long, 125–126, 130–133, 137–139, 169–170, 178–182
Loyalty Islands, 4, 5

Malakula, 8
mestem, 145–146
nao, 160–165, 194
nating, 102–103
negation, 95–96, 114–115, 120; emphatic, 95–96, 103, 166

neva, 95, 102
no, 95–96
nogat, 150
nogud, 186
nomaj, 95
nomo (negative), 95–96; (reflexive), 58

non-countable noun, 52–53
numeral, 29, 39, 52, 53, 54–56; classifier, 56

object, pronoun, 46; zero, 118
obligation, 97
official language, 3
oli, 92, 110–112, 120–121, 168
only, 145
oraet, 194
ordinal number, 55–56
ought to, 94, 100, 116–117

Paama, 15
particularity, 61
part-whole, 70, 128
passive, lack of, 121, 161
past tense, 35, 89, 92–93, 97, 98
Pentecost, 11
perhaps, 143
permission, 99
pidgin, 2, 4; New South Wales, 4; Nigerian, 2
plantation, 2, 3; Queensland, 1, 5; Vanuatu, 5
plural, 38, 44, 51–52, 60, 110–111, 151, 153
possession, 46, 127
postmodifier (of noun), 39, 64; (of pronoun), 31; (of verb), 31, 146-147
predicate, 88–89, 108–109; marker, 93–94, 109–113, 118–120, 166
predicative adjectives, 30
preferably, 146–147
premodifier, 31, 64
preposition, 49–50
prohibitive, 91
pseudo-transitive, 132–133
purpose, 69, 128
purposive clause, 178–179

question, 32; 147–159
quotative clause, 182–184

random action, 74–75
reciprocal, 75–76

reduced form of grammatical marker, 8, 21, 69, 79-80, 94, 99, 127, 128, 129, 130, 188, 189
reduplication, 40-41, 54, 59-60, 72-76
reflexive, 57-58
regardless, 102
relative clause, 66-68, 184
rural Bislama, 8, 44

Sandalwood English, 5
sapos, 94, 189
saye, 150
se, 115-116, 126-127, 149, 151, 182-184
sequential action, 172, 173, 192-195
serial verb, 85-88, 166-172
si, 149-150
similarity, 129-130
so, 195-196
Solomons Pijin, 2, 5, 65
source, 131, 169
South Seas Jargon, 4-5, 6
spontaneous action, 58, 98, 103
stablization of Bislama, 4-5
stap, 35, 98-99
stylistic expansion, 3-4
sud, 94, 100

tag question, 148-149
Tahitian, 6
Tanna, 15
Tok Pisin, 2, 5, 65
too, 144
transitive suffix, 28, 73, 77-82, 85, 87, 132

transitive verb, 28, 86, 117; unsuffixed, 80-81
trial pronoun, 46-47, 48, 57
trigeta, 48
tugeta, 48

unproductive pattern, 44-45, 85-86
until, 134, 139, 187
urban Bislama, 8, 44

variety, 60
very, 145-146
vocabulary, from English 3, 6-7, 11, 12-13, 15-16, 17, 22; from French 3, 6-7, 11, 12-13, 15-16, 17, 22; from local languages, 3, 6, 22, 44
voicing of labial fricatives, 14; of stops, 14, 17, 20
vowel, tense 16-18

-*wan*, 37, 42-43
what, 150-151; (name), 152
whatever, 191
when, 152, 155
whenever, 191
where, 155-157
wherever, 191
which, 151, 152-153, 154
who, 152-153
whoever, 191
why, 154-155, 157-159

yes, 149150
yet, 104

zero pronoun, 49-50, 67, 162

OCEANIC LINGUISTICS SPECIAL PUBLICATIONS

Byron W. Bender
General Editor

Editorial Board

Joel Bradshaw, George W. Grace, Howard P. McKaughan,
Kenneth L. Rehg, Albert J. Schütz

Oceanic Linguistics Special Publications are occasional publications issued under the editorial sponsorship of the Department of Linguistics of the University of Hawai'i. The series consists of independently subsidized studies bearing on the languages of the Oceanic area. The "Oceanic area" is defined for this purpose as the combined Austronesian, Papuan, and Australian language areas. The Special Publications are published and distributed for the Department by the University of Hawai'i Press.

Manuscripts may be submitted to:
Oceanic Linguistics Special Publications
Department of Linguistics
1890 East-West Road
Moore Hall 569
University of Hawai'i
Honolulu, Hawai'i 96822

Publications may be ordered from:
University of Hawai'i Press
2840 Kolowalu Street
Honolulu, Hawai'i 96822

www.uhpress.hawaii.edu

www.ingramcontent.com/pod-product-compliance
Lightning Source LLC
Chambersburg PA
CBHW060604230426
43670CB00011B/1968